AGILE
EXPERIENCE
DESIGN

y Ratcliffe
McNeill

Riders \
VOICES THAT MATTER™

Agile Experience Design
A Digital Designer's Guide to Agile, Lean, and Continuous
Lindsay Ratcliffe and Marc McNeill

New Riders
1249 Eighth Street
Berkeley, CA 94710
510.524.2178
510.524.2221 fax

Find us on the Web at: www.newriders.com
To report errors, please send a note to: errata@peachpit.com
New Riders is an imprint of Peachpit, a division of Pearson Education.
Copyright © 2012 by Lindsay Ratcliffe and Marc McNeill

Acquisitions Editor: Michael Nolan
Project Editor: Rebecca Gulick
Development Editor: Margaret S. Anderson
Copy Editor: Gretchen Dykstra
Production Coordinator: Myrna Vladic
Interior Designer and Compositor: Danielle Foster
Cover Designer: Aren Howell Straiger
Cover Production: Jaime Brenner
Proofreader: Patricia Pane
Indexer: Valerie Haynes Perry

ISBN-13: 978-0-321-80481-5
ISBN-10:   0-321-80481-3

9 8 7 6 5 4 3 2 1

Printed and bound in the United States of America

ACKNOWLEDGEMENTS

We are extremely grateful to everyone who has contributed to this book. In particular, we would like to thank the people who have created and contributed original content in the form of both words and pictures. We are also grateful to everyone who has kindly given us permission to include their thoughts, work, products, or mug shots in this book, and also to those who have given us feedback throughout the process. A big thanks to the team at Peachpit who have supported us throughout this intense process and helped make this book what it is!

Lindsay would like to give special thanks to my hubby, Guy Ratcliffe, without whom nothing would be possible. Your love, support, and constant encouragement have made my dreams come true. To my 'little man' who melts my heart even on stressy days. To my Dad, who kept the faith and always believed in me. The thought of your smile still warms my heart, and I'll miss you always. To my Mum whose strength, perseverance, and determination continue to inspire me. To my brother whose unfaltering pursuit of the good life leaves me in awe. To Marc McNeill, thanks for your inexhaustible energy and passion about all things XD. Thanks for sharing this journey—we make a great team! To Hubertus B and StakenKidney, you are my mentors and muses eternal. To the PufaSistas, the other half of BitchnCharmer, I am eternally grateful for what was, what is, and what always will be. To Andrew, Sarah & Shane, you were there, where it all began, and continue to influence and inspire me. To Claire and my other 'Witches of EastTwick(enham),' you are all amazing and your support and friendship are invaluable. A big shout out to all my good friends and colleagues at ThoughtWorks who have inspired my fresh perspective on design, customer experience, and technology, and supported both of us through this process.

Marc gives a big thank you to Graham Donaghue for giving me the nudge to write this book and to Luke Barrett for his inspiration and support. Thanks to all the ThoughtWorkers, both past and present, who have patiently listened to me rant about the *real* customer whilst I've waved my hands in front of the whiteboard. They've taken me on a journey of agile discovery, from thinking a class was something I went to school in, to having a humble appreciation for the noble art of software delivery. Of this merry bunch, thanks in particular to Alex McNeill, Dan North, Luca Grulla, JM Domaingue, Prashant Gandhi, Jeff Patton, and my fellow experience designers Eewei Chen, Darius Kumar, and Diana Adorno. Thanks to my co-author Lindsay, who agreed to come on this journey and took it to the next level. And finally thanks to my wife, Lindsey, for the patience and understanding she's given me as I've written.

FOREWORD

IN A WORLD
ENRICHED BY
ABUNDANCE
BUT DISRUPTED
BY THE
AUTOMATION
AND
OUTSOURCING
OF WHITE-
COLLAR WORK,
EVERYONE,
REGARDLESS
OF PROFESSION,
MUST CULTIVATE
AN ARTISTIC
SENSIBILITY...
TODAY WE
MUST ALL BE
DESIGNERS.

—Daniel Pink,
A Whole New Mind

As it enters its second decade, the agile movement must continue to innovate and adapt to remain relevant. This book by Lindsay Ratcliffe and Marc McNeill continues a string of agile innovations and adaptations. It brings design back into the software delivery equation. "But, but," agilists might say, "we always do design." But Ratcliffe and McNeill are not talking about module design or database design; they're talking about product design, graphic design, experience design, and more. This level of design *is* one of those things that is "hard to define, but I'll know it when I see it." As the authors say, great design marries a desirable product with an engaging experience, a combination found in Apple's iPhone and iPad, for example.

The early agile movement was a reaction to the problems of waterfall development: splintering of roles, piles of documentation, and little collaboration. The remedies to the problems of waterfall included working in short iterations, reducing the proliferation of roles, slashing documentation, and fostering intense collaboration. But, as it turns out, specialisation wasn't the primary problem— collaboration was. As the agile movement has matured, we've added back specialists as we've learned to integrate them into agile teams. That's not to say that having a more general set of skills isn't very valuable, but in our complex world there is still a need for expertise in certain areas.

Another trend over the last decade has been to show how, in a variety of ways, the statement "agile won't work for or with xyz" is false. Issues with large projects, distributed teams, database-centric products, legacy systems integration, non-greenfield development, specific technologies, and practices like user-interface and experience design have all been addressed by innovative agilists.

Agile Experience Design: A Digital Designer's Guide to Agile, Lean, and Continuous continues these trends by showing how experience design can be integrated into agile products and how designers can be integrated into agile teams. The book delves into the many facets of design and how they can be incorporated to create an engaging experience for customers, and brings the critical issues of design to designers and non-designers alike.

Because, to repeat Daniel Pink, "today we must all be designers."

Jim Highsmith
Executive Consultant and author of the Agile Manifesto and
Agile Project Management

PREFACE

WHY READ THIS BOOK?

This is the book we wish we'd had when we were first introduced to agile methods. We want to show how design and agile are a natural fit together. How bringing together the people who build the products you design with the people who use the products you design will lead to better decisions and better customer experiences. We want to make the experience of designing in an agile environment easier and more compelling. How you no longer need to do all your work 'up front' but work collaboratively and continuously, adapting to the changes that are inevitable in the lifetime of a digital project.

WHO ARE YOU?

This book is primarily aimed at *experience designers* (and related roles) who work in an agile environment. It's for people who are striving to create excellent, customer-centric products and services yet want to be more adaptive, efficient, and collaborative. It doesn't matter if, like us, you have a long tenure as an experience designer and are just coming to agile for the first time, or if you're just starting out as an experience designer.

You'll also benefit from reading this book if you're a *project manager, product owner, developer, tester, or business analyst* working with experience designers in an agile environment. You'll understand more about what experience designers do, what they need, how to get the most out of them, where they fit into the process, and how to collaborate with them.

WHAT TO EXPECT

We're not reinventing the wheel. You won't necessarily find a whole bunch of new techniques. Instead, we've taken some best practises and used them to develop a framework and suggested approach for experience design in an agile context.

There are already plenty of books on agile methods—this isn't another one of those. Instead, we'll give a general overview of agile and then get specific on how to do experience design activities on an agile project. We'll look at the project life cycle and beyond, showing you how to apply experience design to an agile project.

We'll look at experience design as an essential component of a successful, agile, cross-functional project team where customer experience is critical to project or business success. We'll explain why roles are much less important than having the right skills on the project and explore how the different functional roles on a team can collaborate to create and deliver the project vision.

HOW TO USE THIS BOOK

Part One introduces agile—even if you think you know all there is to know about agile, it's still worth reading through to understand how and where experience design fits in.

Part Two is where we'll look at the project process and explore experience design techniques and activities in the context of the agile framework to help you deliver great experiences.

At the end of the book you'll find the Toolbox. Use this as a quick-reference guide to the tools and techniques and how you can adopt them in an agile environment. We hope to add to the toolbox over time on www.agileexperiencedesignbook.com. Let us know your favourite, tried and tested tools and we'll endeavour to share those too.

IT'S A SHARED UNDERSTANDING

Things change. That's a key message in this book. There are a variety of ways that we can keep each other informed of changes to the thinking about agile and experience design. We'll publish and post updates at www.agileexperiencedesignbook.com as and when they occur, but we'd love to hear your stories and thoughts, too.

 TIP

Throughout the book you will also see the lightbulb icon to indicate a tip.

 TOOLBOX

When we refer to a method, technique, or activity in the main part of the book that is described in the Toolbox, you will see the tools icon.

CONTENTS

CONTENTS X

PART ONE

LOOKING AT AGILE AND WHY DESIGNERS SHOULD CARE

REDESIGNING DESIGN 1

"TO BRING ONE'S SELF TO A FRAME
OF MIND AND TO THE PROPER ENERGY
TO ACCOMPLISH THINGS THAT REQUIRE
PLAIN HARD WORK CONTINUOUSLY
IS THE ONE BIG BATTLE THAT EVERYONE
HAS. WHEN THIS BATTLE IS WON
FOR ALL TIME, THEN EVERYTHING
IS EASY."

—THOMAS A. BUCKNER

Over the past twenty years of digital design,
designers have fallen by the wayside as the techies
have taken control. Now it's time for us—the designers—
to change our mindset and get back in the game.

1.1

Printing press.

The design process is stuck in the old world of print: a super conglomerate agency, tangible artefacts, and deadlines. At its worst, it can be a world of ego-driven elitism and tribal mentality. Design needs to be redesigned.

Design is currently driven by deadlines, the points at which ideas, drafts, blueprints, and prototypes are printed, manufactured, and launched. We use the time before the deadline to conceive, produce, and refine our designs. Once the deadline has passed, we breathe a sigh of relief and declare the design to be finished.

This model was born in the industrial era, when we needed large machines, production lines, and schedules to produce tangible artefacts (1.1). We are now in the information age, yet we still apply this thinking and this process to the creation of digital products. Say we develop a new digital product or service, which is considered done at launch. When something new transpires with the customers or the market, we undertake the whole process again from scratch and produce the next generation in exactly the same way. Yet we know that change is inevitable. Change is constant; a self-perpetuating cycle. Human needs change, technology is constantly changing and along with social, environment and political changes, making the cycle of change is an indomitable force.

As digital engineers, we must embrace change: it is the lifeblood of a digital existence. We need to stop fearing change, accept it, and make it a part of everything we do.

CREATIVE HEROES AND IT VILLAINS

Once upon a time, an organisation recognised the need for external design input. A design brief was drawn up, and creative agencies were invited to pitch for the work. The appointed agency started with some analysis activities that they then summarised in a written report. Having completed the analysis, the real design work began. The design team retreated into their creative space and creative magic happened. Some time later they emerged with a fully baked design. After a short period of feedback and refinement, the satisfied client signed off and the designers headed to the pub to celebrate.

This seemed like a fairly good process, and it certainly worked for the creative agency. In fact, at this stage the client was satisfied too, having been impressed by the creative environment of the agency, convinced by the creative team, and wooed by the creative budget that included cocktails and dinner at the venue du jour in town.

Issues arise, after the design honeymoon is over and the design team have left the project. The pain begins when development starts and the Information Technology (IT) manager explains that the amazing designs that everyone is so excited about can't be implemented.

The client could be forgiven for thinking, "IT people are idiots. Why can't they just build it for crying out loud? How hard can it be? Just work harder, longer, faster! Throw more people at it if you have to! If your team isn't capable of doing it, get someone in who can!" Eventually, the project is delivered, much later than expected, with a massively expanded budget, and the execution is only remotely related to the shiny presentation boards delivered by the creative agency.

DON'T SHOOT THE MESSENGER

So what went wrong? From the business point of view, IT went wrong. Everyone knows that IT is notoriously bad at delivering on brief, on time, and on budget. That might have been the case once, but the thing about IT is that it's full of analytical brains, folks who spend their time trying to make the impossible possible. When something doesn't work, IT types try to figure out why it's not working and come up with a solution.

IT was fed up with being the scapegoat. They wanted to figure out what was broken in the delivery process, why it was broken, and how to fix it. Having looked at the process from start to finish, they recognised that the problem lay in the way the software was developed. However, root cause analysis pointed out that the trouble started much earlier in the process, before any code had even been written, in the way that analysis, requirements gathering, and design were done. Invariably, a business dreams up a vision for a product or service and sets expectations with stakeholders and shareholders. Then the design team spends a heap of time and money on detailed design, without necessarily determining if the concept is feasible. Much later, when the IT guys get involved, they plough through the specification documents and are then forced to deliver the bad news: either the product cannot be built in the way it's been designed or it will take much more time and money than originally expected. IT managers are invariably the ones who get shot for delivering this message.

One way IT tackled the problem was to spend a lot more time and effort up front doing technical design and more detailed estimation, but this method had its own drawbacks. So a bunch of smart guys got together and came up with an alternative approach, known as agile. The approach was articulated in the Agile Manifesto, which states that building software better (and building better software) requires an emphasis on "people over process, working software over documentation, collaboration over contract negotiation, and responding to change over sticking to a plan." The simple philosophy of agile and its various derivatives, coupled with elements of lean manufacturing, rocked the IT and project management world.

IT continues to focus its efforts on improving the process for developing and delivering software. This includes everything from techniques and tools to platforms and languages. The latest hot developments include Continuous Delivery, cloud computing, data visualisation, the move from relational databases to NoSQL and functional languages such as Scala and Clojure. Also through movements such as open source IT has embraced the notion that to collaborate is to succeed.

DESIGN IN A VACUUM

By comparison, design as a functional discipline has had very few pivotal changes. While some techniques have evolved with the advent of digital technology, the processes remain largely the same. Perhaps design has not faced the same challenges as IT, or perhaps as designers, we are blind to the challenges we're at the pub celebrating, having left IT to pick up the pieces.

Design as a functional discipline has had very few pivotal changes.

Design has become so wrapped up in its previous successes that it can be ego-driven, elitist, and exclusive. Design is invariably done in a self-referential vacuum of where no other factors are considered. At its best this approach considers the end customers, but sometimes to the exclusion of everything else, resulting in biased designs. Once the design is complete, the outputs are mounted on foam-backed presentation boards or described in heavy design specification tomes. These are then thrown over the wall for someone else to deliver.

While design has been behaving in such a self-involved way, IT and business have been getting cosy. Now design, and to a certain extent the end customer, have been left out in the cold. Business is enamoured with agile, this new, inclusive way of working with developers, which delivers working software every few weeks. These agile guys even write their software requirements as user stories which state who the user is and what his goals are, so the business trusts that IT have their customers in mind.

LIFE AND TIME HAS MOVED ON

The ubiquitous Web has had an unprecedented impact on modern life. Access devices are converging, high-speed wireless networks are almost omnipresent, and the Internet has become a virtual neural network. The digital nature of the Web means that even time itself has a different meaning. In the offline world we strive to meet deadlines driven by the industrial and mechanical production processes of tangible artefacts. On the Internet there's no such thing as a deadline. Instead, there is a notion of a "use by" date, whereby something is hot or not depending on the groundswell of the virtual tribal trend at that moment in time. The Web is ubiquitous and at the same time organic. It is dynamic and emergent, and it continues to evolve following Darwinian theory. If a website is no longer fit for its purpose, it mutates into some enhanced version of its predecessor, otherwise a new cell emerges to triumph.

So if the way we design no longer fits in the real world of business and agile IT, and design no longer fits the organic framework of the Internet, then what is the future for design? Surely this is the kind of design challenge that most designers thrive on. After all, designers are by nature analytical problem solvers; we just use a different side of our brains to solve problems. Certainly a great number of design minds have spent time thinking about and visualising this problem. There may not be a single, irrefutable answer just yet, but thoughout this book we propose a straw man for consideration.

We don't want to reinvent the process wheel. The agile luminaries have done a good enough job of that.

We need to reinvent the way we design and integrate it into the agile process so that we bring design up to date and in line with the information age.

As designers, we just want to get (back) on the bandwagon and come to the party.

A MANIFESTO FOR AGILE EXPERIENCE DESIGN

In this book we explore the digital product development life cycle in the context of the agile project framework and look at how we can inject design into the process. In particular, we will propose a flexible process for an agile delivery project, where experience design is critical to the project or the success of the business.

Let's start with a manifesto for agile experience design that provides positive guidance for approaching digital design within an agile framework.

We'll get into more detail about the meanings behind each of the points in the manifesto as we move through the book. To start with we'll look at how design happens in a waterfall environment, where design has its own exclusive phase. This will give you some context around the need for change, both in the traditional project methodology and in when and how we do design.

Then we'll look at the agile project framework. We'll go into some depth, but this book is not a comprehensive guide to agile; it's a digital designer's guide to being agile. So rather than rehash what other good agile books can already tell you, we'll point out what's different from how you work today, what you need to get going, and what it means specifically for digital designers working in an agile environment. This is the missing book on agile and design.

The aim of agile is to get to code as quickly as possible. By including design in the process we can ensure that the software produced adds value to the business and is desirable to the end customer. There's no point in using software if it doesn't deliver value. So we need to check every decision, every action, and process throughout the product development life cycle and ask, "Where's the value?" We need to take time to understand *why* we're doing the project, *what* value means in context and what that value looks like, and *how* to deliver and measure the value.

A MANIFESTO FOR AGILE EXPERIENCE DESIGN

Agile experience design is

Inclusive rather than elitist

Emergent with direction rather than up front

Integrated and collaborative rather than handed over the fence

Considerate of customer, business, and technology needs rather than biased toward a single factor

MAKE IT COLLABORATIVE, ITERATIVE, AND INTENSE

We'll explore what it means to build an agile team that includes designers and to work in an agile environment. One of the main differences on an agile project is that every team member contributes to product development. On a waterfall project, process functional groups work almost exclusively in sequential phases (more on waterfall in Chapter 2, "The Waterfall Has Dried Up"). On an agile project, a cross-functional team comes together (physically *collocates*) and iteratively develops the product throughout the entire project (1.2).

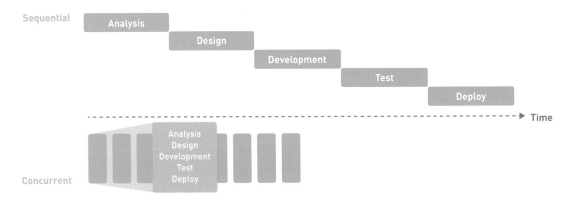

1.2

Sequential versus concurrent project methods.

The initial stages of an agile project are time-boxed and are driven by collaborative workshops. The cross-functional teams attending the workshops might include business stakeholders, senior technical representatives, senior designers, customer representatives, and a project manager. There are many advantages to bringing together everyone who has a stake in the success of a project, but one of the primary reasons is to reach a shared vision for the project as quickly as possible. It's a big ask. Getting so many people to commit so much of their time is not without challenges.

For an agile project to have a good chance of success there must be both understanding and commitment, not only from the immediate project team, but also from the wider organisation.

A cross-functional senior management team within the organisation needs to sponsor the adoption of agile, either for a particular project or as a wider programme of change. The senior management team then needs to push a mandate through the divisional lines to the functional managers where the team members come from.

The aim of the initial set of workshops is to elicit a shared understanding amongst the project team about the business landscape. This sets the context for the project and ensures that everyone understands what the opportunity is and why it's important.

MAKE THE VISION REAL

Once we have gained an understanding of the project landscape, we want to create a vision of success that will guide product development. To create a successful product we need to take into consideration business, customer and technical requirements, and constraints. The product needs to deliver business value, be technically feasible, and needs to be desirable by the end customer. Creating a desirable product does not happen by accident (1.3).

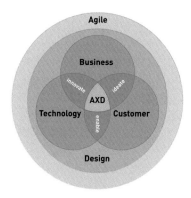

1.3
Agile Experience Design (AXD) considers business, end customers, and technology.

To create a desirable product with an engaging experience, we take the best bits from the most influential design disciplines—design thinking, service design, product design, graphic design, user-experience design—and reapply them in an agile project environment. We'll make design explicit, yet integrated, so everyone knows it's a critical part of software delivery. Design cannot be left to chance and should not just emerge as a by-product of software development. To deliver a compelling, valuable, and desirable experience that hooks customers, converts them, and keeps them coming back, we have to design the experience in a different way.

We'll look at the essential tools and techniques that designers have come to rely on and see how we can sharpen them, adapt them, and adjust them for use in an agile environment. We'll blend design thinking with agile and take guidance from lean manufacturing and lean startup. We'll do just enough to get started and make informed decisions about the direction of the project. We know that the project landscape will change, so we avoid creating "waste" or stockpiling anything that could become obsolete with change.

The project, and ultimately the design, is directed by both business and customer goals, to ensure that we remain focused on delivering value. Designing in this way ensures that arbitrary features or functions won't increase the project time, scope, or budget unnecessarily. We do this in collaboration with the other team members. This might sound like "design by committee," which would have most designers running for the hills, but properly managed this is not the case. The primary role, and therefore responsibility, of the lead experience designer is to use facilitation techniques to drive out the key customer journeys and the design direction, while soliciting input about technical feasibility and business viability.

CONTINUOUSLY DEVELOP THE DETAIL

The aim in the early stages is to explore just enough detail to get to development. It's not about designing or specifying every detail prior to development, because we know that elements will change as we uncover more information. Changes to the final deliverable will be influenced by everything from market conditions, to the competition, to the potential customers. Later, as we dive into development, we'll learn more about the possibilities and constraints of the technology in the context of the application.

The design detail and the user stories (project requirements) emerge together throughout the process. Some stories might emerge first and the designs are based on those stories. Equally, the design direction will influence some of the stories that are written.

Designers continue to build on design detail throughout the development phase. While the product is being built, designers work closely with the business and developers on the detail as user stories are played out. With a comprehensive design vision in place, the design detail can emerge.

On an agile project the build phase is divided into very short chunks, usually one to two weeks, known as *iterations* or sprints. Designers aim to work one or two iterations ahead of the developers to think holistically about the stories in the context of the overall design and to solicit regular and timely feedback about the designs from the end customers. The aim is to test with customers during every iteration, to ensure that the emergent designs are value-based, useful, usable, and desirable.

MAKE THE DESIGN RESPONSIVE

Success doesn't come by blindly spending lots of time, effort, and money in development and then crossing your fingers at launch. Test your ideas with the market as early and often as you possibly can. Get out of the office and onto the streets to get feedback from the target audience. The idea is to succeed quickly or "fail fast."

It's much better to determine early on that your idea isn't going to work than to spend one to two years and a lot of money on an idea that ends up bombing in the marketplace.

These kinds of guerrilla techniques yield quick results and are very effective in directing business success.

Testing with a sample set of customers during design development is essential; however, we acknowledge that design is never truly done. When a digital product or service is launched, it's the start of a new understanding of how customers interact and how they feel about the product. The live environment is the perfect place to measure and analyse how the digital customer experience is performing. With the right tools it's possible to quickly assess what's working and what's not. Then by using techniques such as A/B testing and multivariate testing designers can experiment with design variations, and use the results to optimise the digital customer experience. With the right deployment process in place, changes can be made to your digital service multiple times a day if necessary. This is how we go beyond agile, where design is never done and where the digital product becomes a continually evolving experience that is truly responsive to customers' needs and the changing context in which they exist.

WHAT ARE WE WAITING FOR?

Anyone who's been involved in the development of online (or offline) products and services knows that the keys to success include time to market and perceived value. Agile is all about delivering maximum value in the minimum amount of time.

The traditional design process is outdated and isn't the most efficient or effective path to success. As a profession, we need to redesign the design process to: make it iterative, collaborative, and intense; make the vision real, continuously develop the detail; and make the design responsive.

We also believe that waterfall is not serving businesses well either, so we'll explore how it contrasts with agile and look at the benefits that agile delivers. Then we'll go beyond agile, to the new wave of thinking about product evolution. To do this, we need to change what we mean by "done" and recognise that launch is just the beginning of life for new products. By thinking about product improvements in a different way, and coupling continuous design with continuous delivery, we can reap the benefits of real-time continuous improvement.

THE WATERFALL HAS DRIED UP

2

"THERE IS A REASON FOR THIS MADNESS
AND THAT IS THE WATERFALL."
—ROGER STEEN

Are processes that enforce silo mentality and prevent
change hampering your chances of success? In this
chapter, we explore how the waterfall has all but dried
up and by adopting agile you can create value for end
customers while realising value for the business.

Let's not kid ourselves. The only things that really matter in the digital world of the Web are creating a great product or service experience and delighting your customers.

If you could wave a magic wand and create an e-commerce website with a buzzing community and soaring conversion rates, you'd do it

In this chapter, we'll look at the current state of waterfall project management and illustrate where problems lie. It might mean that, as a designer, you've been focusing too much on the process and administrative work—the process itself is limiting your overall success.

We might not have a magic wand, but we can help you create desirable experiences faster than most designers are used to. In this chapter, we'll deconstruct the Agile Manifesto, and see how it looks to fix many of the problems found in sequential delivery. Then we'll introduce ways to inject experience design into the process to move rapidly from an initial idea to working software that can be continuously evolved throughout the product life cycle.

CURRENT STATE

Done is a past participle of the verb *do*. By definition, *done* means the task of *doing* an activity has ended and the job is complete. This is interesting because this deceptively simple definition has a different meaning depending on the context. Let's look at what it means for offline design and digital design on a waterfall project.

OFFLINE DESIGN: WHEN "DONE"
MEANS SEND IT TO THE PRINTER
(AND HEAD TO THE PUB)

A creative designer who specialises in offline (print) design may be primarily concerned with how best to visually communicate to influence the audience's perceptions. On a project that starts with a creative brief and ends with printed output, the creative designer expends the majority of her effort on the first third of the process. The designs are then passed to the production artist, who prepares the artwork for print. The designer liaises with the production artist at specific review points and also checks and approves the final print proofs (2.1).

2.1
Creative print
production process.

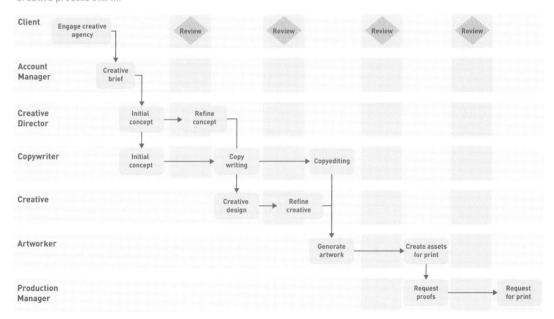

Once the project goes to print it is considered "done." That's when the creative team breathe a sigh of relief and head to the pub to celebrate. It's someone else's job to measure the effectiveness of the design and to see if it produces the expected penetration and response rates.

Most of the activities in the print design process are treated as discrete parts, carried out in isolation by people in different roles with specific skills sets (2.2).

2.2
Print production
process by role.

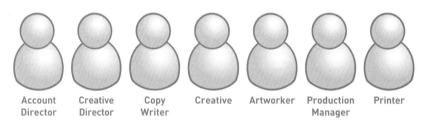

| Account
Director | Creative
Director | Copy
Writer | Creative | Artworker | Production
Manager | Printer |

ONLINE DESIGN: WHEN "DONE" MEANS HAND IT TO THE DEVELOPERS (AND HEAD TO THE PUB)

As Internet technology has improved, the Web has become more of a visual medium, and brand appeal has played a more significant role in customer relationship development, so it was a natural progression to take the offline design process online. As creative designers, we were quite happy with the traditional print process. We didn't know anything different, and who were we (or anyone else for that matter) to change it when it came to designing for the digital environment?

For large online projects, the project method of choice was waterfall, which to the delight of designers, has a specific phase for design (2.3).

Waterfall comprises a series of discrete phases. A phase begins only after the agreed deliverables from the previous phase are completed to the agreed standard and are accepted and signed off by project governance.

Initiation

Concept

Feasibility

Requirements

Analysis

Design

Development

Test

Deploy

A designer's role in the digital world of waterfall is pretty much the same as it was in the offline world. Designers take the documented outputs of the analysis as inputs into the design phase. Toward the end of the design phase, the designers compile the designs into a design specification document. The completed specification is thrown over the wall for developers while the designers head to the pub to celebrate a job well done. Traditionally, designers have had very little input during the build phase.

In waterfall projects a key driver is to lock down the design variables before going into the build phase. Changing the design specification once the build phase is underway is very costly in terms of both time and effort. Therefore, waterfall has a whole change control process designed to manage or prevent all but the most critical changes.

When you deliver a waterfall project, development is considered done when the code is complete and has been sent to quality assurance (QA) for testing. The overall project is considered done when everything that was requested in the requirements document is built, tested, deployed, and proven to work cohesively and without fault in a live environment. It's not an unreasonable approach, as what it measures is project completeness. However, this definition of "done" explains why waterfall projects take so long to complete. All the requirements are analysed, designed, developed, and rigorously tested en masse before being released. This means that the business waits a considerable amount of time for a complete product, and even longer before there is any return on the initial investment.

2.3
Waterfall System Development Life Cycle (SDLC) methodology.

A VIEW OF WATERFALL

Someone, somewhere in the business has an idea.

The idea is turned into documents that are owned by different people, and these documents take on a life of their own.

Product Owner

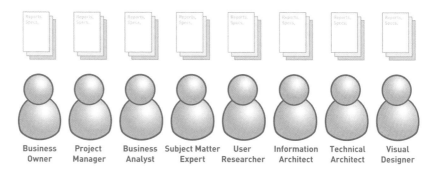

| Business Owner | Project Manager | Business Analyst | Subject Matter Expert | User Researcher | Information Architect | Technical Architect | Visual Designer |

1. Write the first draft.

2. Send the draft to the reviewers and await their response.

3. Update the draft with the reviewers' comments. Send the reviewers the updated document. Await their response.

4. Produce the final draft and send it back to the reviewers. Await their response.

5. Await the completion of supporting documentation, as the final document must be submitted as a pack.

6. Send the document to relevant stakeholders. Await sign-off.

7. Upload the signed-off document pack to the project shared space.

8. Wait for documents to be picked up by the development team.

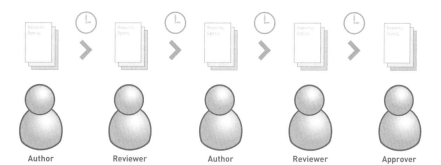

| Author | Reviewer | Author | Reviewer | Approver |

With this process, compromises to the original idea and designs are made all along the way to meet the various deadlines. It's anyone's guess whether or not the idea is realised to its full potential.

Diagram 2.4 shows the steps involved in delivering a project at a global bank once the business has identified a product need. In this sequential process, documentation moves back and forth between different parties, with delays incurred as the parties review and sign off on the documents.

2.4
A waterfall process for product development at a bank.

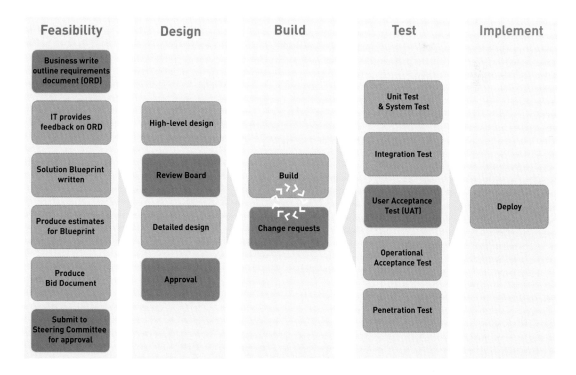

Feasibility	Design	Build	Test	Implement
Business write outline requirements document (ORD)			Unit Test & System Test	
IT provides feedback on ORD	High-level design		Integration Test	
Solution Blueprint written	Review Board	Build	User Acceptance Test (UAT)	Deploy
Produce estimates for Blueprint	Detailed design	Change requests	Operational Acceptance Test	
Produce Bid Document	Approval		Penetration Test	
Submit to Steering Committee for approval				

Working in this sequential way can limit both design and project success.

Design is limited by the design team's ability to translate the business requirements, determined by the analysis team, into a workable concept. Design success is further limited by the design team's time and ability to describe all the design detail and design rationale—the reasons why each design decision was made—in a design specification for the purposes of development. Success is further jeopardised when the design specification is handed over to the development team and left to them to interpret the detail and the design thinking and implement the designs as originally intended while simultaneously trying to wrangle technical constraints.

The sequential process is only designed to go forward.

We get in trouble when things don't go quite as we planned and the feedback loop to correct our direction is disabled. The implications of exclusive project phases are that the project environment is stable and finite, and that once a phase is complete no further changes are made. However, nothing could be further from the truth. When change does occur it has repercussions for every component of a project. Why then is the framework for project success so ill-equipped to deal with change?

The cost of change is compounded over time: It is minimal during the analysis and design phases, tenfold during development, and one-hundredfold post-launch. This perspective and the burden of those figures means that the design has to be thoroughly researched, well thought through, well designed, holistic, comprehensive, error free, and complete by the time it reaches the build phase (2.5).

With such pressure it's no wonder that designers just want to concentrate on design. Surely we have enough to worry about without worrying about technology as well?

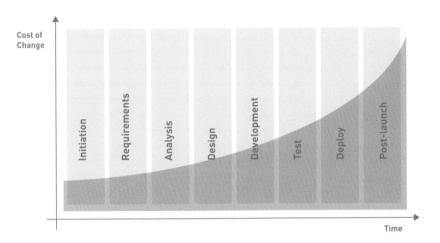

Cost of
Change

Initiation

Requirements

Analysis

Design

Development

Test

Deploy

Post-launch

Time

2.5
The cost of change in
the project life cycle.

AGILE DECONSTRUCTED

In 2001, faced with the challenges we mention above, a bunch of smart guys,
including Jim Highsmith (author for the foreword of this book), got together to
look at "uncovering better ways of developing software by doing it and helping
others do it."[1] And so agile was born.

THE AUTHORS OF THE AGILE MANIFESTO

The original authors of the Agile Manifesto are: Kent Beck, Mike Beedle,
Arie van Bennekum, Alistair Cockburn, Ward Cunningham, Martin Fowler,
James Grenning, Jim Highsmith, Andrew Hunt, Ron Jeffries, Jon Kern, Brian Marick,
Robert C. Martin, Steve Mellor, Ken Schwaber, Jeff Sutherland, and Dave Thomas.
See www.agilemanifesto.org for more details. ▨

1 http://agilemanifesto.org/.

THE AGILE MANIFESTO

Individuals and interactions   over processes and tools

Working software   over comprehensive documentation

Customer collaboration   over contract negotiation

Responding to change   over following a plan

That is, while there is value in the items on the right, we value the items on the left more.

Let's use the Agile Manifesto as a lens over the design process.

A principle difference between waterfall and agile is that agile takes smaller, manageable chunks of work, and uses concepts such as *iterative development* and *test-driven development* to deliver smaller pieces of working software, which delivers value quicker and more frequently.

INDIVIDUALS AND INTERACTIONS OVER PROCESSES AND TOOLS

Software is a social exercise. It should be about people and how they communicate, cooperate, and interact as a team to deliver value to the organisation. The intention of delivering value can be derailed by politics around the correct processes and the appropriate tools. Waterfall teams often have project managers and project officers whose job is to ensure that the project process is being carried out to the letter.

Valuing individuals and interactions means project team members having lots of opportunity to verbally communicate and collaborate throughout the project life cycle. Yet design is often carried out in isolation away from the project team, which drastically reduces interaction and collaboration. Why do designers prefer to work in their private space?

At school we are encouraged to show our workings. Somewhere in the design world this thinking gets lost and as designers we only want to share the finished product with our clients. We fear setting expectations or disappointing if we show work in progress. We get protective. Like a child not wanting her peers to see her work on a test, we wrap our arms around our sketchpads, bury our heads, and don't let anyone see.

Working in a place that is physically removed from other team members affects the project in one way; working closely with team members has a different result.

BUT OUR BEST WORK HAPPENS IN OUR OFFICE, NOT YOURS

A high-tech medical company were developing a new medical device that would enable any medical professional to undertake complex and precise tasks. The IT department decided they needed help to design and build an intuitive interface that would enable nonspecialists to set up the devices and complete complex processes.

A design agency were brought in. They suggested creating personas. The client IT team hadn't heard of personas before and thought it sounded like a great idea. The agency did their research to get a real understanding of how the users did their jobs and distilled the research into the personas. Next they turned to developing the user interface. The design team went back to their cool design offices and then a week later they returned to present their wireframes. It turned out that, despite worthy aspirations to simplify the user interface, they'd gotten the fundamentals wrong.

A week later, after more work in isolation, they presented revised wireframes. They'd also done some creative mock-ups on foam-backed boards. Again, these looked impressive, but the team shook their heads. The designs weren't working; the designers couldn't seem to grasp the complex interactions and dependencies within the process. Budget and time for the design phase was running out. This was becoming a painful process. The client CIO suggested that the agency designers spend a week at the client site and do the designs in their offices. That way IT would be able to see how the designs were progressing as they were developed and ensure that issues could be addressed as soon as possible. The CIO was mildly shocked to be informed that this was not the way the agency worked. After one more presentation, the exasperated client took the design work the agency had produced and let them go.

The CIO brought in a freelance designer who sat beside the development team and interacted with them constantly. He was able to quickly and efficiently produce an interface that worked.

The problem here is that the teams are physically divided and working in isolation with limited interaction. In addition, there were two teams, not one! This lack of interaction results in incomplete understanding and causes inefficiencies throughout the process. This is typical in the waterfall process because it is organised into phases around the functional silos. In an agile process, interactions are plentiful—and it shows.

CAN YOU SPOT THE AGILE TEAM?

If there are two development teams in two rooms, you can tell at a glance which one is agile and which one is waterfall. Two noticeable differences will strike you immediately. The first is the noise. Agile teams are noisy. They talk. They debate. They share ideas. It's part of the how they work! Waterfall teams are careful with each other and speak one at a time, careful to be respectful. Second is the use of *information radiators* (see Chapter 9, "Into Development"). The agile team are surrounded by stuff on the walls: cards, sticky notes, diagrams on whiteboards. The waterfall team works from documents. A performing agile team is more like a social entity than a bunch of individuals. There is a fallacy that the technical team members spend most of their time typing code; product development (even the technical part) is as much thinking, talking, and socialising ideas as it is typing. ▪

WORKING SOFTWARE OVER COMPREHENSIVE DOCUMENTATION

Designers love their documentation. Indeed, more often than not, the deliverables to the client are documents. Formal documents, such as style guides or design specifications, often serve no other purpose than review and sign-off. This ensures that the designer gets paid and a tick can be added in the project process box, but it has very little value of its own.

Take a look at illustrations 2.6 and 2.7. Illustration 2.6 shows a sketch of a customer journey on the whiteboard: the stages, the main events, and which events were a positive experience and which were negative. It takes very little time to produce. It's just a bunch of sticky notes and lines. Everyone on the team is involved in the creation of the sketch and as a result they have a shared understanding and can walk through it with anyone else who might be interested.

2.6
Lo-fi customer
journey map.

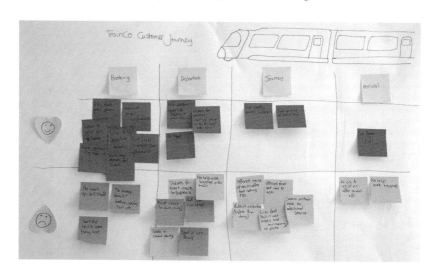

2.7
Hi-fi customer
journey map.

Now take a look at illustration 2.7.

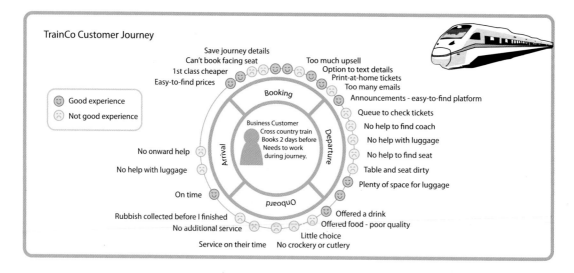

Here a designer has worked on the sketch for hours so that it will look good when presented. And here's the first issue with this approach. It looks pretty, it's been signed-off on. So it can't be changed. And because change is inevitable, as a deliverable it will rapidly lose its value.

There's nothing inherently wrong with documentation. The Agile Manifesto values working software (left) over *comprehensive* documentation (right). It also states (and this is all too often forgotten), "While there is value in the items on the right, we value the items on the left more." So what you should strive for is the right level of documentation at the right time. To work out the right documentation think about your current process and ask yourself:

- How much time do you spend on documentation?
- Who uses the documentation?
- What is the minimum that customers need from the documentation?
- How efficient is your sign-off process? How much time is spent waiting for documentation to be approved? What impact does this have on the project?
- What evidence is there of document duplication? Are different parts of the business documenting the same things?
- If documentation is only for the purposes of communication or development, how polished does it need to be?

Look for ways that you can increase your design time by decreasing the time you spend on documentation. Do a quick sketch and have a conversation with jotted notes rather than detailed documentation.

One reason that waterfall relies on heavy documentation is the sequential nature of the project process. The QA testers need comprehensive documentation from the designer to ensure that what development has built is what was intended. Testing is a separate activity and far removed from the design part of the process. However, an agile project uses test-driven development—testing is completely integrated into the build process. The test, or *acceptance criteria*, emerges alongside the design in the user-story detail. In this way the user story and the accompanying wireframe are all the documentation that is needed to create working software.

30

CUSTOMER COLLABORATION OVER CONTRACT NEGOTIATION

In commercial ventures there's a vendor and there's a customer (although we'll refer to them as clients—see next). When a vendor and a client enter into an agreement to form a working relationship, the contract is there to protect both parties. The client articulates what he wants and the vendor agrees on a time and budget to deliver the client's requirements. If either party becomes dissatisfied during the process, they can refer to the contract to see if there are any breaches of the original agreement and use this a means to claim compensation.

On waterfall projects this contractual agreement is made at the beginning of the process. It is expected that the customer knows exactly what he needs and wants before any work starts. It is expected (contrary to experience) that requirements will not change. There are often furious debates downstream when the customer requests a change and the vendor tells the client that this is a deviation from what was originally specified. Based on the contract, a deviation will extend the launch date and cost more money. Or if the vendor fails to deliver by the agreed deadline, the client may have a case for claiming a penalty against the vendor. All of this takes time, energy, and effort, and it takes the focus away from delivering value. The root cause of the issue is an inflexible philosophy that is not designed to accommodate change.

On an agile project we recognise that the three dimensions of project management are time, scope, and budget. From the outset we gain an understanding of which of these is the most critical. Then we work within these parameters to collaborate on reaching agreement about the right set of requirements that can be delivered within the time and budget available. We acknowledge that we can't know everything up front and we accept that aspects of the project will change.

In other words, change is built into the process. Everyone collaborates on all the activities together.

It's no longer about the business coming up with requirements and then IT doing the estimation, planning, and development. In agile design, IT and the business drive and prioritise requirements, which are then estimated. Based on all this information, we create a plan for what can be delivered. In our experience, it rarely comes down to holding the client to task when a change is requested or holding the vendor to ransom when roadblocks impede progress because everyone is working together to achieve the same goal.

WHAT WE MEAN BY *CUSTOMER*

It is interesting to note the use and meaning of the word *customer* in agile. In the Agile Manifesto, *customer* refers to the client or the business, as is common in the IT world. This sometimes causes confusion, because in experience design we use customer to mean the person who buys from or uses a digital product or service. It's something to be aware of when you are reading agile literature. However, the principle is the same. In the Agile Manifesto, the authors encourage IT to engage and collaborate with their customer—who invariably is the business. In experience design we collaborate with actual customers of the product or service being developed.

In the following example, Tom Illmensee describes the confusion his team felt when Scrum was introduced and insisted on a different use of the word customer. (Scrum is a derivative of agile and can be described as the project management rule book for applying the agile philosophy).

"The peculiar semantics of Scrum were especially confusing at first. In retail, customers were people who bought things like stereos and flat-screen TVs. Not anymore. Agile had changed the definition of perhaps the most important word in our business environment: customers were now internal product owners. [The people we thought of as] customers would now be referred to as shoppers—or users."[2]

Business language backs up our assumption: The employee at the supermarket checkout is called a **customer** service representative; personal **customer** details are held in the bank's **customer** relationship management system; in the electronics store you look for **customer** support, and after completing a purchase, you may be asked to complete a **customer** satisfaction survey.

Since in everyday language a *customer* is the person who makes use of, or buys, products and services, perhaps we need to find a new term for the agile

---

2 Tom Illmensee, from "5 Users Every Friday: A Case Study in Applied Research" presented at Agile 2009.

customer. Reasonable alternatives include client, business, or product owner. It's important to ensure that the whole team are using a common language and that one key word isn't used to mean different things.

RESPONDING TO CHANGE OVER FOLLOWING A PLAN

Organisations seem to believe that products should be planned and designed in detail up front, as though things are not going to change. They employ armies of enterprise architects to devise a road map that reaches five years into the future. Twitter, on the other hand, is barely six years old—it started using Ruby on Rails because that fit the site's purpose at the time. And as Twitter scaled it's moved the back end to Scala. Facebook has been through numerous technologies. Similarly, on the front end, the Facebook look and feel has evolved over time. The site wasn't designed for every eventuality at the beginning because its creators had no idea what those eventualities would be. They iterated.

We'd argue it is far more valuable to iterate your designs on a live product with real feedback than to try to polish something in the lab or rely on research.

This isn't to say you don't need a plan. Wherever your starting point is A and your end point is B you need some semblance of a plan, but keep these points in mind:

- Recognise and acknowledge that your plan is based on what *you know at the time*.
- Don't get too attached to what you have and know. As the Buddhists say, "All attachment is suffering."
- Don't expect to execute your plan 100 percent; as you journey toward point B, things will crop up that will change how you go about reaching your destination.
- If you're not set up to accommodate change, you will find the journey hard going and even impossible at times.
- If you build change into the process and are adaptable and flexible, the journey, and the end product, will be that much better.

CREATING A VISION OF THE END POINT

One of the criticisms of agile methods such as Scrum and Extreme Programming (XP) are that they just take a bunch of requirements, stick them into a backlog, and start writing code against these with no planning at all. While we agree there is value in working software, we believe there is little value if the working software doesn't build the right product for the right people at the right time.

Here's where experience design comes to the fore. No matter how agile the process, we can't just blindly set out on a journey with no idea about where we're headed.

We use experience design techniques to think about the business and the customer, and create a shared vision of what we want to build.

The key is to inform and create a vision that sets the direction for the journey. This is very different from trying to anticipate and specify everything up front before you set off. Remember, however important you think extensive up-front research and design is, the world is moving on without you.

Let's go back in time to 1998 and look at how Google thought of itself in the beginning.

Google Inc. was founded in 1998 by Sergey Brin and Larry Page to make it easier to find high-quality information on the Web. That was their vision. There's nothing there about browsers, phone operating systems, word processors, or spreadsheets. Those are details that emerged on the journey with the vision in mind. It has taken a mere twelve years to go from a "simple" search engine to the Google we know today. In contrast, many enterprises have no idea how to adapt to the changing world. We know of several enterprise projects that are three-plus years into development—a quarter of Google's life—and have yet to deliver any working software or value at all.

We've seen how the Agile Manifesto places a high value on *working software, customer collaboration,* and *responding to change*, and how the waterfall process inherently works against these priorities. Now we'll take our first look at experience in the agile context.

AGILE EXPERIENCE DESIGN

For many organisations, agile offers a welcome, viable, and timely alternative to waterfall. However, as with all change, it is not without critics. One of the main arguments against agile is that while incremental development might be quicker to release smaller chunks of working software, when you combine all the chunks you don't get a cohesive product. Let's start with a metaphor—developing Mona Lisa—which John Armitage introduced in his paper "Are Agile Methods Good for Design?" and Jeff Patton illustrated on his blog agileproductdesign.com.

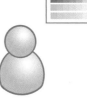

1. Someone in the business has an idea.

2. The development team decompose the idea into stories.

3. Designers say what colours to use.

4. The team deliver in increments, tackling the technically hardest functionality first.

5. They deliver high-quality stories on time and on budget, adding functionality iteratively.

6. Yet the end result is not quite what everyone expected.

The process depicted is far from ideal. Let's see if we can fix it by injecting some user experience.

1. Someone in the business sees an opportunity.

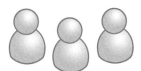

2. A cross-functional team comes together.

3. Everyone has lots of different ideas.

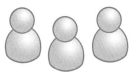

4. Everyone collaborates to reach a shared understanding.

5. They discover new ideas by getting out of the office.

We could use that landscape

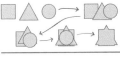
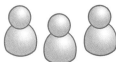

6. Rapid sketching brings the vision to life.

7. With a clearer vision we produce, prioritise, and estimate user stories and create a development plan.

8. Detail emerges throughout the development process, directed by the vision.

9. The result is a useful, usable, and desirable product.

This is not a return to big, up-front design; this is about creating just enough of a product vision that we can set out in the right direction with a view of the end destination in mind. We work out the details as we progress on the journey. The vision can be as simple as a shared set of customer goals that everyone has agreed to deliver on. These goals can be brought to life in rapid sketches and prototypes, but the vision must be created collaboratively and represent the shared view of the project team.

DESIGN IS ALREADY AGILE

One thing that may frustrate experience designers when they hear all this stuff about agile is that the experience design process has always been *agile*, it's just that it has been squeezed into a waterfall phase called design. Experience design has always been about collaborating with end customers. It has always been iterative and emergent. It has always been customer feedback-driven and therefore is accommodating to change. Experience designers tend to have a flexible approach in which they can determine what's appropriate given the project constraints.

Francis Beaudet, Chief Software Architect for Macadamian, wrote:

"In the software world, especially in the past five years, the silver bullet has been agile methodologies.

…Agile is not a process, it's a mitigation strategy…made indispensable by the lack of up-front design. What design brings into the picture, and why it is not just waterfall in disguise, is that design is agile. It's interactive and it's flexible."[3]

There are two key areas where design needs to change to enable its complete integration with agile:

- We need to spread the design effort over the length of the project, rather than trying to do it all up front.
- We need to learn how to collaborate not only with the end customers, but also with the other members of the team to produce the design.

---

3 http://www.macadamian.com.

REDEFINING DONE

Creating agile online customer experiences requires us to redefine what we mean by "done." In the digital world, done means over, out-of-date, past its best—the customers have moved on. The end of the project is only just the beginning for a digital product or service. We need to move beyond the project framework and think about *continuous evolution*. We need to engage in continuous cycle of design, test, and learn and offer constant improvements to the digital customer experience so we keep customers engaged, invested, and loyal—the holy grail for any website. This is where agile, coupled with Lean (see below), starts to shine as a viable alternative to the waterfall process for project delivery.

LEAN PHILOSOPHY

Lean is a management philosophy with roots in the Toyota production system. The philosophy is centred around the main principles of minimising waste (where waste is an activity or inactivity where no value is produced), using automation to remove error and variation out of repeatable processes, and employing *just-in-time* production (creating only what you need based on the information you know at the time). Combining Lean philosophy with the flexible framework of agile puts you in a much better position to recalibrate and reprioritise when conditions change, without compromising on quality or time. ■

Experiences don't stop just because the project has finished. Experiences change over time, due to variations in customer needs, motivations, values, and expectations set by other digital product and service providers—direct competitors and noncompetitors alike. To keep customers satisfied and engaged we need to continuously listen, monitor, and interact with them and be prepared to make changes in line with what we know. We also need to stop thinking about the short-term span of a project and be mindful of the life cycle of a digital product.

THE ONLY CONSTANT IS CHANGE, CONTINUING CHANGE, INEVITABLE CHANGE, THAT IS THE DOMINANT FACTOR IN SOCIETY TODAY.

—Isaac Asimov

PRODUCT VERSUS PROJECT

So what do we mean by *project*?

A project is an effort approved by a business for the purposes of creating— over a limited period time—a product, service, or other predefined result that will deliver a return on the project investment.

Projects have a number of defined dimensions of success, including time, budget, and scope. Projects can be instigated as part of the process of conceiving, creating, and developing a new product for launch. In any new product development process, you'll have both a project manager and a product manager. Their responsibilities are very different. A project manager has two primary goals: ensuring that there are clearly defined project objectives and parameters and that the project team meets the objectives. The role of a product manager is to ensure product success through-out the entire product life cycle, *during and beyond the initial project.*

As one of our clients recently said:

"Project stakeholders expect digital projects to be neatly wrapped up and tied with a bow, but as any entrepreneur in the digital space knows, the project launch is only the beginning."

All too often the differences between a project and a product become blurred. Ask a product manager how difficult it is to get funding for product improvements post-launch and how, despite launching on time, there is still a catalogue of improvements that have yet to be implemented years later.

Look at the products that have stood the test of time because they have evolved and adapted to changing market needs and advances in technology. They may have gone through many different versions since the original launch. Successful products should never be static. Of course this applies as much, if not more, to digital products and experiences as tangible real-world artefacts.

"The immediate needs of the shareholder and the financial mindset of the senior managers have taken precedence over the day-to-day realities of specifying and creating value for the customer."[4]

---

4 *Lean Thinking*, Womack, J.P. & Jones, D.T. Free Press, 2003.

As designers, we must temper what we do in the short-term by keeping our eye on the horizon. We need to think differently about digital product and service development and recognise that it's not done when the project is done. The product launch is only the beginning and there are many more stages a product will go through after launch. Only businesses that continue to innovate in line with customer needs and market forces will thrive.

Digital product success is no longer about meeting the project deadline, or being first to market. It's about creating the right product, at the right time, for the right market, and continuously evolving.

In his essay "Continuous Delivery: The Value Proposition" Jez Humble proposes:

"There are two key components to running a business that depends on software: a vision of how you want to change the world, and feedback from your users, from as early on in the life of your company as possible. The importance of feedback is emphasised by the lean start-up movement, and can be seen at work not only in start-ups, but also on sites like Amazon, Netflix, and Facebook, which are constantly making subtle changes to their sites to increase revenue and improve their users' experience."

Without the vision you don't know what you are aiming for. If you don't know that, you can't measure progress or success. By creating the product vision you can confidently set out on your journey, and by continuously measuring progress you can be sure you're headed in the right direction, even if you veer slightly from the path.

By using smart technology that monitors and measures the digital customer experience in real time, and then acting on the qualitative and quantitative data, we can continuously design and evolve the product to keep up with business, customer, technology, and market advances. That said, to get the most from continuous design we need to continuously improve the live environment. This means automating various parts of the delivery process to enable businesses to frequently deploy valuable, high-quality software to a live environment—which frequently might mean multiple times a *day,* rather than infrequently throughout the year.

By connecting the dots between continuous design and continuous delivery, we truly can exist in a post-project world of continuous evolution.

By monitoring and measuring the customer experience, acting on the real-time data, continuously designing, and continuously delivering to the live environment, we truly can exist in a post-project world of continuous evolution.

IN SUMMARY

In this chapter, we've seen that the waterfall method consists of functional phases strung together sequentially. The success of waterfall projects relies on each functional phase maintaining the intent of the previous phase. From a designer's perspective, this can mean that the product delivered is quite different from the one that was created in the design phase. The designer has little or no opportunity to collaborate and integrate with the engineering team who produce the product.

The Agile Manifesto states that there are major benefits to be realised in working collaboratively and concurrently rather than in a serial fashion. The manifesto is not a complex set of must-do rules, but a collection of preferences that are focused on the creation and delivery of value. We've seen that agile favours *working software, customer collaboration,* and *responding to change.*

By adding experience design into the mix we strengthen the agile proposition, because now we are not only delivering working software at speed, we are also building on a vision that will engage and delight customers.

COMING NEXT

In the next chapter, we'll bust the myth that agile is anti-design and look at where design and the designer fit into agile.

I'M A DESIGNER, WHY SHOULD I CARE?

3

"PEOPLE HAVE ALWAYS DESIGNED THINGS. ONE OF THE MOST BASIC CHARACTERISTICS OF HUMAN BEINGS IS THAT THEY MAKE A WIDE RANGE OF TOOLS AND OTHER ARTEFACTS TO SUIT THEIR OWN PURPOSE. AS THOSE PURPOSES CHANGE... REFINEMENTS ARE MADE...AND SOMETIMES COMPLETELY NEW KINDS OF ARTEFACTS ARE CONCEIVED AND MADE."

—NIGEL CROSS,
ENGINEERING DESIGN METHODS:
STRATEGIES FOR PRODUCT DESIGN

Designers need to care because agile adoption is on the rise and it's a completely different way of working, which requires a new approach and a new attitude toward design.

You might be reading this book because you've crossed paths with agile. Perhaps you're starting a new job with an organisation that uses agile methods, or maybe the company you work for has decided to adopt agile. Like many designers, you probably haven't been too concerned about project management methods before and you may be wondering what all the fuss is about and why you should care.

You need to care because, as organisations look for more effective and efficient ways to deliver projects, more and more of them are adopting agile and derivative methods. You need to understand how agile differs from other working methods: it's one approach that involves everyone on the team, designers and developers alike. How you approach design will change quite drastically as a result of your inclusion in an agile project team. If you don't come to grips with this different way of working, you might find yourself swimming against the tide and pulling in the opposite direction from the rest of the team.

Be under no illusion, like all change, you might feel a little uncomfortable to begin with. You'll probably feel the urge to resist or even revolt; you'll want to revert back to the comfortable world you previously inhabited. Having resisted, revolted, reverted back, and iterated around the process ourselves, we're here to offer comfort and reassurance. As designers, we've survived the transition to agile to become advocates. We have the success stories to prove that agile and design can happily coexist.

IS AGILE ANTI-DESIGN?

Often the first thing designers notice about agile is that there is no design phase. Instead, they see that agile projects dive headlong into development, giving no credence to a designer's belief that design is an essential part of the product development process. What a designer sees are multiple, ridiculously short deadlines where working software is delivered and no consideration is given to the multitude and complexity of the essential design activities. As a result, many designers—believing that design will be severely compromised—go straight into defensive mode.

Agile has openly declared that it is opposed to big, up-front design, which sounds like a criticism of design. This is a position that can leave the uninitiated designer feeling uncomfortable.

Let's add in some context, apply some perspective, and debunk the myth that there's no room for design in agile.

Much of the debate has been about the up-front design of software, so we'll have a quick look at this first and then explore how these arguments apply to experience design.

DESIGN IN SOFTWARE DEVELOPMENT

As we've seen, agile was spurred by a general dissatisfaction with the way that software projects were delivered. Agile moved away from discrete, sequential phases that are function-specific, and instead adopted cross-functional collaboration and concurrent working. Another fundamental shift was to move away from the practise of doing too much of anything—including design—before realising any value. The idea was to do just enough to get started and then refine as we learn more.

This meant that design of the system architecture, which was traditionally done up front and to *n*th degree, was one of the first things to undergo radical change. In his white paper titled *Is Design Dead?*, Martin Fowler explores the "planned design" process, as commonly followed in architectural practice, and compares it to software architecture. Architects draw up the designs and, as they do so, they consider and solve the issues of building design. Once the design is complete, it is handed off to the engineering and construction company who builds from the design.

This is also common practise in software design. Software architects spend a considerable amount of time specifying a system before it is built and then hand over a software design specification to a different team or separate company to build it. This can cause two major issues:

- **It's difficult to address design issues that arise after the design phase is complete.** Since it's impossible to think through all the issues up front, problems will inevitably occur during later phases when the system designers have moved on to other projects.

- **Software architects are no longer developers.** The typical career path for developers starts with writing code. Eventually they graduate to become software architects, who rarely write a line of code. Given the pace at which software development changes, this means that software architects can very quickly become out of touch with development methods and may be less effective when it comes to working out some of the lower-level implementation issues that developers struggle to solve.

The alternative to big, up-front design is *evolutionary design*. Some hard-line devotees of this approach, such as the Extreme Programmers (XP), believe there should be no up-front design. They believe a project should get to code as quickly as possible and that "refactoring" can be done as needed to solve design problems.

LESSONS FOR EXPERIENCE DESIGN

This discussion highlights the use of the word *design* in agile. While the technical community works out how much up-front technical design is appropriate and necessary, we can take some of the same questions and ask them of experience design.

- Does it make any more sense to do all of the experience design up front than it does to do all of the system architecture? Especially when we know and accept that factors that contribute to creating a good experience will change.
- Does it make sense to prolong the period between the initial idea and the time that the business starts to make a return on investment by trying to perfect the product before it is released to market?

Of course not.

Where experience design is considered critical to success we don't believe that projects should start with code, any more than we believe that building construction should start before the concept for the building has been explored.

If that were the case what would the builders start with? Bricks and mortar or with a square foundation? What if the architect designed the building to be made of glass and steel or with a cylindrical form? Would you knock down what the builders have already done and begin again from scratch?

A more effective way of working is to create just enough of a design vision to get started and allow the design detail to emerge by testing, learning, and refining. In the same paper mentioned previously, Martin Fowler concurs by suggesting:

"In order to work, evolutionary design needs a force that drives it to converge. This force can only come from people—somebody on the team has to have the determination to ensure that the design quality stays high."

So is agile anti-design? It's not specifically anti-design, but rather anti-*anything that is perceived to be wasteful or not directly creating value*. So instead of doing all of our design activities in the early stages of the project and then throwing the outputs over the fence to development, we have looked at where we can minimise waste and maximise value, without compromising the quality of the design or the customer experience. The way we do this is to do just enough design thinking to create a design vision that can be tested and validated and then build on the design detail iteratively.

A BIG DESIGN CHALLENGE

IT took the charge and responded to the business need for more efficient and more effective software delivery methods. Now we as designers need to rise to the challenge to redesign design and bring it back in line, and up to speed, with digital development and to inject design into the agile process. We want design to be efficient, effective, and emergent with a vision, but we also want to create engaging and desirable experiences.

The mission of this book is twofold:

- Help designers understand where they fit into the agile process and how to make the most of its advantages.
- Help project managers, developers, and everyone else who is involved in the delivery of software understand how important design is and where it fits into the agile development process.

Design, where it pertains to influencing customer perceptions and consumer behaviour, has traditionally fallen under the purview of the business, or more specifically, the marketing department. Yet it was software developers who created the agile process and so it is fitting that much of the coverage of agile so far has been written by software developers in the pursuit of creating better software.

It's not that agile specifically excludes design. And it doesn't mean that design and the role of designers aren't essential parts of the process. It's just that so far (prior to the publication of this book) no one has really covered design and its role on an agile project.

Experience design is all about solving problems and that requires both logical, analytical thinking as well as creative design thinking.

 TIP

So your first big tip when designing in an agile environment is that you need to create an informed vision for the product/service and use the vision to direct the design detail as it emerges throughout the rest of the project.

When we break down the method for problem solving we can see that it has component parts, comprising a number of related and complementary activities. Whilst the activities might vary depending on the context, the designer, and the design challenges, the process is repeatable.

We first look at the business and end-customer needs and context. We look at different ways to solve the problem, get feedback, and refine the ideas down to one or two that we then explore in increasing detail. This general process is the same regardless of whether you're working in a waterfall or an agile environment. The main difference is that in waterfall all of the above is done in a single phase of the project by the designers working in isolation. However, on an agile project the activities are dispersed through the project and done collaboratively (3.1).

3.1
A design methodology.

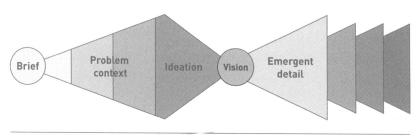

Brief — Problem context — Ideation — Vision — Emergent detail

Start — Launch — Evolution

Agile practitioners recommend getting straight to the business of coding and delivering working software as soon as possible. However, working software is not a means to an end. If the software doesn't add value to both the business and the end customers, then it's just vanity code. So before we get to the part where we are developing design detail we need to make sure that we have an informed and well-considered vision.

The vision becomes the foundation and the framework for the product or service as it is in development.

The vision will not only steer the direction of development, but also keep it on the right path. Informed changes are welcome, but random ramblings from the path are not.

The creation of the design vision can sometimes be overlooked on on agile projects. This is often simply because many agile project managers come from a technical background and are not familiar with the product development process from a business or design perspective. Yet this is a vital part of the process and needs to be included on all projects where customer experience is critical to success. Without the time to consider the business and customer context and then to use that information to inform the design vision, designers struggle during delivery.

Unlike stories, which can be developed in small independent chunks, the small chunks of design are completely dependent on each other to create a comprehensive, consistent, and engaging experience. This doesn't happen by chance. The bigger picture must be considered in advance of having a hungry development army to feed.

Again, this is not big up-front design. The design vision is all about doing just enough to lay down the foundations and set a clear direction. Even Martin Fowler agrees:

"I'm known for being a cowardly XPer, and as such I have to disagree [about getting straight into code detail]. I think there is a role for a broad, starting point architecture."

So the challenge is to understand what constitutes just enough when it comes to design and not falling back into old habits of creating too much detail too soon. We'll explore this in more detail in Chapter 7, "Envisioning Success."

WHERE DESIGN FITS

Here's an awesome picture created by a designer that describes the steps involved in building a website (3.2).

A Web Site Designed
MILESTONES, INVOLVEMENT, IMPORTANCE & TIMELINE

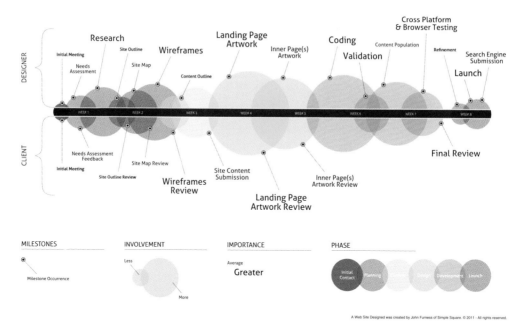

3.2
A website designed (www.simplesquare.com).

Take a look at the time frames and the importance that the creator gives each activity. We don't have a problem with the particular activities; in fact, we'll talk about them in depth later in this book. But we know that this image would be problematic for the agilistas, who might choke on their coffee to see that only one-eighth of the project is spent on coding. That equates to just one week of development for every eight weeks of the project.

Design without content and development is little more than an abstract concept with no value until it is brought to life and used by someone.

Designers might counter the argument by saying that without a customer-centric approach to design, developers can construct a website and populate it with content, but if it fails to engage customers then it equally has no value.

So who is right? Both viewpoints are right, but they are far more powerful when combined. True value is realised by working software that delivers experiences that are customer-centred, useful, usable, engaging, and desirable.

The question that most designers have when they first come across agile is, "Where does design fit in?" There is no phase called "design" on any agile project plan because the activities within a project are much more integrated. The key elements of success on an agile project are in fact integration and collaboration.

Successful design is not done in an exclusive phase, in a vacuum, or even exclusively by designers. Design needs to be an integrated consideration in all project inputs and outputs. It also should be a continuous activity from the beginning of the project (or even before a project is kicked off—more on that later) throughout the life cycle of the project and beyond.

Agile teams are cross-functional; each team member contributes a wealth of knowledge from her functional area. The agile project environment allows the designer to take advantage of the cross-functional intelligence and to use it as inspiration, influence, and a source of design input.

Therefore, there are two answers to the question about where design fits in. If you keep an open mind about design and agile, you will find that you can adopt and make both of these answers work for you:

- Design when required
- Design throughout the entire process

DESIGN WHEN REQUIRED

Adaptive agile borrows from lean manufacturing to avoid creating inventories and stockpiles of stuff that could be wasted if there is no demand.

Don't spend too much time trying to anticipate design demand; instead, put yourself in a good position to react quickly when demand actually arrives.

This means adopting principles like *just-in-time* design and *just-enough* design. Just-in-time design does what it says on the tin. We don't design months or years in advance; we do it as soon as we recognise a need. We do this because, in the current climate, change is a relentless, indomitable force that drives us to look at the way we respond to market need in every arena.

The market is demanding change and it wants it yesterday.

Consumers are almost arrogant in their impatience for change—and they want it cheaper, faster, and better.

They are no longer willing to wait for anything. They have become fickle in their pursuit of convenience. They are loyal only to those brands that deliver instant gratification and woe betide the brand that doesn't deliver on their expectations. If they don't get what they want when they want it, they switch loyalties as quickly as they change their minds.

Fast food may have started the trend for consumer convenience, but it has infected every other consumer market too. The digital space is probably the least tolerant of delay because there are no tangible manufacturing processes that can be forgiven for causing the delays.

This is the primary reason that we don't want to do big, up-front design. By the time a big up-front design gets to market, the market has moved on to the next big thing and no one is buying what we have to sell. We have to become more flexible, more agile in the way that we respond to the market.

"80 percent ready means it's market-ready; 100 percent ready means it's out-dated," said Tony Tomazic, Director of Consumer Innovations at Humana Health Care, at a recent customer experience conference.

Many of us work in or for large corporate enterprises where there are multiple processes to protect the organisation, reduce risk, and make all operations consistent. All this bureaucracy can add weight and fat to the process, making it longer and more difficult than necessary. That's when we need to think differently. Instead of single-handedly trying to steer the oil tanker in a different direction, we need to drop speedboats into the ocean to test the waters and to see what lies just ahead. We need the ability to think and act more like a start-up.

This also means recognising when design is required, when it's not, and how much design is appropriate. If we are launching a "me too" type of product, where the market is well understood and the design patterns are well established, we don't need to spend months researching user needs to ultimately redesign the wheel, when we have one that works perfectly well. In this case, we do just enough learning to understand design and then we adapt and tweak to fit.

We can probably spend a little more time on design in cases where we have a new product in a new market, but we still want to get to market as quickly as possible so we can test, learn, and refine over time while we make money.

DESIGN THROUGHOUT THE ENTIRE PROCESS

Design isn't a phase that we go through. It isn't something that should be executed and given the tick of approval so that we can move on.

Design starts at the onset of a project, or even before the project starts. It is done throughout the project life cycle and continues long after product launch.

We will look in more detail at the agile project process and the opportunities for design involvement over the next few chapters. For now, we'll take a high-level view of how design is developed on an agile project, noting in particular where the experience of the end customer is critical to business success.

STRATEGY
WITHOUT
TACTICS IS THE
SLOWEST ROUTE
TO VICTORY.
TACTICS WITHOUT
STRATEGY IS THE
NOISE BEFORE
DEFEAT.

—Sun Tzu, *The Art of War*

Without considering phases and naming conventions, the following list describes the general activities needed to undertake to develop a product or service (3.3):

- Understand *why* we are doing this. Look at the business problem/opportunity space.

- Understand *who* we are doing it for: the customers who will benefit from the solution to this problem/opportunity.

- Consider *what* the design challenge is and generate multiple possible ideas to solve the problem or suit the opportunity. Refine the ideas down to the most suitable candidates based on the experience equation.

- Dive into *how* you will create the product/service vision, the foundation on which the rest of the product will be built.

- Execute the vision through concurrent design and development practises, using the vision to guide design detail which will emerge throughout the product life cycle.

3.3
A process for
specifying value.

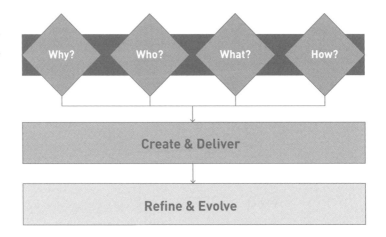

By ensuring that we understand the why, who, what, and how of the product development process, we have a firm foothold that will allow us to move forward with confidence. Keep in mind that we have to spend just enough time on each of those questions to get started.

Once we get into the development cycle of the project, design occurs concurrently with other project activities, not sequentially. We do this because it allows for better cross-functional collaboration. The designers must remember that design affects, and is affected by, most of the project's other functional concerns. To have any real chance of holistic success, we need to take those other functions into account as we develop the design (3.4).

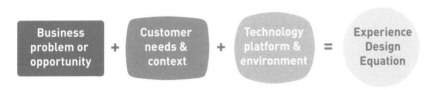

3.4
The experience design equation.

EXPERIENCE STRATEGY

We've looked at where experience design fits into an agile project, but we also want to look at where it fits into the larger organisational ecosystem. In organisations that believe that customer experience is critical and a strategic differentiator, there is tight alignment between business, brand, and experience strategy.

The purpose of any strategy is to give you a game plan. First you envision where you want to get to and clearly articulate the value and benefits that success will bring. Then you take a look at your current position and what is in your arsenal. Then you create a plan, which plays to your strengths while fortifying your weaknesses, that will get you from where you are to where you want to be. Any good leader from history will tell you that your strategy is the difference between success and failure, between winning and losing.

Your experience strategy needs to be aligned with the overall business strategy, and it also should be closely interlinked with other strategic initiatives, including brand strategy. So let's take a quick look at what we mean by each of these (3.5).

3.5
Strategic alignment.

A STRATEGY
DELINEATES
A TERRITORY
IN WHICH A
COMPANY SEEKS
TO BE UNIQUE.

—Michael Porter,
Competitive Strategy
Expert

BUSINESS STRATEGY

Business strategy is the top-line vision for the company. It is the reason that
the business exists and it is there to ensure long-term growth and sustainability.
A business strategy includes the core values, mission, and purpose of the
organisation and is the basis for core competencies and offerings.

BRAND STRATEGY

The brand strategy is driven by the business strategy, but looks at the needs,
desires, and motivations of potential customers to create an appealing and
engaging proposition. Brand strategy is expressed by the brand identity (name,
logos, colours, imagery, and so on), and this shapes and influences both
the internal and external representation of the organisation and its products
and services.

CUSTOMER EXPERIENCE STRATEGY

**The customer experience is the sum of the activities, events, and interactions
that a customer participates in, which stimulates emotional responses and
shapes perceptions and ultimately influences consumer behaviour.**

Customer experience strategy defines the relationship and the interactions between the organisation and its customers across all interactions, touchpoints, and channels. The customer experience is a holistic and cross-functional initiative and requires buy-in and support across many disciplines within an organisation and close alignment to other strategic initiatives.

DIGITAL STRATEGY

The digital strategy determines the customers' experience with the organisation's digital presence, accessed via the Internet.

A digital strategy includes understanding the digital customers (who may differ from offline customers), the company website, portability and mobility, digital marketing, digital and social relationship management, as well as measures and analytics of the digital channel (3.6).

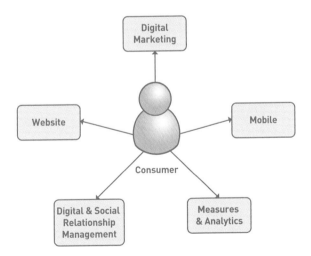

A BRAND FOR
A COMPANY
IS LIKE A
REPUTATION
FOR A PERSON.
YOU EARN
REPUTATION BY
TRYING TO DO
HARD THINGS
WELL.

—Jeff Bezos, Founder,
Amazon.com

3.6
Digital strategy.

The majority of this book looks at how to design digital products within an agile framework. However, we wanted to call out where digital strategy fits into the broader context because customers don't care about organisational structure and channels. They will freely swap between online and offline touchpoints and channels and expect a consistent and holistic experience.

As a digital designer or product owner, it's essential to understand the overall company objectives to ensure that whatever you are creating is strategically aligned. So while you consider digital experience design within the confines of an agile project also think about how you can influence, and be influenced by, other strategic initiatives within the organisation.

WHO ARE DESIGNERS?

Before we get into the details about design and agile, let's first define what we mean by design and look at who traditionally does design. Up to now we have referred to the designer in the proverbial sense. This can be dangerous as it's not uncommon for nondesign people to assume that all designers are equal and that every designer can do everything that uses design in the title. Designers come in many shades and tones and some might have generalist skills, whilst others are quite specialised. To ensure that we're all speaking the same language, let's explore some of the design roles and their respective skill sets (3.7):

3.7
Taxonomy of
Experience Design.

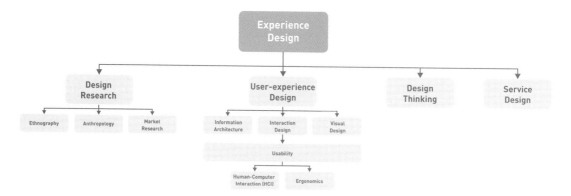

- **User-interface design, interaction design, and usability** underlie much of what we do in experience design today. They in turn were all influenced by human-computer interaction (HCI). The focus was primarily to design for and measure task interaction completion, efficiency, error prevention/recovery, and intuitiveness.

- **Experience design (XD)** is concerned with the design of customers' interactions with products, services, and systems that shape and influence consumer behaviour. Experience design can often involve the creation of experiences that traverses online and offline throughout the entire customer life cycle, and is not limited to software design. Therefore, an experience designer is often polyskilled in user-centred research, interaction and information design, and usability.

- **UI developers and front-end developers** are closer to developers than designers as they spend their time writing presentation layer code. They are often the link between the front end and designers and the back end and developers as they can speak both languages.

- **Information architecture/architects** categorise data or information into a coherent structure that customers can make sense of and find what they are looking for.

- **Visual design/designer** is concerned with the look and feel and the brand elements of a user interface and is most closely related to graphic design. A visual designer considers typography, colour, iconography, layout, image style, and brand development.

- **Design research/researchers** combine disciplines such as usability, ethnography, anthropology, and market research. This combined approach is used to investigate factors that might influence and contribute to the design of a user interface. A design researcher who specialises in research, may, in fact, do no design at all.

For the purposes of the rest of this book, unless we call it out specifically, when we refer to the designer, we mean:

the experience designer who carries a toolkit that includes ethnography, anthropology, psychology, creative design, design thinking, product design, service design, interaction design, information design, and usability.

This designer is responsible for creating the experience that customers have with a digital product or service. Having provided the definition, we hope to inspire more appreciation and a better understanding both amongst designers and non-designers alike.

CURRENT INFLUENCES ON EXPERIENCE DESIGN

There are three other design areas that are worth calling out here because they have had a big influence on experience design as we know it today:

- **Design thinking** appeared on the scene a few years ago and takes the creative approach of traditional design into a business context. The idea is to enable nontraditional design people to use the creative methods of designers to inspire original thinking, more creative strategic approaches, and better product innovation. Design thinking has some great proponents, including organisations such as IDEO and Harvard Business School. Stanford University have even gone so far as to create their own d:school:Institute of Design. It has helped to bring creative thinking and human-centred design into the boardroom and has helped to pave the way for a better appreciation of the value of experience design.

- **Service design** is about creating ecosystems of connected products, services, communications, and environments with people and for people that enable the co-creation of value. Where user-interface design, for example, looks primarily at the user interaction for a single system, service design considers all the links in the customer-provider chain across channels, across organisational silos, across systems. It has influenced how experience designers think beyond the original scope of the website and think more holistically about the customer experience and how the digital channels integrate with the offline channels.

- **Lean start-up** applies the philosophies of just-in-time and just-enough to the business start-up process. It looks to rapidly generate and test business ideas in the marketplace at lightning speed. The idea is to either fail fast—that is, kill the concept that isn't working as quickly as possible, before wasting any time or money developing it further, or scale quick—so for concepts that have shown promise of success in early testing we want to get the "minimal viable product" into the hands of customers so we can test and learn. Of course experience design has always been about testing early and testing often, but lean start-up begins by testing the business case.

DESIGN THINKING

by Deborah Kneeshaw, founder of Sydney Design Thinkers

Design thinking is a way of thinking and doing which combines the creative techniques used by designers with rigorous business practice. It differs from conventional approaches in several key aspects:

- Design Thinking looks at each project within the context of the bigger picture, embracing complexity and systems thinking, in order to produce sustainable solutions rather than short-term fixes.

- Design Thinking emphasises the needs of customers, end users and stakeholders, and designs solutions based on their needs.

- Design thinking practitioners produce multiple original ideas, which are tested at an early stage.

- Design Thinking is highly collaborative and inclusive and provides a powerful vehicle for teams to work together creatively. Ideas then go through several iterative rounds of refinement, usually involving customer feedback, often before detailed implementation.

Design thinking is a practical innovation tool that can be successfully used to either improve or invent services, products, systems, and strategy. It is useful when creative approaches are needed, whether it's at a micro level to simply shift perspective on a minor challenge, or at a macro level to solve the "wicked problems" of the 21st century. New challenges and situations that have not been encountered before, such as global warming, and that require new ways of thinking. ▪

IN SUMMARY

As a designer, you need to care about agile because adoption of this process is increasing, and it delivers concrete benefits to businesses and customers. You need to take some time to become familiar with agile because the process is quite different to how you have worked in the past. Contrary to what you might have heard, agile and design can happily coexist and, once you understand and have practised within the guidelines, you can adapt them to ensure that your projects take advantage of the opportunities that both design and agile have to offer.

As designers, we have the opportunity to reinject design back into agile projects. We need to create a design vision that will direct the emergent detail. Creating the design vision is not a return to big, up-front design but rather a just-in-time approach to laying the foundations and setting the direction for project development.

There are many design disciplines, but for the rest of this book, when we say designer, we mean the polyskilled experience designer who draws from many different disciplines to create the ideal sequence of interactions to influence perceptions and behaviour.

COMING NEXT

In the next chapter, we'll look at agile project management and how a cross-functional team, collaborating on iterative development, can yield better quality results faster. We'll look at tips for designers working on an agile project and tips for project managers and other team members working with designers.

SETTING THE SCENE 4

"COMING TOGETHER IS A BEGINNING.
KEEPING TOGETHER IS PROGRESS.
WORKING TOGETHER IS SUCCESS." —HENRY FORD

Let's begin our journey into agile by understanding what makes agile different from other working methods and how all of this affects designers.

Success. Now there's an interesting word. By definition, success means the accomplishment of desired aims or goals. Achieving success is the holy grail of any business or project. The pursuit of success is the reason businesses invest time and money; it's the reason we take risks. This book is about design and we want to look not only at what makes design successful, but also how the involvement of designers on an agile project contributes to the overall project, and ultimately business success.

In this chapter, we'll take an initial look at agile project management, communication styles, rituals, processes, and environments and then talk about ways to improve the chances of both design and project success by integrating design and designers into the agile project framework.

AN AGILE EXPERIENCE DESIGN PROJECT

To get an idea of experience design on an agile project, let's think about what's needed to get us from the start to the finish. Creating a mental model for these activities makes them easier to understand and apply, so we've grouped them into the following five stages (4.1).

4.1
Iterative activities grouped together with the agile project framework.

PROJECT ACTIVITIES NOT DEFINITIVE GATES

There are no hard and fast rules about where you should start or when you need to move on to the next set of activities. In fact, you might repeat some activities in each phase, iterating, testing, and building on previous learnings. Rather than being prescriptive about how long and when, we recommend a more lean and agile approach. Just do what you need to do and then move on. If you find you're missing information at any given point, you can simply iterate through the activities again and build on your initial findings.

DISCOVER—ASK WHY

We look to gather customer, business, and technical insights that will provide us with the customer and business goals and identify opportunities for inspiration, improvement, and innovation. Often, you'll find stakeholders entering the process assuming they already know the answers to the *why* and *what* questions. Great if they do! Your objective is to get their thinking out on the table to be understood and agreed to by *all* the stakeholders. Equally, there may be some scenarios where nobody has really stopped to ask *why*. The idea sounds good on paper, but why should anybody care? Who are the customers and why might they use it? What do they *really* want and need? If we can't answer those questions, we're not ready to think about the *how*. There's no point in pulling together a plan if the fundamental proposition isn't going to fly.

Gather customer, business, and technical insights that provide insight into customer and business goals and identify opportunities for inspiration, improvement, and innovation.

ENVISION—ASK WHAT

Now that we've identified the customer and business goals, we can ask what we need to do to meet them. We don't want just one solution at the start. We're looking for a design vision, a direction for the product, with the full knowledge that this may change as the product evolves.

We place the customer at the heart of our design thinking to produce a multitude of ideas to create different opportunities.

We rapidly test these ideas with the people whose lives will be touched by the product we build for them. Those that are promising we'll elaborate on. Those that are duds we'll kill early and cheaply.

The key to our approach is not to spend months thinking. The market is moving on. The decision on how far to go will depend on the context and the maturity of the business. If you're a start-up, you don't have the luxury of testing ideas in a closed environment. You want to get stuff to market as soon as possible and adapt as you go. If you have an established product in an established marketplace, you may wish to build a prototype to test your ideas before committing to costly development.

ELABORATE—ASK HOW

With a design vision in mind we now look to do just enough to start development. We elaborate on the vision and plan what we'll need to do to get a product into production as quickly as possible. We'll agree on a first cut of the project scope: what the desired customer journeys are, sketches to illustrate screens, and user stories that are estimated and prioritised.

DEVELOP—LET'S DO IT

Agile software development is a social activity. No longer does the designer throw artefacts over the fence in the hope that they may be delivered; in the agile process the designer is a member of the team. She works closely with the business analyst to clarify the stories just ahead of when the code is written. Indeed, sometimes the developers start coding *before* the design is done.

We think about the critical path and, as in lean manufacturing, produce our design inventory just in time.

Clearly, we can't always work in this way; we may need to iterate our ideas before coding starts. Alongside the development iterations we're spiking design options, working up different options to test and validate in a safe environment outside the main development effort. Testing is key. Usability testing is not a formal procedure done at the end of the project; it's baked in from the start.

EVOLVE—CONTINUE TO IMPROVE

Once your product is in the hands of your customers, you can really start *learning* how to make it better. Up to this point you only have a bunch of hypotheses about how good it *could* be and how it *should* work. The idea is that you release the first cut of your product and then continuously enhance it, learning what works and what doesn't, and evolve the product to make it ever better.

Unlike the past, when software was brittle and the cost of change meant you had to get it right the first time, today software really is *soft*. Focus on what is important to your business and to your customers and get something to market fast and early, even if it's just a pilot beta with a small, invited panel of trusted loyal customers, and let real behaviour and customer feedback inform your decisions.

You then seek to continuously improve your product through a process of test and learn.

You can learn subjectively through usability tests, customer surveys, and the like, and objectively through analytics, split testing, and so on.

IGNORANCE
IS THE SINGLE
GREATEST
IMPEDIMENT TO
THROUGHPUT.

—Dan North, Agile
troublemaker,
developer,
originator of BDD

REMOVING UNCERTAINTY

Think of a time-boxed period where we do just enough to get the project started. Or changed. Or cancelled. We want to create models that we can test and validate at speed. We want to produce a design vision of where we want to go and elaborate on that vision to get us going.

When we start a project it looks something like this (4.2).

The line of uncertainty

4.2
The line of uncertainty.

There's a line of uncertainty. In fact, we can only really be sure of three things:

- Change is inevitable and things will go wrong.
- We can't know what will change and what will go wrong.
- When things go wrong or change is required, it will cause us pain and suffering.

Rather than being oblivious to these truths, producing a watertight vision that everyone believes will be delivered in its entirety, or trying to second-guess how things might change or what might go wrong, we should create an environment in which we can explore areas where we have the greatest uncertainty and try to mitigate the risks. Based on this principle we have two options:

- Do just enough *that is good enough* to provide us with a direction that we all agree is the right one based on the information available today.
- Be ready to kill the idea early or change, *pivot*, when the available information tells us this is the right thing to do.

When thinking about a project, we need to be mindful of those three questions— *why, what,* and *how*—before we *do* or *evolve.* So let's overlay those questions as a funnel on top of the line of uncertainty (4.3).

4.3
Using the model to reduce uncertainty through the product development life cycle.

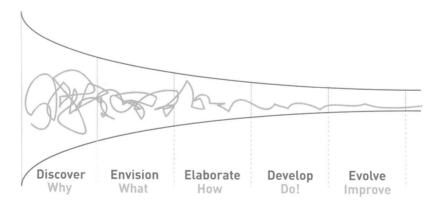

Discover	Envision	Elaborate	Develop	Evolve
Why	What	How	Do!	Improve

Unlike the familiar approach to interface design, which can take a leisurely approach to *what* to build, and agile, which is quick to focus on doing the actual build, agile experience design brings together the best of these two approaches, providing a framework to remove uncertainty and do the right thing.

ACTIVITIES, NOT A PROCESS

We use this framework of *discover, envision, elaborate, deliver, evolve* to reduce uncertainty. Don't look at this as Gantt-chart-driven phases with deliverables due before the next phase can commence. These are activities to clarify thinking and product direction, not a prescriptive process. They may happen at the same time; you discover and envision new ideas as you develop. You may spend only a day in research, and a couple of days distilling your insights into a vision and elaborating requirements to start development. How you work will depend on the team and your environment. Take this framework as inspiration and adapt it to what works best for you, continuously improving as you evolve.

THE LAST RESPONSIBLE MOMENT

Whenever you start work on a project there are choices and options that you'll make on the way. Of course you want to make the right decisions. But the right decisions will be based on having the right information, and at the beginning of the project, it's unlikely this will be the case. It's easy to give yourself a false sense of security by basing your design work in detail on assumptions.

Here's an old joke: *A man is driving in the countryside and is lost. He asks a farmer for directions and the farmer says, "If I were going there, I wouldn't be starting here."*

People often think there is only a right decision or a wrong decision. What they miss is the no-decision option. Sometimes we don't need to make a decision at that moment. It is possible to defer it to a later time, when you'll know more and be able to make a more informed decision.

In his book *The Toyota Way,* Jeffrey Liker describes how Toyota developed the Prius. With a tight time frame and a vague goal of developing a "fuel-efficient, small-sized car," the team:

- Tested over 20 different suspensions simultaneously.
- Worked on 80 different hybrid engines before whittling them down to one.
- Started with twenty designs and then, through a design competition, selected two that were revised based on feedback before a final design was chosen.

The point is that the team didn't fixate on one particular solution too early. In fact, they simultaneously pursued a number of different options to rule out the bad and go with the good. Sure, there was a short-term cost, but greater rewards were reaped later.

It's all too easy to decide on a particular direction and get fixated on it.

Thinking about our process we could continue to explore different options and only decide which one to take at the last responsible moment.

Beyond that moment the option expires (4.4).

4.4
Defer the decision until
the last responsible
moment.

This is one of the most fundamental concepts in agile experience design. Don't make decisions unless you have to. Don't spec out the user interface in detail until that detail is required.

AGILE TEAM STRUCTURE AND THE ROLE OF THE DESIGNER

As organisations recognise the advantages that agile can deliver, we're increasingly seeing agile and its derivatives as the delivery project management tool of choice. This is especially true in the commercial world of digital product development, where the promises of early working software and a flexible, scalable process that enables an adaptive approach to product development is very attractive.

The world of digital product and service development is one where customer experience is critical to business success. Despite this, the role of experience design has been somewhat underrepresented on agile projects to date. Agile project managers apply project patterns and team structures that are applicable for software delivery projects.

But when the focus shifts to be more experience-centric, those patterns need some adjustment.

We're here to inject design back into experience-centric agile projects.

So let's have a look at the typical agile team and the role design plays in an experience-centric project. Rather than trying to inject designers into the team, we'll look at a couple of different project requirements and cross-match them with the applicable skill sets, to help agile project managers get the right people for the job. We'll explore options including "design pairing" to increase efficiency, quality, collaboration, and knowledge sharing, and then finish this section with a look at how to avoid some of the pitfalls of cross-functional teams.

SILOED FUNCTIONS VS. CROSS-FUNCTIONAL TEAMS

Most organisational structures are made up of functional silos, and lines of reporting follow functional expertise and authority. In general, there are only two opportunities for cross-functional collaboration. One is at the very top, where the heads of each functional division collaborate on the strategic direction for the organisation. The other is on projects, where expertise from each functional area is required to contribute to project success. However, even within projects, prior to the advent of agile, each phase was assigned to separate functional group of specialists and generally executed and delivered in sequence.

One problem with this approach is it can introduce functional bias. This is where a functional team, undertaking their functional project phase, pulls the project in a particular direction relevant to their area of expertise, without considering other functional areas. The subsequent function receives the outputs from the previous phase, and with limited appreciation for the previous functional expertise, then pulls the project in a different direction, adding alternative bias toward their own functional area (4.5).

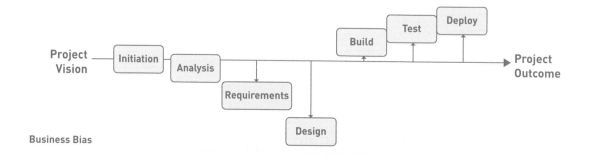

4.5

Potential functional
bias on a sequential
project.

The best way to avoid this situation is for cross-functional teams to collaborate to create a solution. Agile uses the cross-functional team approach primarily because it offers many advantages, including:

- **Efficiency:** A collocated team comprising functional experts collaborating to reach a common goal will succeed far more quickly than a team separated by function, acting in a sequential manner.

- **Knowledge sharing:** The communication, team learning, and knowledge sharing process is much more efficient in a cross-functional team. Furthermore, members of the cross-functional team then cross-pollinate knowledge and communication with their original functional group.

- **Innovation:** By bringing together people from diverse backgrounds you're providing the stimulus for multidisciplinary thinking, a potential catalyst for increased creativity and innovation.

- **Holistic success:** A cross-functional team is more focused on a common directive rather than siloed functional success.

However, bringing a bunch of people together from different backgrounds, disciplines, and areas of expertise and just expecting them to get on with it, get on well, and be successful is a tall order. A cross-functional team needs both a strong leader (not manager) and members of the team to be self-directed. To be self-directed, roles and responsibilities need to be clear and individuals and the team need to be empowered to make the right decisions at the right time. They also need to share a common directive or vision.

THE TYPICAL AGILE PROJECT TEAM

In most books about agile you'll find an amorphous description of the agile project team. This is because agile is less prescriptive about who does what and is more concerned with getting the job done. In his book *The Agile Samurai,* Jonathan Rasmusson suggests that "roles blur on agile projects and they are going to be expected to wear many hats…there are people who know what needs to be built…and people who can build it…agile is less concerned about who plays what role and more worried about the right roles being played." [1]

It's much less about roles and much more about activities and the appropriate skills to do the activities. This means that a developer can write tests or undertake analysis of a user story with a product owner without other team members getting territorial. In common practise though, for reasons of efficiency, individuals stick to the activities that they have expertise in. But when a blockage in the delivery pipeline occurs, team members can apply themselves to other functional activities with which they are not traditionally involved.

THE ROLE OF THE EXPERIENCE DESIGNER ON AN AGILE PROJECT

The responsibility of an experience designer (or design pair) on an agile team is to create the design vision and drive the design direction for the experience that a customer will have when engaging with a product, service, or whole system.

So what do all these cross-functions and blurred roles mean for design and designers? Well, in the same way that a developer still writes code, and analysts still analyse information, designers still design. It just means that potentially, where time and skills allow, designers can also do other activities and other team members can get involved in some aspects of design. But don't let this put

1 Rasmusson, J. The agile Samurai, The Pragmatic Programmers, 2010.

you off. This doesn't diffuse quality or undermine the expertise of the designer; we still have a very important job to do. Let's look at that in a bit more detail.

The responsibility of an experience designer on an agile team is to work alongside the product owner and business analysts to create the design vision and design direction for the customer experience and define what will be built. The designer also works alongside the developers and testers to figure out how it can be built. You have the whole team or specific members or functions within a team who can input to design and help with problem solving.

Once the design vision is drafted, designers are then responsible, again with other team members, for the design detail. With a design vision in place, the details can emerge throughout the life cycle of the design development. However, and this is where we diverge from some more purist views of agile, design detail should not be emergent without a design vision to hold it all together. It is absolutely essential that time is spent before development of the experience layer on thinking holistically about the design vision.

Create a design vision that will provide focus for the rest of the design activities and guide design detail as it emerges.

SKILLS VS. ROLES: TIPS FOR PROJECT MANAGERS

There are a number of distinct skill sets that come under the umbrella of *design*; non-designers might be forgiven for thinking that all designers do every sort of design. However, that is not the case and a project manager who makes that assumption will be in as much trouble as one who believes that all developers know how to code in Java.

The best way to avoid problems and make sure that the team have the correct competencies and capabilities is to think about the skills needed rather than thinking about the roles. What's the difference? "The designer" is a role, but there are many different areas that a designer might specialise in (4.6).

content analysis **interaction design**
user research rapid prototyping ethnographic research
user-experience design product design
guerrilla testing **sketching** usability testing
user profiling ideation **collaborative design**
process flows information architecture
visual design competitor analysis GUI design
service design **design thinking**
customer journey mapping

You can see from the word cloud that a broad range of skills is available, and even if you don't necessarily understand what each of those skills involves, you can probably appreciate that it's hard to find all of those skills in a single designer. Some of the skills listed above are not exclusive to designers either. Talk to all the people on the team to see who has skills and experience in particular areas (4.7).

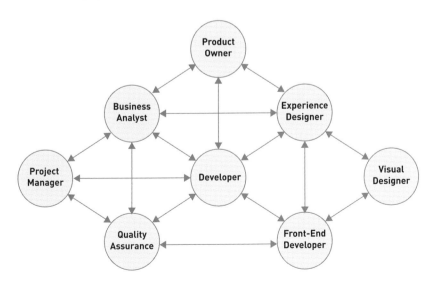

GENERALISTS VS. SPECIALISTS

Which is better: generalists or specialists? The answer depends on the breadth and depth of the problem. The deeper the problem goes into a specific area, the more it requires specific skills and the more you're likely to need a specialist in that area.

A specialist is someone who concentrates primarily on a particular subject, activity, or field, and his expertise is based on years of experience dedicated to that particular cause. A generalist is a person who has competencies in one or more fields.

In his book *Ten Faces of Innovation,* IDEO General Manager Tom Kelley describes "T-shaped individuals," who he says, "enjoy a breadth of knowledge in many fields, but…also have depth in at least one area of expertise."

Pabini Gabriel-Petit, Founder, Publisher, and Editor in Chief of UXmatters, provides the following definition: "User experience design takes a holistic, multidisciplinary approach to the design of user interfaces for digital products. It integrates interaction design, industrial design, information architecture, visual interface design, user assistance design, and user-centred design, ensuring coherence and consistency across all of these design dimensions. User experience design defines a product's form, behaviour, and content." And he goes on to suggest that "a UX designer is, by definition, one example of a T-shaped person."

Whether you decide to plug for a specialist, a generalist, or a T-shaped person the key is to match that person's skills with the understanding of your project's requirements. If you have limited understanding or limited budget, then the safest option is to find a generalist and set his expectations. A good generalist will let you know if additional expertise in a particular area is needed and will even help you build a case to justify the additional resource if necessary.

GIVE UP CONTROL TO GAIN CONTROL

Designers are used to controlling all the aspects of a design, from the start of the design phase to the end. Since the dotcom era, some of the more enlightened organisations have recognised that it is not enough to do design in a vacuum. Instead, they recognise and embrace the notion of customer-centred design: the idea that the design should be focused on the customer's wants, needs, and context of use. If the process is truly customer-centred, then customers should be involved throughout the design development. From the outset, where you spend time understanding the customers' world: who the customers are, what they do and how they do it, to getting them involved in collaborative design or user testing throughout the process.

So the point here is while it's good to understand the users of the system and their context, it's equally essential to add the business and technology concerns into the mix too. Now we're not expecting that on top of being experts in design that designers should also become business experts and technology experts. We are, however, advocating that designers collaborate with business representatives and developers throughout the project life cycle. This collaboration, together with the continued application of user-centred design methods will help to ensure that any designs deliver business value, provide an engaging and desirable experience for the customers, and are feasible from a technology point of view.

It's not enough to just engage with these different stakeholder groups at the onset of the project; you need to be in constant consultation with them throughout the project. As you know, things change frequently in design, and so too they change frequently in business and technology. The design needs to be continuously recalibrated to reflect the fluid nature of the age in which we live.

AVOIDING PITFALLS: TRIBAL BEHAVIOUR

Projects would be great if it weren't for the people, right? Team dynamics can make or break any situation and all the benefits of collocation definitely ring true when the team members play nicely together. However, for teams to work well together, the individual team members must all contribute to or buy into the vision and feel that they are making a worthwhile contribution that is valued by the other team members.

Having a collocated team can help to break down tribal behaviours associated with functional groups, as the functional group identity is not preeminent in a cross-functional team. However, to avoid tribal behaviour it is important that each of the functions is represented and not disadvantaged. DK Matai, writing about digital tribes, says:

"The predominant characteristic of tribes throughout time is the need to share and to communicate ideas, thoughts, observations and views."[2]

TRIBAL IDENTIFICATION

Janelle McGuinness, Head of eBusiness at an international direct retail bank

By nature, individuals have a "tribal" identification with their particular discipline and are often protective of the teams they have come from. So when they are thrown into a new cross-functional team they may not fully appreciate the skills and perspective of other specialists. Whilst each team member can provide opinions and suggestions, to keep delays to a minimum it should be clear who has responsibility for decision making in particular areas as well as deciding when to escalate, and to whom. Ultimately, making the team responsible for their collective success, and rewarding the team—not individuals—helps to ensure the teamwork necessary to achieve the desired outcome. ▪

Tribal behaviours can still occur where team members are in a functional minority and escape back to their home tribe whenever they can for a sense of belonging. Or the opposite can occur when team members are in a functional majority and form a clique to the exclusion of some of the minority functional team members.

While team dynamics are ultimately the responsibility of the project manager, it's obviously the individual team members who contribute to the dynamic. Be mindful of tribal behaviours and avoid reverting to tribe when things don't quite go your way.

---

2 Digital Tribes: Rising Asymmetric Power. DK Matai, Chairman, Asymmetric Threats Contingency Alliance (ATCA).

THE AGILE PROJECT ENVIRONMENT

This chapter's opening quote perfectly summarises the work ethic that we want to explore in this chapter. Henry Ford is of course famous as the proprietor of Ford automobiles, but he also invented the assembly line used in car manufacturing. The assembly line is an excellent example of essential teamwork, where each member contributes to the delivery of the vision. But almost as important as teamwork is an environment in which the team can work together.

A SHARED WORKSPACE IMPROVES INTERPERSONAL AND PROJECT COMMUNICATION

We have already said that to improve chances of success design should not happen exclusively in one phase, or be performed exclusively by designers. We also recommend that design not be done exclusively in a creative environment. To make design inclusive, integrated, and continuous it must also be collaborative and therefore the designers need to be collocated with the rest of the team. A face-to-face conversation is usually the most efficient form of communication, especially when time is of the essence. Therefore, project communication is most efficient when the team members work in a shared space.

Where teams are collocated there is no need for complex project reporting tools as the wall becomes the project dashboard and the project repository. Design artefacts work best when they are shared and understood by the rest of the team. Rather than burying design detail in documents that no one ever has time to read, design artefacts in an agile environment are displayed on the wall as a constant visual prompt to the whole team.

WHERE DOES A PROJECT TEAM CALL HOME?

Life on an agile project can be quite different from that of other project structures. To facilitate "individuals and interactions over processes and tools," it is preferable to have shared project space where the team members are collocated. Ideally, this is in a single space or a group of spaces in close proximity.

COLLOCATION IS KEY

Collocation is a critical success factor on an agile project. It makes sense for functional teams working on the same project to sit together. So of course it's going to make sense for cross-functional teams who are working on the same project to sit together. The key benefits are efficiency and quality of both communication and problem solving.

Collocation is key for cross-functional teams delivering a project together. Benefits include efficiency and quality of both communication and problem solving.

To be truly effective, collocation requires a certain amount of discipline from the team members. Complex thinking takes much longer when the thinking process is constantly interrupted or there are too many distractions.

Here's a summary of the key benefits of collocation of cross-functional teams:

- Closer physical proximity
- Shorter feedback cycles
- Less time spent traveling between floors and sites
- Less time spent in less frequent but longer-duration meetings where individuals benefit from only a small proportion of the total meeting time
- More rapid establishment of team building, familiarity, and trust
- Cross-functional problem solving, rather than solutions that are biased toward one particular functional area
- Tribal behaviours break down where functional groups are not prevalent

DISADVANTAGES AND PROBLEMS WITH COLLOCATION

We don't want to be idealistic. Collocation of cross-functional teams isn't for everyone or every project, so what follows are some of the main issues that come up and ways that you can solve them.

SEPARATION FROM FUNCTIONAL TEAMS

If an individual has a stronger sense of belonging to a functional group than to the project team, especially if he is in a minority on the project team, he may be reluctant to separate from the functional team. You won't solve this problem by decree; instead, acknowledge the importance of the functional tribe and allow the individual the opportunity to reconnect with his functional group. This could mean letting him attend his functional group weekly meeting, which was established long before the project team, or allowing him one day a week to work with his home-team environment to reconnect and reestablish his position in the group. Be cognisant of the fact that if the individual is having tribal issues, it might have nothing to do with the project and everything to do with his own tribal politics. He might feel that his position or value will be undermined by sustained periods of absence from the tribe.

WORKING ON MULTIPLE PROJECTS AT ONCE

Where certain capabilities are in scarce supply or where a particular functional role is not required full time on a project, some individuals may need to work on multiple projects simultaneously. Regardless of project utilisation though, individuals still need to feel that they are making a worthwhile contribution and that their contribution is recognised by the team. Simple gestures such as confirming or acknowledging a team member's attendance prior to his arrival on the project site are worthwhile. Arrange an adequate space, even if it's a "hot desk" for him to work at while he is on the project site as opposed to having him crash at someone else's space. Confirm his requirements prior to his arrival—there's nothing worse than having a limited window of opportunity and then finding that other essential contributors are unavailable.

RESISTANCE FROM THE FUNCTIONAL GROUP MANAGER

There will always be the insecure middle manager who thinks you're trying to poach his team and who doesn't understand the need for collocation. First try reason and logic. If that doesn't work, try to appeal to his better nature and reason that it's necessary for the greater good of the organisation and its customers. If all else fails, then escalate. Appeal directly to the manager's direct boss. If you've gone as high as you can go and he's not giving in, you've probably got bigger problems than getting individuals to collocate.

WHEN COLLOCATION IS NOT POSSIBLE

Collocation is ideal but not always possible. Just because you can't collocate the entire team doesn't mean that you should abandon agile. You can adapt and adopt and do the best you can with the opportunities and constraints that you have. There are many reasons why you might need to work in a more distributed fashion. It could simply be that parts of your team (functional areas, for example) are located elsewhere in the region, country, or world and the cost-benefit ratio of moving the teams to a single location is too high.

Again, the wheres and hows of collocation are probably the primary concern of the project manager, but in cases where you're the person or part of the team who cannot be collocated, here are some ideas to make your project life easier:

- **Up-front collocation:** If you can't be there for the whole of the project, is it possible to attend the initial part (inception) where the team come together to build a shared understanding of the project? If you can't have the whole team attend the inception, can you delegate to one or two individuals who will be responsible for imparting the key messages to the home team on their return?

- **Part-time collocation:** If you can't be there for the whole of the project because you have commitments elsewhere, can you consider part-time collocation? You can agree on the frequency and duration of your involvement with the other team members who need your input and the project manager.

- **Videoconferencing:** If you can't be there in person, can you attend remotely via videoconferencing? You don't need any fancy equipment; a free Skype account and a webcam work quite effectively.

- **Instant messaging:** One of the key benefits of collocation is being able to get an answer from the team when you need it. If you can't be there in person, consider using the next best thing, such as instant messaging. Don't rely on e-mail as it can take too long to get an answer, plus you can't always see from e-mail if a person is actually available. If you have a complex issue, you can use instant messaging to invite a team member to attend a videoconference.

- **Collaborative tool sets:** We've spent a fair chunk of this chapter talking about the collaborative workspace and the value of the visual wall. This is not such a great metaphor if you have distributed teams. There are any number of virtual collaborative tool sets available, such as Mingle from ThoughtWorks.

- **Collocation at each site:** Where you have distributed teams it still makes sense to have team members collocated on each of the project sites so they have the benefit of working together.

- **Adjusted work schedules:** You might need to consider adjusting the work schedules, especially if your distributed teams are in different time zones. This will ensure that no one team is persistently disadvantaged.

Stick with agile practices—you might not be collocated, but it shouldn't stop you from adhering to some of the other agile practices and tools such as using a card wall and daily stand-ups.

AGILE PROJECT COMMUNICATION

Communication, as with design, doesn't just happen by chance. Agile places emphasis on verbal communication and interaction rather than documentation. Therefore it's essential that everyone on the team understands the communication objectives and protocols. It's important to be clear about how each function and individual is expected to interact, and deliver and communicate outputs to the team and the wider business.

Agile takes a no-surprises approach. The general principle is when something needs to be said, say it. It's better to say it when you see it, rather than potentially compounding an issue by ignoring it and hoping it will go away. The earlier a possible issue is dealt with, the better the chances of recovering from the situation with minimal impact. As a result, there are a number of communication protocols that agile project teams use to provide ample opportunity for insight into the team and individual progress:

- **Feedback** is a way of communicating with individuals on the team to help them improve competency or social interaction. The structure is based on Pendleton's rules[3]—what was done well, what was not done so well, and what could be improved. The main objective is to provide the opportunity for growth in a positive and constructive manner.

- **Stand-ups** are a team communication protocol used within the development phase. They are short, succinct daily meetings that keep the team informed of progress being made, current and intended activities, and any roadblocks.

- **Showcases** provide the opportunity to demonstrate and get feedback on the working software at the end of an iteration or sprint. Showcases are often attended by stakeholders from beyond the core project team.

- **Retrospectives** are the team version of feedback. They provide a measured forum for looking at aspects of the project that went well, those that didn't go so well, and those that might be improved.

TEAM COMMUNICATION AND SETTING EXPECTATIONS ABOUT DESIGN AND AGILE

Designer's perspective: If you're a designer who has never worked on an agile project before, it's worthwhile getting to know the project manager before you start. This is your opportunity to let the project manager (PM) know that you're new to the agile environment and that you'd like to know generally what's expected of the project team members. You might discover that you're not the

---

3 Pendleton D, Schofield T, Tate P, Havelock P. The Consultation, An Approach to Teaching and Learning. Oxford: Oxford Medical Publications, 1984.

only newbie. Often, a project team consists of members with varying degrees of agile experience and that should be of little concern. If the PM is aware there are agile newbies on the team, then he can dedicate some time to covering the process and the protocols. He may choose to run informal agile coaching sessions, or even assign an agile coach to the project to help the newbies get up to speed.

While you're getting to know the PM it's also worth asking what experience he has with agile projects with a design component and how he has integrated design with development. If the PM has only worked on delivery projects that did not have an integrated design, ask if he already has a plan for integrating design activities and design tasks and, if not, if he would be willing to work with you to make a plan. If the PM does have design and agile project experience, ask him how he intends to include design activities and tasks in the plan. Allow him time to explain the process and make notes about any areas of concern. At the end of his explanation relay any concerns you might have about the process, pointing out the possible impact to the project if the concerns are not addressed. Again, ask if he would be willing to work with you to address the concerns and adjust the plan accordingly.

Project manager's perspective: If you're a project manager, spend some time getting to know your designers and understand what their agile experience is. As with all functional team members, if the designers have only worked in a waterfall-style project environment, the agile framework for design might take some getting used to. You make need to make provisions for agile training or for an agile coach to work with the team.

If you haven't had experience with design on an agile project, ask if your designers have. If they have agile experience, take the time to understand what they need and what specific design tasks and activities they need to do, but also look out for the other project activities that will either affect design or that will be affected by design.

If neither you nor the designers have had agile design experience, take some time to understand the tasks and activities that the designers consider critical and invite them to help you plan how to incorporate them into the project.

Obviously you have bigger concerns than just the designers on the team, but it's certainly worth canvassing the other roles to see who else has worked with designers on an agile project. Run a mini-retrospective with the designers to uncover what worked well in the past and what didn't work well. By identifying pains early on hopefully you can avoid problems and functional conflict biased by a poor prior experience. Look for opportunities to get cross-functional team members working closely together to improve collaboration. It's essential that business analysts work closely with the designers to uncover the user stories and the narratives.

At the beginning of the project you'll need to communicate with the entire team about everyone's roles and expected responsibilities. Let them all know how you expect design to be integrated and how collaboration is everyone's responsibility. The project will suffer if even one of the functional representatives doesn't pull his weight. Let the project team know how design tasks will be tracked and how they will feed into development.

Also communicate the project plan, highlighting to the entire team where functional activities should occur so that the whole team can decide what is relevant to them and what they need to do about it. So, for example, a lead developer might decide that he doesn't need to attend the wider business design review meetings, but he might want to attend the customer-review planning sessions so that he can agree to the scope of development work for customer testing.

AGILE PROJECT MANAGEMENT

There are many books and training courses on agile project management, but to our knowledge there are none that address the management of design and design activities on an agile project. This is a major oversight in our opinion, because good design does not happen by accident. Design needs to be baked into the process, thought through, planned, and managed.

Traditionally, the designer or design team takes care of the design management, where design activities are contained in a design phase. When design is tightly integrated with delivery, as it should be on an agile project, then the agile project manager must be much more actively involved with design management. Where this is not the case and design is treated separately to the rest of the team, design can become a bottleneck because design and development are working to different priorities and schedules.

Agile is quite a different way of working for designers, and integrating design with delivery on agile projects is a fairly immature process for agile project management. Therefore, there needs to be a bit of give and take on both sides for it to work.

MANAGING DESIGN AND DESIGNERS: TIPS FOR AGILE PROJECT MANAGERS

If you're an agile project manager, or even a lead designer on a team of multiple designers, you'll need to help the designers and other team members understand the collaborative design approach, collocation, and communication methods. Expect some resistance to start with, as humans by nature are opposed to change. However, the key to successful adoption of this new way of working is to offer it as a flexible framework, then any good, self-organised team can adopt and adapt the approach that is best suited to them and to the project.

To determine whether you have the correct design resources for your team, you need to consider a number of factors, including:

- Is the user interface/customer experience critical to the success of the project or organisation?
- Is the product or service well-established in the marketplace?
- Is the brand well-established in the marketplace?
- Will the product/service attract high traffic?
- Is the product being released into a mature market, with lots of competition?

The more questions that you answer with yes, the more you need to increase the volume of design effort. You also need to understand what kind of designers you need on your team.

You'll need to ascertain what the designers know about the agile process, tools, and techniques, and, if necessary, run some introductory sessions. You'll need to help them understand how they fit into and feed the development life cycle.

More importantly, you'll need to help them understand that design is no longer all done up front. This may well be one of the biggest challenges for the designers: working out how to create a design vision and then letting the design vision emerge throughout the development process.

SUPPLY AND DEMAND

Once you've determined what kind of designers you need, you need to think about when to get them involved and for what duration. As a general rule, you'll probably need more design involvement at the beginning of the project than you will at the end. This is not to be confused with big, up-front design. The difference is that there will be a finite number of design challenges on any project, and once the solutions for the design patterns have been established, the details can be applied by the business analysts and developers as the user stories are played out (4.8).

4.8
Experience design involvement on an agile project.

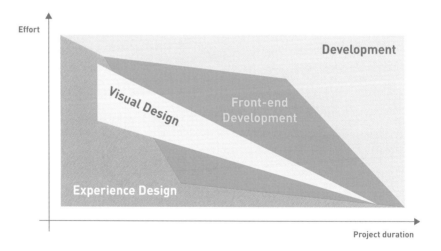

Effort

Development

Visual Design

Front-end Development

Experience Design

Project duration

Ideally, the lead experience designer should be on the project from the start, especially where customer experience is critical to success. However, you probably won't need to introduce some of the other design resources until later on. Visual designers may not need to get involved until the general experience design direction has been set. Equally, front-end developers may not be needed until after some of the initial visual design work. Although the front-end developers can start the HTML structure in advance of any CSS and visual presentation layer work, and they can also help test design concepts in presentation layer code, so it can be fruitful having front-end developers around earlier.

WHEN YOU NEED TO BRING IN DESIGN HELP

Cross-functional teams are all well and good, but what do you do when you're lacking capability in a particular functional area that is essential? As with all projects you have to beg, borrow, steal, or buy it. However, agile is such a different way of working that it can be difficult to plug people and resources into the process. Most of the agile project pains we hear about involve agile teams having to work with service providers who are not agile. Incompatible methods and processes can create a world of hurt for everyone.

If there's no design capability within the project team and you need to outsource it, choose a design organisation or individual who is flexible. It doesn't matter if they don't have agile project experience, but they must be willing to work on-site with the project team, collaborate to develop the design throughout the process, and produce design artefacts that are lightweight and facilitate conversation, rather than rely on heavy documentation. Determining the design credentials of your design supplier is essential, but you also need to consider the process and cultural fit. Here are some things to consider:

- Talk to the designers/design manager before they start on the project to get an understanding of how they like to work.
- Ask them if they are willing to collocate; if not, think very hard about whether they are the right supplier.
- Ask if they intend to work on your project full time, and if not, how they will ensure their availability during critical decision-making points.
- Ask about their experience collaborating with business stakeholders and developers throughout the process. If they have no experience, probe deeper about their willingness to collaborate.

Don't be convinced by suppliers who tell you that they need to work at their offices because they have the kit and the support they need. No matter how great the intent at the start of the project, the relationship will break down over time. Designers who work off-site tend to want to produce pixel-perfect designs before revealing anything. No matter how quick they are, it's still wasted effort producing pixel-perfect designs if they are wrong. It is much more efficient to work in a low-fidelity way to start with and to get frequent feedback about work in progress so that the designer can adjust and adapt as he goes. Also, it takes much longer and much more effort to send an e-mail with attachments and words to explain the design intent than to have a quick face-to-face conversation.

The same can be said when you source design capability from within your organisation. You really need the designers to collocate with the project team for the duration of their involvement. If you get any resistance, remind them that you're not asking them to make a permanent move away from their department. Most designers understand the benefits within a very short period of time.

MANAGING DESIGN AND DESIGNERS: TIPS FOR DESIGNERS ON AN AGILE PROJECT

Agile project managers are not the taskmasters and shepherds that other project managers need to be; they are more like leaders. Agile projects are much more self-directed and agile teams are self-organising. An agile project manager does not need to assign tasks to team members because they can do that for themselves when they are ready to work on the next thing. Instead, the role of the project manager on an agile project is to:

- Inspire and motivate the team and to help them focus on the project vision.
- Remove blockers or anything that is impeding the progress of the project.
- Ensure that communication is free-flowing.
- Promote the use of the agile principles, tools, and techniques.

As a designer, the project manager should become your new best friend because he can help you communicate to the rest of the team about the value of design and how it affects the success of the project. But before he can do this, he needs to understand the value, the activities, and the effort required, and you need to help him with this. Get to know your project manager and understand what experience he has had in managing agile projects with a design component.

If you're new to agile and the PM has experience managing design on agile projects, talk to him about his previous projects to understand where design activities fit in and how to work collaboratively with analysts and developers.

If you're new to agile and the PM has no experience managing design on an agile project, talk to the PM about what you aim to achieve with design and how you have worked previously. With his agile experience and your design experience, you should be able to come up with a plan that will work for you both. You'll have to adjust and adapt; try to be flexible and think creatively about the design process. Remember, you don't have to compromise on design quality because you're changing your approach. The more you can help him understand about design and what you need, the more he can help you and help the rest of the team help you.

If you're experienced in design on agile projects but the PM is not, then simply help him understand what has worked well in the past and what did not work well. Tell him about some of the problems you had that blocked your progress so that he knows what to look out for. If the project manager is aware of potential issues like this he can make it happen, which takes some of the pressure off you.

If both you and the PM have experience with design on an agile project, then happy days. Well almost—it's still worthwhile having a conversation and making sure that you have matching expectations because, as we've mentioned, there is no one-size-fits-all agile process. Compare notes about what worked well in the past, what you would like to keep doing, and what that caused problems.

 TIP

Ask the PM to help get content from outside providers to populate a design. This helps everyone.

DESIGN ACTIVITIES TO BUILD INTO THE PLAN

These are design-orientated activities that you may wish to build into the project process and planned for:

- **Regular end-customer feedback** is about engaging with end customers to find out what's not working in the design so that designs can be adjusted before they are developed. Techniques range from "guerrilla testing" to formal lab-based testing, and the time and effort increase accordingly. Ideally, feedback should happen as frequently as possible, such as once an iteration for one to two cycles, or multiple times an iteration where the iterations are longer.

- **Regular feedback from business stakeholders** who may or may not be directly involved in the project team. This gives everyone who has a stake in the design the opportunity to give input and feedback about the designs. These meetings will likely need to happen once or twice within an iteration.

- **Frequent interaction with developers** to ensure that the design ideas are feasible and also to get input about what the technology can do to enhance the designs. These need not be formal meetings but the conversations need to happen frequently.

- **Frequent interaction with business analysts (BAs)** to ensure that the designs cover all the user stories and that the user stories describe the full extent of the design. Again, this is not a formal session, but conversations need to happen regularly—multiple times a day.

- **Interaction with QAs** on the project to make sure that the tests reflect important interaction, visual design, and usability criteria too.

- **Cross-functional conversations** can encompass all the points listed above. When BAs, designers, and developers all need to have conversations with the business, it makes sense to have these conversations once and have cross-functional input. Discuss with a representative from each functional area to find out the most efficient way of discussing areas of common ground.

IN SUMMARY

In this chapter, we looked at the agile experience design project process and how design and designers fit in. We looked at what this means for designers who are new to agile, and for agile project managers who are new to design.

COMING NEXT

Now that you have a high-level understanding of the agile process, we're going to look at the specific activities you need to do to get ready to start.

PART TWO

HOW TO DESIGN COMPELLING EXPERIENCES AND DELIVER THEM—QUICKLY

GET READY TO GO 5

"ALL MEN DREAM: BUT NOT EQUALLY.
THOSE THAT DREAM BY NIGHT IN THE DUSTY
RECESSES OF THEIR MINDS AWAKE TO FIND
THAT IT WAS VANITY: BUT THE DREAMERS
OF DAY ARE DANGEROUS MEN, FOR THEY
MAY ACT THEIR DREAMS WITH OPEN EYES,
TO MAKE IT POSSIBLE."
—T.E. LAWRENCE

Before we start on a project, we need a rapid and
intense process for getting collaborative and setting
up for success.

In the previous chapters, we looked at the philosophy behind agile. We talked about why design in its current incarnation is likely to become an endangered species and made a case for doing design differently. Now let's turn to the practical question of how to make this a reality. In this chapter, we'll look at how we are going to get a new agile project successfully started. We'll introduce how we gather the right people together in a focused, time-boxed, collaborative, and workshop driven process to drive out our requirements before development starts and gain an understanding of why, what, and how we'll proceed.

IDENTIFYING THE PROBLEM— AND THE SOLUTION

We begin each new agile experience design project with a process of discovery, envisioning, and elaboration to consider the following questions:

- What problem are we trying to solve?
- What market opportunity are we trying to exploit?
- What will make our idea a fantastic product?
- What will the solution look like?
- How will we build it?

We start with a bunch of assumptions, the first being the assumption that there's a problem or an opportunity that the project will address. The team rapidly gathers insights about the people, the system they interact with, and the nature of the problems they or the system have. We validate these insights as quickly as possible, then develop a set of solution assumptions. Again, we test these in a rapid and collaborative process. The sooner we kill ideas that have no traction, the less risk there is for the project. Through an intense process of workshops, game playing, design thinking, and getting out of the building, we can remove uncertainty and ambiguity from our thinking and set the project on the right footing.

HOW DO WE DO IT?

We want to do just enough work at the beginning to remove uncertainty and clarify what the business (and customers) need. We do this by getting the right people together to make it happen. What follows are the key elements for getting our ducks in a row before we move into build.

GATHER THE RIGHT PEOPLE IN THE SAME PLACE AT THE SAME TIME

The importance of gathering all the key stakeholders and team members at the outset cannot be overstated. From them will emerge a common understanding of the problem to be tackled and its potential solutions. This understanding must be common not only to the various areas of the business itself but also to those implementing the solution (both designers and IT).

This means having business, design, and IT representatives in the same place at the same time—and not just any representatives, but those empowered to negotiate and set direction. Much time is lost in traditional analysis when analysts and designers play the role of go-between, caught between opposing and uncompromising business stakeholders with conflicting views of both the problem and the "correct" solution. This approach short-circuits such potentially unprofitable expenditure of effort.

Perhaps surprisingly, while this level of hands-on involvement is sometimes resisted by the business and designers, it becomes one of the most engaging aspects of the process. There is quite simply something very compelling about seeing a solution evolve in front of your eyes in response to your feedback. In addition, it is rare that any member of the combined team has as complete an understanding of the problem at the outset as that which the process uncovers. This makes it a learning experience (sometimes a profound learning experience) for everyone involved.

EMPLOY A HIGHLY ITERATIVE AND FEEDBACK-DRIVEN PROCESS

Complex problems don't yield to a single pass. Instead, an understanding of their nature (and the nature of a solution) evolves over a number of iterations (or cycles) during which we:

- Model the problem.
- Reflect on that model.
- Revise the model in response to external changes (beyond the combined team) and internal changes (the business changing its mind as the solution evolves).

This process is highly iterative and based around the evolution of highly tangible models which drive increasingly detailed levels of feedback from the participants.

In turn, as the models evolve to incorporate the steady stream of feedback from the team, the team's level of ownership and buy-in grows proportionately.

KEEP YOUR EYE ON THE GOAL

Businesses and customers have something in common. They have *goals* they wish to attain. They reach these goals by performing *activities* that may comprise multiple discrete *tasks*. To accomplish these tasks they may use *tools*. So, for example, you have an overarching goal: you need to work to earn money. That's like your business goal. But you've also got a more discrete goal: to get to work on time. To accomplish this goal you'll need to complete a number of activities: leave home (which encompasses tasks such as open door, shut door, and lock door) and travel to work. To accomplish this activity you can employ a number of different tools: you could walk, cycle, take the bus, train, or taxi, or drive your car. You don't need to decide which tool to use to accomplish this goal days in advance, you can leave this decision until you need to make it.

This is fundamental to agile experience design: focusing on enabling customers to accomplish their goals in pursuit of the overarching business goals being met.

BASE DECISIONS ON OBSERVATION, NOT JUST THE SPOKEN WORD

How do you know what people want? When you ask questions, you may get the answers they think you want to hear. People don't always behave the way they think they do; the way they behave can be significantly (and materially) different from how they say they operate. Often the best way to get to the truth is to see it in action. This means getting out of the building, out of the meeting room, and observing people in their workplace, where they shop, where they will use your product, where they will interact with your service. Being lean and agile means that the whole team get out and do this, bringing back their findings to share and analyse together, rather than taking it secondhand in a PowerPoint presentation from a third-party researcher.

CENTRE IDEAS AROUND VISUAL COMMUNICATION

Rather than being something that sits outside the process in a design studio, in this customer-centred approach design becomes a central pillar to support the process. We develop ideas based on the understanding of the customer. We then use design to bring the ideas to life, starting with the Sharpie and sketch-pad or marker and whiteboard before increasing the fidelity of the design as required. Momentum and ownership grow from feedback that is rapidly incorporated and reflected back to the contributors. Using design deliberately appeals to the visual nature that many of us have (a picture being worth a thousand words).

FOCUS ON VALUE AND IMPLEMENTATION COST

The business needs to be in an informed position if it is to make decisions about where to focus time and effort. The two key metrics for any area of the solution in development are the business value it will bring and implementation cost it will incur.

IF THERE IS ANY ONE SECRET OF SUCCESS, IT LIES IN THE ABILITY TO GET THE OTHER PERSON'S POINT OF VIEW AND SEE THINGS FROM THAT PERSON'S ANGLE AS WELL AS FROM YOUR OWN.

—Henry Ford

Clearly the earlier you're in the process, the greater the variability in any estimates of either metric (as the number of assumptions being made is larger). Despite this, even at the early stages, this is valuable information. This balance between cost and value can be iteratively developed as an evolving business model throughout the process rather than a static business case. With the people who are going to build the solution as part of the process, estimates for the implementation cost should be more reliable as they will be responsible for its success.

KEEP ACTIVITIES TIME-BOXED AND RAPID

Once we have the right people in the room, we need to keep them engaged and focused. Establishing momentum and ownership is an important aspect of the process. In return, reasonably high demands are made on the time and attention of participants, particularly at the beginning. To manage this effectively and drive progress, activities are time-boxed and concentrated, often using models to share understanding. How long will depend on certain variables. If there is little ambiguity in the problem space and the solution is well understood, then there is no reason why you shouldn't be able to elaborate your thinking and be in a position to start development in a couple of days. But more generally, depending on where you want to get to, it's going to take between one and six weeks.

It's probably fairly clear by now that the iteration, and so evolution, of tangible models is central to the process.

Models are representations of real-world things that help simplify our thinking. The models form the basis around which the team communicates and collaborates.

The team creates and owns the models. They represent, at any given time, the team's collective and common understanding of the problem domain as well as potential solutions. What may be less clear is what these models are and why we've placed such emphasis on them.

THE ROLE OF MODELS
IN THE PROCESS

The importance of models to the process stems from the fundamental role they play in everyday life. We use mental models for economy of effort (for which read: attention). Attention is one of our most precious assets when it comes to dealing with the world at large; it's scarce and we use it sparingly.

Take a look at the figure below (5.1).

5.1
Mental models in action.

Most people see a white triangle overlying three circles and a second outlined triangle. But it could equally represent three Pac-Men and three angled brackets. Our brains choose the simplest model available that manages the complexity and explains the data. We don't expend further effort or attention.

Models are powerful in this way. They promote simplicity and clarity, and they can be used to focus on the most relevant aspects of any information, dispensing with irrelevant detail.

In general, if we can map input from our senses to a mental model, we do. Once mapped to a model, we can use that model's predictive power to explain and control our environment. We don't have to invest further effort (attention) in explaining the input—the model does that for us.

This is tremendously useful. For example, consider a model that explains the action of gravity on objects. It predicts (among other things) what happens when an object is thrown or dropped. This particular model has remained unchanged for some time (as gravity has been pretty constant in its behaviour). But a model is only useful while it continues to be predictive. If, tomorrow, we found ourselves on the Moon, our Earth-based mental model of gravity would be inaccurate. The general theme would be the same (things still fall), but the parameters would be different (they don't fall as fast). Fortunately, we're ruthless with such models. They only have value if they are helpful in predicting actual outcomes (this is where they save us effort). To track this, we constantly test and refine any model we use. In general, refinement is sufficient (the Moon's gravity is simply less than the Earth's, not fundamentally different) but on occasion we need to completely reject and reformulate a model (for instance, if we found things falling upward).

5.2
The key
"test and refine" cycle.

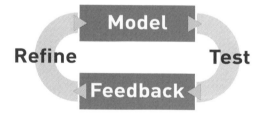

This cycle of "test and refine," shown in Illustration 5.2, driven by a central model or models, is the heart of the engine that drives the communication and collaboration that is so important to this process—and it couldn't have had a better proving ground. Clearly, in a team context, the models used can't be housed in someone's head—they need to be external and available for scrutiny by all—while at the same time being sufficiently lightweight and flexible to incorporate the changes that will inevitably occur.

Here are some examples of the types of models we might use. The first models are symbolic, abstractions of reality. The latter, for example prototypes, are more physical in that they are a more tangible visual representation of reality (**Table 5.1**).

We use these models to structure thinking and share our understanding of problems and solutions. Agile experience design places an emphasis on this *sharing*.

That means engaging the right people at the right time to identify problems or opportunities and develop feasible and compelling solutions. Next, we'll look at who you need to engage, when they need to be engaged, and what they will do.

TABLE 5.1 Models that drive understanding of a problem and reduce uncertainty

MODEL	DESCRIPTION
Prioritised list	Provides a simple but very useful understanding of the relative importance of any number of items (business objectives, requirements, story list, and so on).
Financial model	Models the costs and benefits associated with a particular solution; often forms the financial basis of any business case and is likely to be based on a number of explicitly stated assumptions.
Business model	Deconstructs the key elements of a business proposition.
Process model	Articulates the key business process(es) being considered. Frequently both an "as is" process model and a "to be" process model will be created.
Customer model	Indicates who are we designing for, what they do, and how will they do it. Often captured as either empathy maps or personas.
User stories	Offer short descriptions of what the application should do from the customer's perspective.
Story map	Offers a model for arranging stories according to customer goals.
Information architecture	Provides a model of organisation and structure of digital content.
Comps/scamps	Illustrate design thinking, ideas, or layouts in quick, hand-drawn sketches (scamps); provide detailed blueprints of how designs will appear (comps).
Storyboards/wireframes	Model customer interactions and page layouts; a more tangible model that will drive out more representative feedback.
Prototype	Takes the sketches, scamps, storyboards, and wireframes and adds greater fidelity to the look and feel, potentially demonstrating a working, interactive version of a concept that anyone can try, understand, and see how it would work.
Code	Remains at the centre of the "test and refine" approach; the most tangible of the models available.

WHO DO WE NEED?

It's important to ensure the involvement of four key groups of participants:

- Core project team
- Senior business stakeholders
- Point experts/subject matter experts (SMEs)
- Customers

Getting the right people in the same room at the same time is one of the defining characteristics of the agile experience design and is critical to its success.

A single individual may belong to more than one of these groups. Given the commitment we're expecting from the participants, it's important to give them adequate advance notice so they can clear their schedules. Better for them to be free and then we politely inform them that they are no longer required than them not being available when their presence would be critical.

CORE PROJECT TEAM

The core team is split into those who are content focused and those who are process focused.

WHO'S ON THE CONTENT SIDE?

In an agile project, the key content role is the product owner. This is the person who sets the vision and product objectives, manages the product ROI, works with the team to prioritise the backlog, and collaborates with the marketing team to position the product in the marketplace. A challenge the designer often faces with the product owner is the focus on delivering features and functions as expressed by the product backlog with the focus of the experience being lost in the process. With this in mind, it's important for the product owner to pair with the experience designer to ensure design integrity over feature bloat.

Other content team members include representatives from the business, design, and implementation teams. They have day-to-day responsibility for defining and delivering the solution and therefore must be empowered to make decisions and provide feedback to drive progress. The process will be severely hampered if the core team lack the authority to set direction within the context of a workshop.

WHO'S ON THE PROCESS SIDE?

The core process team consist of the process facilitator to lead, direct, and drive the process, and practitioners to support the model creation and produce artefacts. Almost certainly this group will include an experience designer and a developer. Other roles are illustrated in the below table. Note that these are roles rather than people; thus, one person could be responsible for several roles. The experience designer might facilitate and drive creative direction, for instance, while the business analyst is project manager, and so on (**Table 5.2**).

TABLE 5.2 Roles and responsibilities on the core team

ROLE	RESPONSIBILITIES
Facilitator	Leads workshop sessions; facilitates discussions; keeps process on schedule.
Product owner	Serves as the ultimate decision maker from the business side; drives product direction; prioritises work effort.
Experience designer	Maintains focus on customer experience; leads sketches, screens, wireframes; performs guerrilla testing; leads customer research activities, contextual inquiry, and so on.
Business analyst	Provides business and competitor insights; produces stories; ensures nonfunctionals are captured.
Visual designer	Defines creative direction and visual identity.
Developer(s)	Ensures that the direction pursued is feasible; estimates requirements and assumptions for how these are arrived at.
Project manager	Manages expectations; provides an umbrella to shield the team from unnecessary distractions; pulls together the plan.

WHAT LEVEL OF COMMITMENT IS REQUIRED?

The core team is the workhorse of the approach, with the greater burden being taken by the process side. On the content side, the core content team need to commit to each workshop and the daily stand-up.

SENIOR BUSINESS STAKEHOLDERS
WHO ARE THEY?

These are the individuals sponsoring the project—those responsible for realising the business value through whatever solution is implemented. There should be involvement from at least one senior stakeholder on the business side and one on the implementation side (usually IT). This is a minimum. Often, more than one area of the business will be intimately concerned with the successful outcome of the process; senior stakeholders from each area should be included. If these key individuals are not brought into the process, its value is significantly lessened, if not completely undermined.

WHAT LEVEL OF COMMITMENT IS REQUIRED?

By default, the senior stakeholders should be present at the kick-off for each week and at the showcase and retrospective which conclude the week. In addition, they are welcome to attend any of the remaining workshops and will, most likely, be called on to provide ad hoc input from time to time (to clarify direction, prioritise options, and so on). Also, where the focus of the process is on business strategy they are likely to be required as point experts (see below).

POINT OR SUBJECT MATTER EXPERTS

WHO ARE THEY?

These are individuals with specific subject matter expertise relevant to some portions of the analysis and design but not all. For example, senior stakeholders are nearly always point experts with respect to the business objectives and business case. An industrial hygienist might be an SME for a workplace safety tool, as they tend to be knowledgeable about the *content* of the product.

WHAT LEVEL OF COMMITMENT IS REQUIRED?

In general, point experts can expect to attend one or two workshops as appropriate together with a level of offline ad hoc follow-up. Clearly, this can vary.

CUSTOMERS

WHO ARE THEY?

These are the people whose lives will be touched by the product you're developing. Given that the success of the product ultimately lies with their adoption and usage, it makes sense to engage them early in the process, to test concepts and validate thinking.

WHAT LEVEL OF COMMITMENT IS REQUIRED?

Customers may be involved in different ways:

- Observed as they work or behave
- Interviewed as they work or behave
- Participatory in design workshops
- Customer testing

Commitment will depend on the activity and location. It may be tempting to engage the customer too much, but after a while you can face the law of diminishing returns. Get input early on, then test ideas and concepts as they become more concrete.

THE SPANNERS IN THE WORKS
WHO ARE THEY?

A pig and a chicken were opening a restaurant. "What shall we call it?" asked the pig. "How about 'bacon and eggs,'" said the chicken. The pig gulped and looked aghast. "We can't go with that," he said. "I'd be totally committed, but you'd only be involved."

These people are the chickens. These are the people who appear when you least want them (typically when you're almost done with whatever you're doing) and tell you "you can't do it like that." They throw their spanner into your well-oiled engine and smash it to bits. They are the legal people who tell you that your decision to let your community self-moderate will not fly in this organisation—you need to build out complex moderation workflow with supporting roles. They are the global human factors department who want to review your research and refuse to buy into your fast and furious approach. Who else?

- Training
- Security and compliance
- Marketing
- Technical architecture
- Other project teams
- Facilities (getting permission to stick stuff on their precious walls)
- Agencies (getting the agencies you've got on retainer to play this sort of way can be a challenge, especially when your location is distant from their studio or offices and they dislike traveling)

WHAT LEVEL OF COMMITMENT IS REQUIRED?

It's paramount to identify these individuals and communicate to them from the outset what you're doing, how it differs from what they are used to, what they can expect from you, and what you can expect from them. Often, just being invited to get involved early on is sufficient to keep them on your side. Asking them to drop by the project war room informally first thing, at lunch, or at the end of the day enables them to understand what's going on and raise issues early so they can be tackled before they become risks to the process.

THE TRUTH VS. THE HIPPO

Sometimes it can be hard introducing agile into a culture where review and sign-off by stakeholders from across the organisation is the norm. This can be especially so where leadership expect to be presented with a choice of different design treatments to select from. *'We like the third option you presented. The first just didn't do it for us, but there are certain elements of the second that we'd like worked in…'* And you go back to your studio and make the changes and your job's done and *their* job's done. In agile we don't make these choices just at the beginning of the project; there are design decisions to be made throughout the process. And more often than not, there's not much time to make them—certainly not time to circulate them through dozens of different executives for approval. In environments like this, the role of the product owner becomes even more important. The product owner must be established as the truth, the mouthpiece through which all decisions are made in a timely fashion and with whom responsibility lies. Where design is critical, the product owner pairs with the experience designer or creative director who own the integrity of the emergent product. They prevent the HIPPO (high-paid person's opinion) throwing a spanner in the works. For this to be successful of course, the HIPPOs must be identified and made to understand how the rules of the game have changed. ▪

One of your first tasks when starting a project is to map out all the stakeholders who have an interest in what you're doing. Once you've identified them, the next step is to decide how and when to engage them. Inform them of the process and how it is different. Then for many a feeling of being engaged is as important as their actual engagement. This may mean inviting them to showcases, and inviting them to specific workshops as required.

HOW ARE WE GOING TO STRUCTURE OUR TIME?

Now that we've identified the people we're going to need, we need some structure and planning to make the best use of their time. You'll see the activities to be undertaken described in detail in the following chapters. Whilst these may seem linear, the process is actually iterative and overlapping. So over the span of a few days or a few weeks you'll start gathering insights on the nature of the problem, identifying multiple potential solutions, refining these, and discovering whether they resonate with customers. The goal is to elaborate the solution in just enough detail to commence building an initial minimum viable product.

WHAT DOES A DAY/WEEK LOOK LIKE?

The context that each team finds itself working in will vary from project to project, but there is a reasonably standard shape or pattern to the days and weeks that comprise the process. These patterns provide a starting point and can be adapted by the team in light of their particular situation. It's also common for the appropriate pattern to vary over the course of the project itself. Whether you're seeking insights, envisioning, or elaborating to start, this collaborative workshop–based process can be followed. Once the project is in full flow, it moves into a more structured delivery process.

SHAPE OF A WEEK

Here's the default starting point for a week (5.3):

	Monday	Tuesday	Wednesday	Thursday	Friday
09:30 – 11:00	Weekly Kick-off	Workshop	Go where the customers are	Workshop	Workshop
13:00 – 14:30	Workshop	Workshop	Workshop	Workshop	
17:15 – 17:30	Stand-up	Stand-up	Stand-up	Stand-up	Showcase

5.3
Example of the weekly schedule.

The week is topped and tailed by a workshop that sets the week's direction and then showcases and reflects on the week's output, respectively. Use of a formal retrospective (an opportunity for the entire team, including senior stakeholders, to reflect and feedback on the process itself) is invaluable in continuing to adjust the process both in terms of content and the practicalities themselves and often immediately follows the showcase. We've put one morning of getting out of the building in this schedule to illustrate; as you discover insights, there's likely to be more of this than when you're looking to elaborate and build the initial story map and story backlog.

SHAPE OF A DAY

The default day consists of workshops in the morning and afternoon. These are deliberately timed at 90 minutes. Due to the time-boxed nature of the process, the workshops are fairly intense activities and pretty tiring for all involved. Experience shows that teams in a workshop context tire significantly after an hour and a half and certainly after the two-hour mark.

Keeping the workshops short helps to ensure that they are focused and respectful of the significant commitment made by the participants.

It also allows the process team a balanced amount of time to consolidate their findings. The aim is to establish a cycle whereby the output from one workshop can be reflected back and confirmed in the subsequent workshop. In this manner the team can see their feedback incorporated in almost real time. It underlines a sense of ownership in the output and establishes a feeling of momentum with respect to the process.

During the week, all (or some) of the team may go out to spend time with the customers. Typically, this happens in the mornings. Insights they capture on these field trips are brought back and synthesised on the wall in the afternoon.

The daily stand-up is a dedicated reflection point for the day. It provides an opportunity for the team to review the progress made and issues arising, and to set or tweak the agenda for the coming day (much as the formal retrospective at the end of the week does for the weekly cycle).

THE WAR ROOM

The ideal place to collocate your team for discovery, envisioning, and elaboration is in a large room, commonly referred to as a war room. The name is likely taken from the Cabinet War Rooms, the command centre of the British government during the Second World War. During their use, the cross-functional forces of the Army, Navy, and Air Force occupied the Cabinet War Rooms. This ensured collaborative intelligence was applied to the war strategy.

The war room provides a hub where the team can collaborate. Critically, it will have plenty of wall space to stick artefacts on and whiteboards or flip charts to explore ideas together.

OUR WAR ROOM

Linda Luu, Customer-Centred Design Project Lead, Life Insurance, BT Financial Group

The project war room broke down any barriers to communication across all levels of the organisation! We had the general manager, product managers, IT, and underwriters popping into the room for an update and to share ideas throughout the project—it was a great way to quickly collect valuable feedback without booking meetings and asking people to think long and hard.

At the project team level, we practically lived and breathed over each other and it was fantastic! Being collocated meant we were able to say, "Hey, I'm stuck" or "I've got an idea!" and "What do you think of this?" while drawing wireframes and process maps to articulate what we were thinking. No more lengthy e-mails and PowerPoint drawings! In fact, the collaboration was so powerful that I feel like I've known the team for years...it's hard to believe it was only three months and we achieved so much depth in that time.

Our war room allowed us to stick up quotes and other visual artefacts collected during our exploratory research. This was a consistent reminder about who we were designing for and allowed us to leave our personal opinions and biases outside the room. ▪

WALLS ARE THE NEW DESK AND DASHBOARD

Dave Gray, founder of XPLANE and coauthor of *Gamestorming,* is often quoted as saying, "The wall is the new desk" and talking about creating a meaningful space (5.4). Among the reasons why a wall is great for collaboration:

- Wall space is more abundant than desk space.
- Everyone can gather around a wall with a certain degree of comfort.
- The orientation of the wall is the right way around for most people.
- It is a shared space that everyone can view and everyone can contribute to.
- It belongs to no one in particular and no one person can take ownership.
- Walls typically don't come with chairs.

ON MONDAY THE WAR ROOM HAS SPARTAN WHITE WALLS. BY WEDNESDAY IT IS COVERED FLOOR TO CEILING (WINDOWS AND WHITEBOARDS INCLUDED) IN VISUAL ARTEFACTS AND DIFFERENT-COLOURED STICKY NOTES.

5.4
Design ideas emerging
on the wall.

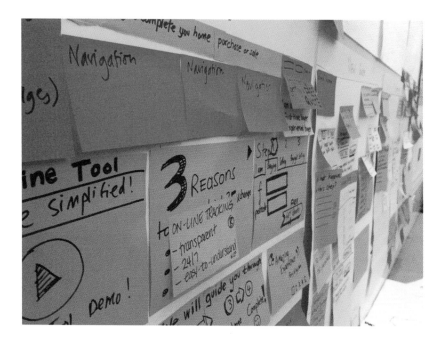

On that last point, "walls typically don't come with chairs": you're probably wondering why this is a good thing. Chairs by their very nature are objects designed to make people more comfortable and relax. Therefore, the energy output from someone sat in a chair is typically low. However, standing implies a certain amount of urgency and it also means expending a certain amount of energy.

The wall (or whiteboard) is an excellent medium for visual communication (look at any typical national art gallery—it has hundreds of walls!). You can use the wall as your easel: simply attach a drawing surface (flip chart or magic chart paper or a whiteboard), grab some pens, and away you go! Or you can produce your artefacts elsewhere and then use the wall as your gallery to facilitate a shared understanding within the immediate team and beyond. In this way it becomes an information radiator; anyone can, at a glance, get a feel for what is going on, and it is a living, breathing document.

WE'RE TOGETHER, WHAT NOW?

HOW TO BEGIN?

So you've brought together your merry band of stakeholders. They're in the war room, it's 9:30 Monday morning, and everyone is looking to you to kick things off. As soon as possible you need to get the most senior dude you can find to rally the troops, to put his stamp of authority behind the exercise, to say how important it is that everyone works together, frees their diaries of time, and contributes to the success of the process.

Now make sure everyone knows why they are in the room. It's introduction time, but let's add a twist. Don't just go around the table and ask for people to state their name and their role—look to understand why they are there and how engaged they are likely to be:

- Who are you?
- What do you do?
- Why are you here?
- What do you want to get out of this?

If they can't answer the final question, are unsure, or say that their boss told them to attend as soon as possible, you need to confirm whether they need to be here. Then understand where they are coming from and engage them accordingly.

WHY ARE WE HERE?

Now that we all know each other, by name at least, we need to get everyone on the same page on the business objectives. What's the project all about? Why is it important? What are the business goals we're looking to achieve? Rather than diving into spreadsheets to look at the business case, or PowerPoint slides that show the market opportunity, get the team engaged. It's time for an icebreaker. This isn't a "let's all have a laugh and feel good about each other" icebreaker; this is about starting the process with a collaborative exercise that everyone can contribute to. You'll find a whole bunch of examples in the Toolbox at the end of this book.

 TIP

When you've got a room full of people introducing themselves, sketch out a plan of the table and record each name on the plan. This aide-mémoire will help you address everyone by name—if they don't move around!

And now we go out and come back: discovering, envisioning, and elaborating. And that seems like a good place to move into the detail of each of these.

IN SUMMARY

This chapter has set the scene for the rest of the book. We've talked enough about the philosophy and the reasons why; now we begin to shine the light on how.

We introduced a model that the forthcoming chapters will hang from: discover> envision>elaborate>develop>evolve. For this model to work effectively we need to identify the right people and get them working together from the outset. This means:

- Get the right people in the same place at the same time.
- Be highly iterative and feedback driven.
- Be goal oriented.
- Go out, observe, and experience human behaviour and the problems you wish to solve; don't just listen to what people say.
- Use visual design to elaborate on your thinking and share ideas.
- Stay focused on value and implementation cost, the art of the feasible as well as the art of the possible.
- Be time-boxed and rapid.

COMING NEXT

With the scene set and a project in the making, the following chapters plot a path from taking a nascent idea into a product and beyond. Whilst these chapters are linear and sequential, that doesn't mean that in practice you need to do these things in this order. Think of the next three chapters—discovery, envisioning, and elaboration—as a buffet from which you can pick and choose elements that will help clarify your vision, reduce the uncertainty and risk of building the wrong things, and focus on building delightful products that engage your customers. To that end, we'll commence with discovery.

AGILE
DISCOVERY

6

LE MIEUX EST L'ENNEMI DU BIEN.
(THE BEST IS THE ENEMY OF
THE GOOD.)

—VOLTAIRE, *LA BÉGUEULE*

Do just enough research to get started. Customer
insights, business intentions, and technical
implementation. Get out of the building to test
assumptions and remove your ignorance.

In this chapter, we'll look at how research can be integrated into an agile project. We'll take a leaf out of the lean manufacturing book and consider how it's possible to do just enough to provide insight, direction, and vision to a project whilst avoiding the waste of building inventories of knowledge that we know will change. We'll look at how we can rapidly understand the problem space, remove uncertainty and ignorance, and work towards getting our product to market at the earliest responsible moment.

GETTING STARTED

We undertake research to learn more about the business, the customer, and the technology so we can remove uncertainty and unknowing from our thinking. We want to learn just enough, just in time. How we go about this will depend upon the time and resources you have to hand. In the same way that every product is different, and every team is different, so the process will be different. It's hard to mandate a cookie-cutter methodology. You'll have to feel your way around. Before we get into the details of discovery, there a few principles worth spelling out:

- Do it only if it will make a difference.
- Do just enough and no more.
- Iterate, iterate, iterate.

WILL IT MAKE A DIFFERENCE?

Always ask yourself, will what I'm doing make a difference? How will what I'm doing benefit the outcome of the final product? When we start a project, we enter a world of uncertainty and unknowns.

The purpose of discovery and research is to uncover what we don't already know.

If the output of your work does not have a direct and material impact on the quality of the final product or the ability to deliver it, then you must ask yourself, do I really need to do this?

JUST ENOUGH AND NO MORE

User-centred design has its roots in academia, and academia is based on backing up assertions with valid and reliable research. More often than not this rigor is overengineered for most digital or commercial projects. We should apply the Pareto principle to research and discovery:

20 percent of our effort will yield 80 percent of the results.

Do just enough and do it continuously.

Just enough means doing only what is required to move on to the next step of the process. It means thinking in terms of days rather than months. The key is to effectively prioritise your time.

Focus on the areas of greatest uncertainty that need the earliest answers.

The evolution of your discovery should move through the question stack:

- **Why?** Confirm why the project is important. Confirm that it will deliver value both to the business and to the people whose lives it will touch (the "who").
- **What?** What goals will it deliver on? What are the measures of success? What will satisfy the needs of (and delight) the customer?
- **How?** What do you need to do to realise those goals?

ITERATE, ITERATE, ITERATE

Don't assume that you'll get all the answers to all your questions in one go. Think about the critical path, about what you're uncertain about, and focus on that first. Treat your research as an iterative exercise. Make assumptions and treat them as hypotheses to go and test.

You needn't have completed your research before design and development start; they can be undertaken in parallel. Prioritise your effort to test the most critical or riskiest assumptions that will have a large impact on the lives of your customers or on your business model. If those assumptions are validated, strive to get a minimum viable product into the hands of your customers. You can then iterate based on the insights you glean from actual usage.

Paul Buchheit, the creator of Gmail, had a big question: how to make it easier to find e-mails. He built the first version of Gmail in a day. It was launched internally and was a success. Google iterated the product from there. It was in beta for five years before Google finally removed the beta logo. ▪

THREE I'S OF COLLABORATIVE DISCOVERY

There are three pillars of focus that will help you in your agile discovery. These align to the different stakeholders in the project:

- Business *intentions*
- Customer *insights*
- IT *implementation*

As a designer, you'll probably be comfortable with customer insights, but you may not be used to thinking about intentions and implementation. This is because we tend to work in functional silos.

Agile experience design provides a means for breaking down these silos, starting projects with a short period of collaborative discovery to get *all* your ducks in a row: business, design, and IT (6.1).

Successful software development is an inherently social and shared experience. Agile looks to democratise the decision-making process.

The activities within the three pillars are concurrent, shared, and iterative. A cross-functional team work together, getting out (often physically out of the building) then returning to share their findings in a collaborative space.

What follows is a description of these pillars before we address the question of what to do with it all.

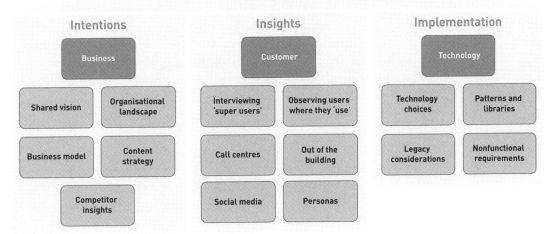

Envision, elaborate, develop, and evolve

Intentions

Business

| Shared vision | Organisational landscape |
| Business model | Content strategy |

Competitor insights

Insights

Customer

| Interviewing 'super users' | Observing users where they 'use' |
| Call centres | Out of the building |

| Social media | Personas |

Implementation

Technology

| Technology choices | Patterns and libraries |
| Legacy considerations | Nonfunctional requirements |

6.1
Pillars of collaborative discovery: the three *i*'s.

DO YOU REALLY NEED TO GO OUT?

In large organisations there's a good chance that many of your questions can be answered internally. Someone, somewhere may have done the research you're proposing, particularly when it comes to big topics such as competitor research and market segmentation. Spending a bit of time on your intranet may save commissioning research that's already out there.

You'll also find secondary research on the Web from which you can develop hypotheses. Firms like Forrester, Gartner, and Nielsen provide a wealth of (paid-for) data, although their abstracts are usually free. If your budget is limited, the U.S. Census Bureau and the Pew Research Center publish their data for free. You'll often find insights published in presentations by others on SlideShare. Google trends can provide you with precisely that. And if you've got an existing product, you can always mine your usage logs. Chances are you've got a web analytics tool on your existing website. Use that to understand how customers interact with your current proposition. ■

BUSINESS INTENTIONS

As designers, if we can understand the intentions behind the project, we'll be better placed to make reasoned and balanced decisions. With clear business intentions you can avoid meandering up a creative cul-de-sac that doesn't support the business objectives, drivers, and underlying business model. When it comes to prioritising features and functionality, you'll have clear justification for the importance of good visual and interaction design as differentiators, efficiency generators, or providers of a competitive advantage in the marketplace if those are the business intentions. When design is critical to the product's success, then that puts you in the driver's seat. But if it's not, if the business *intention* is to solve an immediate problem in the least amount of time at the lowest cost, then you are inevitably going to have to compromise your design. This is a hard truth, but it's better to know this early on before your design work gets rejected.

DISTILLING THE INTENTIONS INTO A VISION

A business vision helps keep the product development true to the needs of the business.

A project without a vision is like a rudderless ship. A clear vision from the start is essential to the success of a project.

The vision is a simple articulation of what the final product will look like and how the product will touch the lives of its ultimate recipients: the customer or the user.

TOOLBOX

Check out Product Box, Elevator Pitch, and Trade-off Sliders.

When Google started working on a calendar, they started with a clear vision. It's a simple PowerPoint slide with two points and six bullets. One of these was that it must be *"Drop-dead simple to get information into the calendar"*—that's hardly a requirement to be proud of, but it was a vision. It's a statement of what the product would mean to the end customer and will help maintain focus and vision from the start. It was a point of reference to refer back to when scope or design decisions had to be made. For Google, the proof of this approach was in Calendar's success. Just eight months after launch, it was beating MSN's calendar market share.

THE BUSINESS MODEL

Whilst the vision is aspirational, it needs to be supported by a business model that illustrates how this will be achieved. This need not be a document that is signed off on before the project starts; rather, it should be a living canvas on the wall, something that can be referred to and updated as you discover more. The Business Model Canvas engages all areas of the business in this process (www.businessmodelgeneration.com).

This useful tool enables you to quickly and collaboratively explore and capture all the critical dimensions of a traditional business case on a single, poster-sized sheet of paper. Even if the business have created a business case prior to the project team coming together, it's still worth running a short, time-boxed business-model canvas session so that the business can validate their thinking and the whole team can understand the bigger project picture (6.2).

6.2
The business model canvas. It can be downloaded at www.businessmodelgeneration.com.

Key partners	Key activities	Value propositions	Customer relationships	Customer segments
Third parties, suppliers etc.	Things we need to do to make the proposition happen.	The problems we are solving, the needs we are meeting and the value we are offering to customers	How we will interact with customers and maintain the relationship	The customers we are targeting
	Key resources Things we need to haveto make the proposition happen.		**Channels** How we will reach the customer	

Cost structure	Revenue Streams
The costs associated with supporting the proposition	What customers will pay and how revenue will be generated

ORGANISATIONAL LANDSCAPE

Creating ideas and great design is one thing, but are you doing it in a vacuum? How does it fit into the larger organisational context? As much as you look out, be mindful of looking within and ensure your thinking is aligned to the broader organisational objectives. This often means engaging with parts of the business that you've not previously worked with.

It's vital that you discover as early as possible all the stakeholders that have a vested interest in the success (or otherwise) of your product.

Having an understanding of the organisational landscape will prove invaluable as you remove blockers and ensure your design is aligned to both the overarching organisation and the personalities who could derail it. When you're considering a multichannel, multi-touchpoint solution, it becomes even more important to identify the stakeholders and bring them together to focus on the customer journey across the touchpoints. You may be building an incredible digital customer experience, but if it isn't aligned to the offline touchpoints such as delivery and returns, then your goal of creating a compelling and consistent brand experience is unlikely to be fulfilled. Find the people that matter. If they are not available or are unwilling to be available, flag this as an issue early on.

CONTENT STRATEGY

When it comes to a digital product, content is king. Without content there's little reason for customers to engage in your digital experience. It's vital to get your content strategy identified early on. Consider your communication style and tone of voice. Are you an expert, neutral, or strongly opinionated? What do your customers want and how do they want to consume it?

Content is multimedia and includes text, images, video, games, widgets, feeds, and so on. Where is your content coming from and who is generating it? Do you have the capability in-house or are you outsourcing to third parties? Are you commissioning content from specialists? Do you have the kind of experience that can support and accept consumer-generated content? Can you support links and feeds from other content sources? How will you keep your content timely and fresh? Where will you store it and how are you going to access it? Furthermore, how will you let your customers know about the depth and breadth of content that is available to them?

Leaving content to the last minute can result in rework and compromised design. Great design is only as good as the real content that customers will see in the final product. For example, a product page of vacuum cleaners may look good in your demo, but how will it look when it is a page of vacuum cleaner parts? Lorem Ipsum placeholder copy is easily included, but how will real copy impact the design?

COMPETITOR INSIGHTS

It's easy to get caught up in the need to innovate and be the first to market, but often a better strategy would be to "fast follow" competitors and "magpie" from other market leaders. This will have a bearing on how you focus your research activities. Often, it means taking what others do and making it better. For example, there's no point in reinventing the wheel for utilitarian interfaces when it's a known problem with tried and trusted solutions. Understand what competitors—both direct and indirect—are doing to come up with solutions that take the best from these. Focus your research efforts on areas where you're uncertain of a solution and the results will be valuable to the business. For "hygiene" you need only follow fast and ensure your product is usable (6.3).

	Low value	High value
Unknown solution	Rapid discovery to validate	Discovery to differentiate
Proven solution	Fast follow	Fast follow and discovery to validate

6.3
Where to focus your research effort.

LEARN FROM OTHERS' MISTAKES

Remember www.boo.com? It seems like such a long time ago now. It was the height of the dotcom boom; boo.com was a clothing retailer getting all the press. Central to the proposition was a virtual avatar who guided you through your shopping experience. At the time we were working on an online wealth management tool for a financial services company. The use of an avatar was a promising idea, something that could shepherd customers through the landscape of complex financial products. The concept got a good response in focus groups. But this wasn't good enough. We did some usability testing of boo.com. We gathered insights into its usability issues, but more importantly, learned that when people saw the avatar concept for real, the response was entirely negative. This could have been due to boo's execution of the concept. But it was enough for us to decide that it would be a risky "nice to have" and that there were better ways to impart advice than through an avatar. ■

CUSTOMER INSIGHTS

PEOPLE IN THE WILD

TOOLBOX

See Ethnographic Research, Me and My Shadow, and Contextual Inquiry.

What do your customers want? What do your users need? Rather than going with assumptions based on what you think, get up out of your chair, get outside, and *test* those assumptions with your customers *in the wild*. Experience what life is like on the shop floor, in the branch. Talk to customers. Look for problems that people have today, identify the sticking plaster and chewing gum they hold solutions together with, and work these ideas with them to come up with something better.

YOU ARE (PROBABLY) NOT YOUR CUSTOMER

Unless you're building a tool that meets your own specific needs, you are rarely a representative customer/user of the system you are designing. New users will be beginners, but when you're immersed in the detail it's hard to think like a beginner. We've seen developers get overly possessive and defensive about the way they've implemented a feature. It's an eye-opening experience for them when they see a user struggling to complete a task that they thought was so clear and obvious.

HOW CAN SHE NOT KNOW THAT?

Sue is a research analyst. She is a domain expert. She gathers information and data from the market and enters it into the system. She produces reports that are issued to the market. She loves her job, she loves research, she loves talking to people, she loves working with numbers. She hates technology. Or, more to the point, she hates the technology that she uses to produce her reports. She particularly hates it late at night when she loses all the work she's done in the last hour because she tried to execute too many commands at the same time. Or the following morning when she discovers the report that was published has errors in the numbers.

Sue has been with the company for fifteen years. Reports are created using Microsoft Word. Over the years, IT have developed a bunch of macros and Visual Basic scripts that support their production. There's a separate application for converting charts and tables from that system to Word. Sue selected that data from her charting system. She moved her mouse to the menu bar. She selected Edit > Select All. She then used her mouse to minimise the screen. In Word she went to the menu bar and selected Edit > Paste.

Fifteen years, and Sue had no idea that those eight mouse movements could be done with four keyboard shortcuts. ■

Accepting that you are not the user, we need to find someone who is. When building an internal product the typical approach is to find a proxy, someone who is close to the system, who knows how it works and can describe requirements based on real user need. In seeking such users, teams tend to focus on one of two types of "super users":

- **Type 1** super users have constructed a world of workarounds and are happy with the current reality. They are beyond seeing pain points; they are comfortable with the as is and feel challenged or threatened by anything new. With something new, they fear becoming a novice again and losing their super-user power.

- **Type 2** super users once worked on the front line but now live in head office. They are deemed by management to be best placed to describe requirements, but they often tell a selective view of their experience. They shape their requirements based on memory and what they know the business objectives behind the project are, not what the current user needs or goals are.

Engaging these users is usually better than no user contact at all, but be mindful that they are unlikely to paint a complete and true picture. For that you need to get out and observe what's really going on.

BE THE FLY ON THE WALL

What people say and what they do are often quite different. When questioned, people struggle to remember details, and it is the details that are likely to uncover the greatest insights. So the art is to unobtrusively observe them in their environment.

Start by observing users or customers engaging with your organisation. They could be traders on the trading floor, bank tellers in the branch, call centre staff, or customers in the stores.

When observing employees, ask their permission or explain what you are doing. Be as unobtrusive as possible. You'll need to find your own balance between observing and asking open-ended questions:

What did you just do? Why did you do that?

Look for job aids they have produced to make their lives easier; the sticky notes around their monitor, the notebook they refer to.

Observe customers from a discreet distance. Where possible, frame hypotheses that you want to test or specific questions you want to answer rather than hoping to learn something from just watching. For example, when self-service checkouts were introduced into supermarkets, uptake was low. Was it because the user interface was overly complicated? Were there cultural reasons, or perhaps a fear of technology?

We observed customer behaviour through the checkouts. It soon became obvious that the volume of the voice instructing customers on using the machines was too loud. The phrase "bagging error" across the four machines was quite audible at other checkouts and was intimidating customers. Interviews with customers as they exited the store confirmed this hypothesis. The volume was turned down and footfall through the checkouts went up.

WALK IN YOUR CUSTOMER'S SHOES

You might not be your customer, but that doesn't stop you from becoming your customer.

If you want to understand what the customer experience is like, why not experience it for yourself?

Think like an actor: get yourself into the mindset of your customers and then go and experience the customer life cycle for yourself. Think and behave like a customer and go through each of the phases of the relationship, from research to purchase and beyond. See from your customers' perspective what the experience is like.

This is exactly what Kevin Peters, the president of North American retail for Office Depot, did. He wanted to know firsthand about the experience that customers were having in his stores—not from executive reports and business intelligence. He went incognito into over 100 stores across the United States. What he found didn't tally with the reports he'd read and the presentations he'd seen. He saw customers walking out of stores empty-handed because they couldn't find what they wanted. He has used this direct research method as the catalyst for pushing organisation-wide change.

 TOOLBOX

See Ethnographic Research.

YOUR CALL MAY BE RECORDED FOR TRAINING AND QUALITY PURPOSES

Your customers talk to you all the time. The key is to listen to them when they have something to say, not just when you choose to listen. Talking to the product owner is essential, but it will only give you a high-level understanding of the intended customer experience and their perceptions of the current weaknesses and opportunities.

Listen directly to what the customers are saying and experiencing for themselves.

Make time to visit the call centre and spend time with the contact centre managers, the customer service agents, and customers.

CONTACT CENTRE MANAGERS

The role of the contact centre manager is to provide an efficient and effective team for dealing with frontline customer enquiries. Most contact centre managers have targets related to performance, call queues (waiting time), call duration (handling time), quality of resolution, and customer satisfaction. Contact centre managers are useful in a couple of ways.

They will give you deep insights into current issues and trending queries because the manager will be monitoring both calls and the service team throughout the active service period. If there is a trend or a known current issue, managers want to know so they can quickly disseminate the knowledge throughout the team so they can deal with the enquiries efficiently. Managers are also essential because they can give you access to the customer service agents.

CUSTOMER SERVICE AGENTS

These people are the front line of service for the organisation and deal with customers all day, every day. If there is one group of people who know what customers feel about the organisation's product/service/experience, it's these guys. They are a highly valuable and often overlooked resource. If you have time and permission from the manager, the way to get the best from the service agents is to first run a focus group and then, second, double-jack with them on calls.

Focus group: Ask for a handful of service agents during an off-peak time, and get them away from their desks in a room together. You'll soon be inundated with anecdotes, stories, complaints, and issues—all valuable insights to work with.

Double-jacking: This is listening in on calls that the agents take as they happen.

CUSTOMERS

Once you join the call queue and your service agent starts answering calls, this is your opportunity to listen to the customers firsthand. It can be a little frustrating, as you can't ask the customers to explain their comments. It's also difficult to listen to customers while watching what the service agent is doing; the key is to take copious notes about the following:

- Listen intently for each customer's question, complaint, or issue. Make note of the topic and the detail.
- Listen for urgency, tone of voice, and emotion as well as topic and content.
- How does the customer sound when she begins the call? Is she already frustrated and annoyed? If yes, is that because of the original issue she was calling about or is there an added element of frustration because of the phone channel experience she's just had?
- How quickly and efficiently is the customer's question or issue dealt with?
- How does the customer's emotional response change during the course of the call? Does it improve or decline?
- Does the customer have an opinion or suggestion for improving the product or service?

Contact centres are now becoming multichannel. Not only are the customer service agents manning the phones, but they are potentially also using other technologies such as instant messaging, screen sharing, and even video chat. Make sure you're able to experience those other channels in use, too.

TIME TO LEAVE THE BUILDING

Will real customers use your product? Time to get your jacket on and leave the building. Go out and find them and talk to them. "But what about our segmentation!" we hear you cry. "We pay our market research company good money to find our target audience to attend focus groups!" Indeed you do. And we're not suggesting that you stop doing that. What we *are* saying is that you may be able to test some of your riskiest assumptions quickly and use more formal research methods to validate the details. It's about doing just enough to get started, then continuing to do it throughout the life of the project.

WHERE WILL YOU FIND THIS STRANGE SPECIES SOME CALL "USERS"?

To begin with, they don't sound as strange if you use the warmer term *customer*. But how do you find them? You could hit the sidewalks and coffee shops and hunt for people that may fit your target market. Unless it is really broad and generic, this is unlikely to give you the most reliable results. Go where your customers hang out. If you're working for an organisation that has a bricks-and-mortar channel, you're in luck. Get yourself down to your retail outlets and observe people shopping *in situ*. Talk to them as they come and go. Equally important, observe and talk to the staff. They are a gold mine of ideas, insights, and inspiration borne from their interactions with customers and often with their frustrations with their employer.

Be aware that when doing observational research it's easy to take your preconceived ideas and prejudices out into the field and let them cloud your judgment. Identify these beliefs before you go out so that you can recognise them when they occur.

THE MILLION-DOLLAR MARKDOWN

We were working with a retailer to develop a new supermarket stock control system. At the end of the day, the staff marked down prices on the short-life items, such as sandwiches.

Using a handheld scanner with a belt printer, the staff would scan each item, print the label, and stick the label on the item. Well, that's what the process was *supposed* to be, but this took time (20 seconds per item) and when you have a whole shelf to do, it's a chore (12 items takes four minutes). It was far easier to just write down the new price on a "discount label" with a marker pen and stick it over the barcode (whole shelf in less than a minute).

Where's the problem in that? In fact, three minutes of waste (waiting time) has been eliminated. Well, it becomes a problem when the customer takes the item to the checkout. The markdown label covers the barcode. The checkout colleague tries to peel it off to scan, but it doesn't peel cleanly. So she manually enters in the SKU and the markdown price. This takes 2 minutes *for one item and* the queue has grown *and* because of the "one-in-front" policy, another checkout lane has to be opened *and* suddenly that small problem at one end of the value chain is replaced by a bigger, costlier one at the front end.

Had we not observed this we would never known that bulk-price markdowns on the handheld device was not a "nice to have," it is million-dollar requirement. ■

TAKE A DEEP BREATH—THEY WON'T BITE

For many of us, the idea of walking up to a complete stranger and engaging her in conversation fills us with dread and fear. Nothing we write is going to change that, but there are some things you can do to make the process less scary. The first thing is to plan the interview, be prepared, and have a framework that you can work with. Know what you're looking for and what assumptions you're looking to test.

Have a practised opening line and don't forget to smile. After approaching a few people, this will be as natural as saying "hello" to your colleagues at work, and it will probably evolve as you start discovering some common themes.

Briefly explain what you are doing (for example, developing a new product) and say what it is. Tell her that it's in the very early stages, but you want to get some feedback to see if it's the kind of product that she might be interested in. Your first question should be easy and put the person at ease. During the interview:

- Use phrases such as "Can you tell me a bit more about that?" or "What do you mean by that?" to clarify points.

- Avoid closed questions that demand a yes or no response.

- Summarise what the person has just said by repeating her response in your words to help maintain the dialogue.

- Give her time to think. There's no such thing as an uncomfortable pause in an interview!

- Don't ask hypothetical questions or enquire about wish lists. You're interested in facts.

- Keep the dialogue going by visibly showing interest; nod your head and say "uh–huh" to show you are listening.

- Keep the conversation on track. Acknowledge the customer's point then bring her back to the subject at hand ("Can we return to what you were saying about…").

- Try taking notes with sticky notes. As the interviewee makes interesting points, jot down each key message, one per sticky note.

- Pair with a colleague (a developer or a business analyst). You ask the questions and they take the notes.

At the end of the interview, remember to thank the person for her time. If she has been particularly accommodating and insightful you could invite her to become part of the customer development panel that you use on an ongoing basis to get feedback.

Use the camera on your phone to take copious photographs. Audio recording can be useful and video can be invaluable when you are alone and want to share insights with others back at base. Be mindful that editing it to be useful in future presentations will take time; be wary of promising to deliver video insights from your research without knowing why and what value it will bring. And don't forget that if you're going to use video for anything other than your own personal use, you'll need to get the subject's permission.

 TIP

Using icons on sticky notes can further simplify the process: happy or sad faces for emotions, a lightning bolt for a pain point.

SNOOPING SOCIAL MEDIA

Like it or not, your customers are talking about you. Right now they are chattering about your customer service, about how you #Fail. You don't need a social media strategy to do something about this; you can start by listening. Save a Twitter search for your company name including negative terms such as "sucks" and #Fail or just your products.

ONE DAY OF TWEETS ABOUT A BANK WITH THE SEARCH TERM "SUCKS" AND "#FAIL"

AA: Wow, *****. Your site **sucks** more than usual today. Errors everywhere, "our site is slow right now" notices, won't accept transfers… Ugh.

KJ: I'm pretty sure ***** just lost about 200 customers that I know of lol..only thing that **sucks**..is actually switching banks!

DW: Dear @*****, Monumental **#fail**. Over 30 hrs since we can access our accounts and you are going to charge fees when we can't transfer $.

AS: Btw ***** mobile banking as well as online banking was down for the day. Guess that's what happens when u charge monthly 4 debit card. **#Fail** ▪

You don't need to engage in dialogue with the customer (and there can be inherent risk with that approach if you don't have a strategy and resources to support the inevitable overhead), just listen.

- ▪ What issues are customers are facing?
- ▪ What don't they like about your product?
- ▪ What do they like?

It's not just Twitter; use other social networking tools, Facebook, special interest forums, chat rooms, blogs, and so on to listen to your customers. These can also be a valuable hunting ground for participants in customer research and for inviting people to participate in closed betas. Anyone who follows your brand is likely to be a passionate advocate and an obvious person to recruit in developing your product.

PEOPLE ON PAPER: PERSONAS, ROLES, AND GOALS

Collecting insights about people and their behaviour will help inform the design process, but these insights are fragments. Personas are "pen portraits" that bring these to life through composite users or customers of a system, service, or product. They humanise the requirements and enable you to think about user or customer needs and goals, and the context of their usage.

In 2005, Forrester surveyed vendors who conducted ethnographic research to develop personas. They found that on average four personas were created based on 21 interviews at an average cost of $47,000. (One vendor produced eight personas based on 100 interviews for $500,000. No comment.) This costly and time-consuming persona development is not required when product development is close to design and when the evolving product is being continuously tested with real users. In this case, a high-level persona should suffice.

Focus upon what's important: why customers are interacting with your brand as well as their roles, goals, needs, and wants.

Keep the number of personas to a minimum, or at least prioritise between primary personas (your most frequent, valuable, or critical users) and secondary personas (who will be considered but are not the core audience). When building a customer-facing application don't forget the internal users—operations, administrators, and so on who are also personas that interact with the product.

Take a large sheet of paper and divide it up as illustrated on the following page (6.4).

- **Characteristics:** In the top section list the persona's name, role, and characteristics. (You don't need to create a full backstory, just a few words to give the picture.) Provide the persona's reason for using the existing and/or new product and a few words about what the persona's values are or what he values most.

Name Characteristics Use	Goals
Pains	Desires
Scenario (motivation, context, and environment)	

6.4
Persona template.

- **Use:** Capture the persona's technical ability, familiarity with technology, and frequency of use. For example, Mike has used computers for 20 years on a daily basis but only for e-mail and word processing and is not tech-savvy.

- **Goals:** List the persona's goals, what he wants to achieve using your product. There may be a few of these; try to denote which ones he might do most often and which ones might be most important.

- **Current pains:** List reasons why trying to fulfill these goals is painful today. This might be using your existing system or a new product where customers are feeling pain from using something other than your system.

- **Needs, wants, and desires:** List the persona's needs, wants, hopes, and desires for achieving their goals in a new and improved way. Both the pains and the needs and desires will suggest opportunities for your product.

- **Scenario:** Very briefly, describe a scenario that tells why the persona is using your product. Think about the trigger, the reason why he will be attracted to your product or service and what will drive him into action with it. Remember the old maxim that a half-drunk bottle of water in a desert is worth its weight in gold, but on the streets of a city it is worthless trash. Even the best of products will deliver little value if they consider only the customer, and not the context in which they apply: time, demand, and usage.

IMPLEMENTATION

It may surprise you as a designer to see a section about technical implementation.

If you're going to succeed in an agile way, you have to get over any animosity you have toward technology. After all, you are building a technology product.

A significant part of an architecture degree is spent understanding engineering. Similarly, with a decent product design qualification you'll study manufacturing processes, probably electronics, and gain an understanding of basic engineering principles. To work on a technology project with no care or understanding of how your designs will be implemented is bordering on negligent. We don't mean that you need to understand code itself, but it's important to comprehend what the *art of the feasible* is, otherwise the *art of the possible* is only dreaming.

SHE WHO SHALL REMAIN NAMELESS

We once worked with an information architect who, when the conversation turned to how pages would be rendered by the content management system, said, "I'm out of here. I don't do technical. I've got some wireframes to build." ■

The world of IT has for too long been immersed in the *how,* with little consideration of the *what* and *why.* Designers have to stop wishing that the technologists could build what we desire; they've got to be part of the process. Collaboration benefits both groups: IT learns more about the customers and the rationale for your design thinking, and passionate developers can give you insight into new technology that you might not be aware of.

PATTERNS AND LIBRARIES

Developers may propose basic UI libraries to work with. Understand what these are and work with them. We worked with one client who went live with a new site that had been designed with little input from the developers. Rather than using standard HTML controls for simple searches, the client built custom JavaScript controls. Whilst these were more aesthetically pleasing—with rounded corners and a more "designed" look— they didn't actually work. They took longer to load and were not accessible. A short time later the client retrofitted the site with standard controls that performed better and were more intuitive to the user.

TECHNOLOGY INFLUENCING DESIGN

Remember pre-Web 2.0? The common pattern for search was a search field and a call to action. Wait and a search results page would be returned, probably with pagination. That's the model you would have worked with. Unless you worked closely with the developers and could benefit from their insights into technology, specifically AJAX, it's doubtful you would have proposed a "find as you type" search experience where, as the user types characters into the search box, results are automatically returned and refined. Why would you have thought to do anything other than a pagination of sorts? It's doubtful you'd have designed "more" results as Facebook does. Don't think that as a designer you have all the ideas for optimising the customer experience. There's power in the technology and developers love to play and experiment with new ideas. ■

TECHNOLOGY CONSTRAINTS

Anything is possible. We shouldn't be constrained by technology, right? In the 1960s, we put men on the moon; today's washing machines have more computing power than Apollo 11. The only things that constrain us are time and money.

What we call technology constraints are really budget constraints, and they are real. What looks great in a demo may be a nightmare to implement. Is it really worth all the time, effort, and expense of building a custom widget when there's a perfectly good (but not so pretty) standard tool that will do the job just as well?

Any developer will tell you that, from a technical point of view, there are two primary constraints that they have to work with:

- Vendor products
- Legacy applications

As a team, it's important to have these constraints out on the table as early as possible. We may strive for the art of the possible, but if this is just not feasible with legacy systems, it's futile to get attached to, or dwell in, creative blue-sky thinking.

DO AS THY VENDOR INSTRUCTS

Ascertain early on whether a vendor product is being considered by IT and, if so, what the constraints of the product framework are. Take part in product demos so you can understand the design opportunities and limitations and also spend time with the vendor to ask specific questions. Better still, be part of the vendor production selection process so you can steer the evaluation away from a focus on feature comparison to how they fit into your domain and how they will enable customers to realise their unique goals.

THE WORLD OF LEGACY PAIN

As soon as you start interfacing with legacy applications, the complexity (real cost) of a project will inevitably rise. Here are some things to consider from the outset that will help determine whether the costs outweigh the benefits:

- What functionality is required? (Often processes have developed around the legacy application.) By taking a fresh look at the actual business requirements, much of the legacy functionality can be retired.
- Is it possible to pick off the highest-value features first and build interfaces for those, leaving the rest of the legacy system for infrequent or low-value tasks?
- Is there an opportunity to rebuild core processes as part of the replatforming to make a more convincing ROI?
- Is it possible to do a skunk-works project outside the legacy system to demonstrate the value of tackling the legacy applications?

NONFUNCTIONAL REQUIREMENTS

There's a whole bunch of requirements you'll need to discover before the project starts. This is the unsexy stuff that doesn't have a design, or, if it does, it will probably be a design constraint rather than an opportunity. When working with the developers, you need to understand nonfunctional requirements (sometimes referred to as *non-functionals*). The "ilities" include areas such as:

- **Security:** Information should be protected against attack. This will be tested through penetration testing.
- **Scalability:** The technology needs to be able to grow as the volume of users and functionality increase.
- **Performance:** This may cover both speed and concurrency. It refers to how quickly information must appear to the user on a call to action and how many users will be using the functionality at the same time.
- **Reliability:** No one wants the product to be unavailable when there is demand for it, yet there is often a cost associated with "365/7/24."
- **Capacity:** What volume of users is the product expected to serve? How many records will the product need to store?
- **Accessibility:** This is more in the realm of the experience designers (and is often something they will champion). In most countries there are legal obligations to ensure that products do not exclude people through design.

Why do you care? Let's take retail banking as an example. Security is clearly of primary concern. How will security be implemented and what is the related customer experience? The technical solution will directly affect how the customer interacts with the application. The technical solution may be "two-factor authentication": the customer knows something, and he has something. What does that mean in practice? If we leave this to the engineers, it's likely that the customer experience will be compromised. After all, the engineers' key concern is security. In the two-factor authentication example, the result was major banks in the UK adopting a pocket calculator–sized device into which the customer entered a card then a PIN number. Then, finally, the device displayed a security number for him to enter into the website. Hardly an anytime, anywhere experience.

BRINGING IT ALL TOGETHER

We've described the parallel streams of activity conducted by functional experts looking at the technical context, the business context, and the customer context. The aim is to gain a shared understanding as quickly as possible. Sharing won't come about through keeping our insights in notebooks and devoting a large amount of time to preparing presentations on what we found. We need to use the insights as we gather them. As a shard activity we do this through the use of a shared space—the wall and by regular checkpoints so we know where we are.

THE WALL

Your team has spent the morning in the call centre. You've observed people using the systems, and listened in on calls. You've jotted notes in your Moleskine and taken copious photographs on your phone. You've got a bag full of sticky notes from your interviews. It's time to download them all onto the wall.

This is a process of taking key facts from your research and writing them down on sticky notes using a marker pen and sticking them on the wall.

The words must be visible from a distance, one fact per sticky note. The note focuses the mind—you can't write much on it and the idea will be to arrange them in a meaningful way. Here are some tips to help you in this process:

 TIP

If you have sticky notes from interviews, you are one step ahead. Label them with the initials of the customer or stakeholder.

- Download the information immediately while it's still fresh in your mind.
- Write one idea, issue, or theme on each sticky note in marker pen.
- Read the sticky note that you're writing out loud for other team members.
- Add a reference code to the note to help remember where the information came from. This is particularly useful once you start grouping the notes.
- As you write each sticky note, ask yourself or each other the short question, so what? (See the sidebar.)
- Lay the notes out on the table or wall, identifying themes and affinities.

SO WHAT?

What you are looking to understand is why this particular point is important. What is its relevance to this project, the end customers, and the stakeholders? What can we learn from it? How does it relate to the other points? By asking "so what?" for each note as you write it, you will start to automatically build up an affinity map by grouping together notes that have similar answers to the question. When you have a big group of related notes, use an index card to give them a heading summarising the answer. Then ask "so what?" about the group heading, and there you will have your insight. Write these insights on A4 sheets of paper and place those above the group of notes. These insights will guide and influence the direction of the project. ▪

Once you have the data on the wall, it will serve two purposes. First, as a team you'll gain a shared understanding of the *problem space* (the challenge and activities around it) and be better informed so you can ask the right questions and make the right decisions. Second, it acts as an *information radiator*; anyone who is interested in the work can view it and quickly appreciate the landscape.

This involves a new way of working for some executives. They cannot rely on an executive summary being presented in the boardroom if they understand that there is inefficiency and waste in that process. They are paying the team to take time out to create a document to serve their vanity. A trip down to the war room will speak volumes in a far shorter time frame.

 TOOLBOX

The Toolbox at the end of the book provides examples of the tools you can use to bring it all together.

CHECKPOINTS

The team has daily checkpoints to share what they've learnt each morning or at the end of the day. At the end of a set period, maybe a couple of days or a week, the team have a showcase where they collate their findings and present them back to the stakeholders. This may be in the format of a presentation (where the time spent preparing it does not interfere with discovery activities) or "walking the wall," sharing the process and insights from the material displayed on the wall.

IN SUMMARY

One criticism from the experience design community is that agile can be a bull in a china shop, charging headfirst into building without checking the facts first. The agile community can retort that the value of design is only in working software. By applying a lean and agile mindset to research and discovery, it is possible to do just enough research to start the project successfully rather than be paralysed by research inertia. The three *i*'s—intentions, insights, and implementation—provide a framework for doing it in a lightweight and collaborative way, bringing back the findings to a shared project space to analyse and synthesise the findings.

COMING NEXT

In the next chapter, we'll turn to envisioning: using the insights and findings from discovery to rapidly explore design options. We'll look at how the team can use sketches and design to help create a vision, a shared visual understanding of the goal, and in turn use this understanding to reduce product uncertainty and test ideas to ensure you're building the right product for the right people.

ENVISIONING SUCCESS 7

"IN THE AGE OF ABUNDANCE, APPEALING ONLY TO THE RATIONAL, LOGICAL, AND FUNCTIONAL NEEDS IS WOEFULLY INSUFFICIENT. ENGINEERS MUST FIGURE OUT HOW TO GET THINGS TO WORK. BUT IF THOSE THINGS ARE NOT ALSO PLEASING TO THE EYE OR COMPELLING TO THE SOUL, FEW WILL BUY THEM." —DANIEL PINK, *A WHOLE NEW MIND*

Adding creative and design thinking back into the project mix to help create a vision of business success.

Agile has long been associated with utility and functionality, and it does a great job at delivering these quickly and efficiently. Agile and the practises of XP are synonymous with an anti-design attitude, because in the process of designing up front no actual value can be realised by either the business or the customer, and by the time you have got to market the world has moved on.

However, we believe that there *is* room to include a creative process in the agile approach and that combining agile with lean and design thinking is powerful. In this chapter, we'll look at what it means to create product and business success by doing just-in-time design thinking. You'll learn how to take the insights we've discovered to inspire rapid innovation, which is validated with customers and becomes the design vision for elaboration and development.

The difference between project/business success and failure is about whether you get the:

right product (business, technology, and design)
to the *right people* (human-centred approach)
at the *right time* (lean and agile)
with the *right experience* (human-centred design).

The right product means looking at the factors that will make one product stand out from another, and in such a complicated marketplace, these are the elements of good design.

From a design perspective a successful product:

balances *utility* (does it fulfill a physical need?),
desirability (does it fulfill an emotional need?),
usability (can I actually use it to meet a need?),
and the *experience* (am I valued as a customer?)
before, during, and after the purchase decision.

CREATING CREATIVE

There's a difference between design and creativity. You can't be a designer without creativity, but you can be creative without being a designer. Anyone with the right aptitude, attitude, can be creative. It's worth remembering that:

- Inspiration rarely comes in a flash of blinding light.
- Design is not done by some magical creative with mythical powers.
- Good design does not happen by accident.
- Good, simple design is rarely simple to create.
- You needn't be an artist to be able to design.
- Creativity is a natural ability.

A DESIGN THINKER'S PERSONALITY PROFILE: EMPATHY, INTEGRATIVE THINKING, OPTIMISM, EXPERIMENTALISM, AND COLLABORATION.
—Tim Brown, CEO, IDEO

When starting a project with a shared space and shared goals, Tim Brown's requirements of *optimism, integrative thinking, experimentation,* and *collaboration* are inherent. What about empathy?

We can't necessarily choose our project team members based on their empathetic qualities, but we can engender a sense of empathy for the customers we're creating the products for by getting to know them a little bit better; we explored the discovery techniques for understanding customers in the previous chapter.

So in our project team we have the right people ingredients to get creative, but how do we get them involved?

FROM PASSIVE RECIPIENTS TO ACTIVE PARTICIPANTS

One of the major factors that sets a well-oiled, agile project apart is the degree of stakeholder engagement, the level of feedback, and the ability to accommodate change. Project stakeholders have the opportunity to become active collaborators and participants in the delivery of the product.

With complex customer experiences touching multiple parts of the organisation, no one person can create a compelling solution in a silo.

It will *have* to be a team activity with participation from many perspectives, including the customer.

That level of participation and engagement begins in advance of development during the discover and envision activities. The diagram below shows how participatory design comes together. Rather than basing the solution on the direction of the expert (often in their functional silo), participation is core. All stakeholders are involved; the project team and customers become partners in the process and inspiration comes through continuous idea generation rather than idea evaluation. After all, customers are the people whose lives will be touched by the design of the product, so it makes sense to engage them to help create the solution.

7.1
Success accelerated through design-led participation.

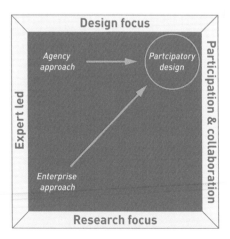

CHINESE WHISPERS

Have you ever played the game Chinese whispers, where someone whispers a message to someone else who whispers it to the next person until it has gone full circle, and the original person laughs at how badly distorted the message has become?

The diagram below shows the communication chain at a B2B company we worked with. The voice of the customer was nine mouths away from the developers who were implementing features and functionality. The primary channel of communication between the product company and their customers was through the sales channel—their sales force to the buyers. The product was being bloated with more and more features. Yet when we asked the end customers, they said that the product was a cumbersome necessity that they would badmouth at every opportunity. ◾

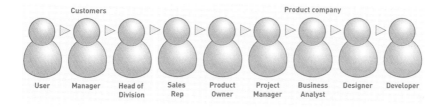

Customers   Product company

User   Manager   Head of Division   Sales Rep   Product Owner   Project Manager   Business Analyst   Designer   Developer

WHAT ABOUT DESIGN BY COMMITTEE?

If you've experienced the horror that is design by committee you may be shuddering at the notion of collaborating on design throughout the life cycle of the project. Let's be clear: participatory design does not mean design by committee. With participatory design, participants can make suggestions and add ideas into the mix. These are then objectively assessed to make sure that they meet the needs of the customer and the business and that they are technically feasible. Design by committee is more likely to occur when contributors:

◾ Get personal or subjective, rather than objective.

◾ Try to push their agenda or bias the outputs toward their functional area.

◾ Lose sight of the design vision.

GENIUS IS
ONE PERCENT
INSPIRATION,
NINETY-NINE
PERCENT
PERSPIRATION.

—Thomas A. Edison

As the designer, your job is to keep the group true to the vision and steer the group in the right direction. You are also the voice of the end customer when the customer cannot be represented. And if that isn't sufficient, *get out of the building* and back up your assumptions with data.

MAKE IT HAPPEN

We have a team who is ready and willing to collaborate. We've a shared space. We've discovered issues and opportunities. Now we seek solutions. Let's look at what's involved.

We're looking for ideas to set the course, a vision. Undoubtedly, the product that hits the market will be significantly different from the one you envision in these early workshops. What we seek here is some inspiration, creative ideas that will set the direction. If you sit in a meeting room hoping that will come by chance, you'll probably be sitting a long time. Luckily, there are lots of exercises you can do to provide that stimulus in the hope of creating that "random collision" of thoughts that might spark great ideas.

COLLABORATIVE IDEA GENERATION
by Damien Read, General Manager of Propositions, BT Vision

There are many times in a company's product development cycle when you need to pull yourself out of the day-to-day pressures and provide an environment in which many ideas are generated—you'll often be surprised how many new and different thoughts or themes emerge. This has happened many times in my career in digital television and requires a different mind-set and approach from the normal pinball of working.

A team with diverse perspectives always produces the best results. The first principle is location: it has to be a venue where the participants can feel that they are away from the norm. There are some great "innovation spaces" that you can rent on a daily basis. Also ban BlackBerries—they're a major source of distraction and should be checked in at the door!

The participants should also be carefully selected; you want people with as many different perspectives on the problem as possible and there is no harm in having external views. However, you don't want too many people as you also need to create an atmosphere of "no opinion is a bad opinion." Setting the atmosphere at the start of the session is paramount. You risk people clamming up if their first few ideas are ridiculed. Make a point of writing every idea down and giving all of them your full attention. Squeeze every idea out of the group by throwing ideas and stories into the melee: "What about x? I know it's mad, but what do people think of that?"

Then pause and enter the vetting phase. This only works if you have clear criteria by which to assess all the brainstorm ideas. Classic bucketing and prioritisation is the obvious approach and all you need is a whiteboard. Finally, it's important to provide all the participants with feedback—people need to see that their ideas were noted and debated no matter how small. This approach has worked several times over the last few years but needs thinking about and planning. In fact, I am hosting a session this Friday on the subject of how the connected home will affect TV over the next 5 years. I'm taking the team to a great space in Soho with the promise of sushi and a few good bars afterwards for additional motivation! ▪

SET THE SCENE FOR ENVISION

Brief your session participants well. For the sessions that follow, the participants need to be able to free their minds to think creatively. Make sure everyone is committed for the duration of the session, with phones on quiet and laptops closed. Remind them not to be constrained by what they already know. Don't worry about business, market, or technology constraints for now. We want to go wide and generate as many ideas as possible. We want radical ideas, crazy ideas, blue-sky ideas, greenfield ideas. We don't want to criticise, judge, or critique, and we need to respect other people's ideas and opinions. Every idea counts at this stage and no idea is a bad idea.

"WHEN SOMEONE SEEKS," SAID SIDDHARTHA, "THEN IT EASILY HAPPENS THAT HIS EYES SEE ONLY THE THING THAT HE SEEKS, AND HE IS ABLE TO FIND NOTHING, TO TAKE IN NOTHING BECAUSE HE ALWAYS THINKS ONLY ABOUT THE THING HE IS SEEKING, BECAUSE HE HAS ONE GOAL, BECAUSE HE IS OBSESSED WITH HIS GOAL. SEEKING MEANS: HAVING A GOAL. BUT FINDING MEANS: BEING FREE, BEING OPEN, HAVING NO GOAL."

—Hermann Hesse, *Siddhartha*

Siddhartha is a difficult quote to include in a book that places such importance on starting with clearly defined goals. But during the process of envisioning you need to let go of what you know and what you think you need and want and be open to new ideas. This enables you to realise new goals that you would otherwise not have realised.

I DON'T WANT TO GET TO A SOLUTION TOO EARLY BUT...

We often hear this from businesspeople starting out on an agile journey. We're identifying as-is pain points and they come up with an idea but feel compelled to shut it away because getting to the solution too early is somehow a bad thing. If you come up with ideas and potential solutions at any part of the product development process they should be positively welcomed. In fact, the more options for solutions we can generate the better; they become options that we can explore at a later date. The important point is not to get too attached to any one idea or solution too early on. ■

LET'S GET WARMED UP

At this stage, many participants might feel quite apprehensive. It's a large group of people, some of whom haven't worked together before. They don't want to make a fool of themselves or expose some area of weakness. If you've talked about being creative but they don't consider themselves creative, they might be wondering how they can make a hasty exit.

The key is to *think* creatively, and thinking is something that everyone in the room is capable of. It's not about designing and how well you can draw. Quite the opposite: if you can draw a box, a line, and a stickman, that's all you need to do. In fact, give everyone a pen and a piece of paper and ask them to first draw a line, then to draw a box, then to draw a stickman and have everyone hold up their pictures and confirm that is the level of drawing ability that got them their jobs in the first place.

THE KILLJOY

One of the challenges in this process is stakeholders who come to the session with preconceived ideas of what the solution will be, closing their minds to any alternative, better options that may come out of the process. That's not to say that having prebaked solutions is an issue. What *is* an issue is the inability to see any other solutions to the problem. Key to dealing with these types is ensuring that they know what to expect; even if they already have ideas, you'll be starting from scratch, and letting them see that their ideas have been listened to and will be returned to later. Get it on a sticky note on the wall as soon as possible, then move on. ■

Before you get into the exercises, do introductions and a warm-up exercise. The warm-up exercise is designed to set everyone at ease and get the creative juices flowing. There are plenty of good examples on the Internet, but an old favourite, especially with limited time, is the shoe exercise. Show the group a shoe and then go around and ask each person in turn to name a use for the shoe *other than to wear it*. Keep going until ideas have been exhausted.

START WITH TODAY'S CUSTOMER JOURNEY

In the previous chapter. we introduced the persona. Now let's walk through a day in their life as a customer journey. How do they interact with your (or competitors') products or services to accomplish their goals (7.2)?

A customer journey is a way of illustrating in a flow every touchpoint, every activity, and every interaction the customer has.

7.2

Example of a customer journey map.

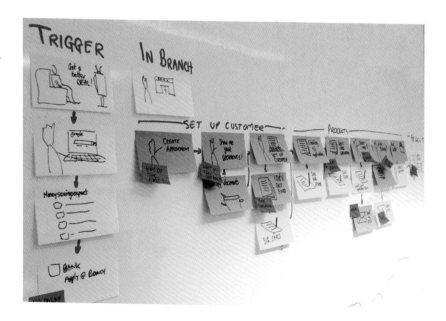

For each persona, start by identifying the persona's interactions with your organisation. Identify the corresponding internal processes that support these interactions—they may be human or system processes. Then consider the emotions and experiences that arise for the persona through the process. You are then ready to look for moments of opportunity.

VALUE-STREAM MAPPING

Value-stream mapping is the lean manufacturing version of customer journeys. The point of difference though is that with value-stream mapping you're looking to uncover the waste in the process—what's taking up time yet not adding any measurable value. The general idea is that you first map out the current state. Next you apply timings to how long the actual activity of creating value takes and also how long the process takes in-between each activity. Then analyse the output to see if you can increase value and decrease waste and then you create the future state value-stream map. ■

SEIZING THE MOMENTS OF OPPORTUNITY

As we map out the journey we identify moments of opportunity. We use different-coloured sticky notes to denote a pain point, an opportunity to differentiate, or a moment of delight. These could be found in issues with the current journey, or (more positively) opportunities to innovate, do things better, or even completely differently.

Be sure to call out where and what the different customer touchpoints are—all of the ways that a customer can communicate or interact with an organisation. This could be advertising, bills and invoices, e-mail, customer service, Web, live chat, direct sales, among others. Even if you're tasked only with designing the website, it's good to cover the touchpoints to see how everything interrelates for the customer. You could even add heart-shaped sticky notes to depict moments of customer satisfaction. Chances are the customer will see you as one organisation and will want the experience to feel like that too, not a bunch of siloed, disparate services.

Pain points on the customer journey may include:

- Manual workarounds
- Sources of customer frustration
- Uses of legacy technology
- Points of high customer attrition
- Sources of customer complaints

Differentiation denotes an opportunity to innovate, to do something different, to make the product stand out from the crowd. Can you take a customer goal and realise it in a completely different way?

Missing features are steps, tasks, or features that the customer journey lacks. If these could be addressed, the journey could be significantly improved.

IDEA GENERATION

Now that we've identified moments of opportunity, it's time to think about how they might be addressed. To generate ideas we need to think about different styles of thinking. What we're looking for at this point is *divergent thinking*, a concept attributed to the psychologist J. P. Guilford in the 1950s. In his description of divergent thinking he talks about four characteristics:

- **Fluency,** the ability to rapidly produce lots of ideas.
- **Flexibility**, the ability to consider different approaches and different options.
- **Originality,** the ability to think differently about a problem.
- **Elaboration**, the ability to think through the details of the idea and take it to the next step.

The converse of divergent thinking is convergent thinking, which we will look at shortly.

So the idea of divergent thinking is to go as wide as possible and to generate as many ideas as you can as quickly as you can. There are lots of tools and techniques for generating ideas, some of which we've listed in the Toolbox at the end of the book. Here are five to get you started.

BRAINSTORM

Present the topic and get everyone to think of ideas to solve the design challenge. As a facilitator you can either write the answers on a whiteboard or flip chart or have the participants write each new idea on a sticky note. Get participants to build on one another's ideas until everyone has run out of ideas.

Also try it in reverse. Instead of thinking about how to solve your problem, think about ways to cause the problem.

Successful brainstorming depends on basic rules being followed:

- Don't judge—every idea could lead to something else.
- Respect your team players.
- Go wild! The crazier the better.
- Go for volume.
- Build on other people's ideas.
- Stay on topic.
- Stick to one conversation at a time.

HOW MIGHT WE?

If we've identified a list of problems or opportunities, we could start the process by asking direct questions to drive a solution. For example, for a travel website we could ask:

- What is a better ticket-booking flow?
- What social strategy will make the site more sticky?
- What travel-planning tools do we need?

The problem with asking questions like these is that they are already pointing us in a specific direction.

Tim Brown talks about how IDEO uses the question *How Might We? (HMW)* to frame the company's ideation process. Stressing *we* is important, as this is a collaborative process. Rather than constraining thinking within the boundaries of the problem as above, using *HMW* gives the team "flexibility to release [their] imagination…while providing enough specificity to ground its ideas in the lives of their intended beneficiaries."[1]

For the travel website, the stated business problem is low online conversion rates. Through the discovery process and customer journey mapping we have identified a number of broader issues that are contributing to low conversion rates. These include:

- Jack, a key persona, is a recently retired teacher who is not particularly tech savvy and is quite anxious about computer viruses, phishing, and identity theft and feels more comfortable completing sales on the phone.

- Louisa, a completer-finisher food scientist, who doesn't feel confident that everything she wants in a holiday is included in the final sale price and prefers to talk to someone in person.

Rather than starting with the boundary statement *what will improve online conversion?* we use our insights and the *HMW* question:

- *How might we…* increase confidence in the security of personal and financial information and help customers feel safe in making a purchase online?

- *How might we…* support customers better and increase visibility of the sales inventory during the quotation process so that customers are more self-assured that they are making an informed decision with no hidden extras?

You can see from these examples how it is no longer just about online conversion but also about the perception of the customer experience. By phrasing the questions in this way, you have a clear focus but with a broad scope for exploring solution options.

---

1 Tim Brown, *Change by Design*.

WHAT IF?

On a similar track, you could simply ask *what if* to give a different frame and dimension to the challenge. Here are a few examples:

- What if we had to deliver this tomorrow?
- What if the budget was unlimited?
- What if we were constrained by X?
- What if we had no constraints?
- What if it was to be nominated for an award?
- What if it was to have social impact?

ROLE-PLAY

Let's get physical and instead of writing or drawing your solution, act it out. Divide up into small teams and work out the roles. Devise the outline of the plot or story and do a quick rehearsal ad libbing the dialogue and the action. Then present your show back to the group.

OPEN FOR IDEAS

Seeking ideas, inspiration, and an understanding of what customers want needn't be a one-way street. Customers are no longer just passive recipients of products who have little choice in what they use. They are keen and eager to get involved. Increasingly, brands are inviting their customers to engage in their product development. As well as getting valuable insights from customers, companies also see this as another way of building the brand and creating social buzz. Unilever, Procter & Gamble, Johnson & Johnson, and Kraft all have websites that welcome customers to submit ideas and innovations to work together on.

An early proponent of this customer collaboration was Dell and their IdeaStorm. In three years IdeaStorm had harnessed over 10,000 ideas and implemented over 400 of them. IdeaScale is an example of a vendor platform that lets you set this up as a service.

Lloyds TSB, a UK bank, introduced an "innovation exchange" on which ideas generated by staff were traded. Bank staff who contributed (by submitting ideas, comments, votes, reviews, and so on) were paid "bank beanz." This currency enabled them to invest and speculate on ideas. Staff could cash out for real-world rewards such as shopping coupons.

REFINE

In these exercises we've generated lots and lots of ideas. Now we have to distill them down to a few choice ones that we can progress to the next level. This is where we apply convergent thinking. Where divergent thinking was about throwing the net wide, convergent thinking is about narrowing ideas down to a select few.

TAKE IT TO THE VOTE

How you do this will depend on the kinds of exercises you ran, but one of the quickest and easiest ways to narrow down thinking is to get the participants to vote on the best ideas. If you have a large number of ideas, give participants three sticky notes and ask them to put them on their preferred ideas. A variation on the sticky note idea is to use fake money and ask participants to "buy an idea."

ENTER THE MATRIX

Another useful way to prioritise ideas is to use a matrix. Draw up your matrix by listing your evaluation criteria in horizontal columns across the top of the chart and list your ideas in rows down the left side. Decide on your scoring mechanism and then give each idea a score against each of the criteria. Add up the scores and see which ideas come out on top.

FILL THE BUCKETS

A quick way to narrow down choices is to group ideas into buckets or categories. As with the matrix, decide on your evaluation criteria or bucket title and then get the group to agree which bucket the idea belongs in. Be careful not to have criteria that will narrow the list too fast. Don't be tempted to jump into categorisation based on feasibility or budget at this stage. Instead, have positive categories like most desirable, most playful, most imaginative, most original, most usable. Once you've filled the buckets, you can narrow the lists down further by voting on items from each bucket to carry forward and elaborate.

EXPLORE

This is when we start to get a little bit more focused. We want to take the ideas that we have narrowed down and add the next layer of detail. This is about extending the thinking to make sure that it has legs and is actually more than just an idea but a concept that is worth pursuing.

ENVISIONING A BETTER CAR INSURANCE EXPERIENCE

When moneysupermarket.com developed its new car insurance process, it didn't start with a specification document and a list of requirements to build from. It started in a meeting room with people from the business, designers, and IT drawing pictures. They took personas as input and walked them through the flow of the process. They developed different journeys for the different personas (think the difference between a budget-driven, carefree young driver who has just passed her driving test and a brand-loyal, cautious, detail-hungry 60-year-old) and together mocked them up into pen-and-ink drawings of screens representing different scenarios. In a couple of days, they had an initial concept that they could test with real customers (7.2).

7.3
Rapid wireframing at
Moneysupermarket.

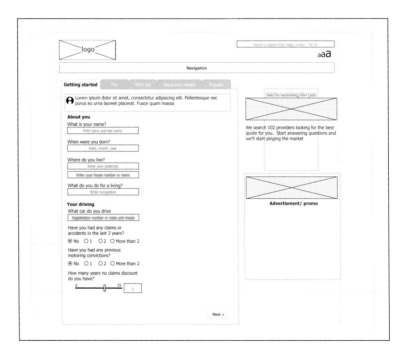

Some of the ideas that the team were excited about fell flat with the consumers; in fact, they were seen to detract from the experience. These were immediately descoped, allowing the team to refocus on areas of the proposition that were seen to be more successful.

This meant that just before development started, the team had a vision of the product they wanted to create. It was supported by user stories that were estimated and prioritised. Whilst some of the stories and detail changed throughout development, the vision as articulated in the initial sketches in the collaborative workshops was by and large implemented. With the product vision and the design direction in place, the team started development and launched a new product that went on to beat the competitors and significantly increase conversion rates. The key point here is that the process was participatory and included everyone from senior executives to operations staff and customers whose lives would be affected by the product. Another key point is that creative thinking and design made all the difference. The basic utilitarian insurance product is nothing more than a form with a bunch of questions and a results page that lists insurance quotations. Seen like that (as you might when you look at any IT-developed insurance form) you can see why online insurance products fail to engage customers and why online conversion rates might be so low. Instead, the moneysupermarket.com team put their feet in the shoes of their customers and developed a really engaging (and successful) car insurance form (7.4). ■

7.4
The finished product, an evolutionary improvement.

SKETCHING OUT SOLUTIONS

There may be many different solutions to the problem. By nature we're conservative and get attached to our first solution. By forcing ourselves to come up with multiple solutions we can break this conservatism. Six-up sketching is a great way of doing this. Have the team or a small group brainstorm six different ways to answer the question, "How might we…?" and then rapidly sketch out thumbnails of the different ideas on a single piece of paper. These may be process steps, screens, interactions, journeys. The key thing is to do multiple versions.

After generating six ideas, the team should then debate which is the best idea given everything you know about the customer and business goals to date. Once you have decided on an idea, take it to the next stage. This time we want to magnify the thumbnail and draw the next level of detail on a single page (7.5).

Repeat this for each of the moments of truth or for each of the design challenges. When you have most of the key moments sketched up, present back to the team for further feedback. They will have new ideas that spring from your new ideas. That's how idea generation works. Simply modify the sketches or add sticky notes to remind you to do it later.

7.5

Example of a
6-up sketch.

I CAN'T DRAW

Give a young child a pencil and a sheet of paper and she will not hesitate to start drawing. Do the same to an executive and she will stop, think, wait. Drawing doesn't come instinctively to executives—it's a painful process. And even then they will find it hard to be spontaneous. There's a great exercise for getting people started. It was developed by Luke Hohmann and it's called *Product Box* (see the Toolbox at the back of the book).

Participants in a workshop have a blank box and are asked to write on it key messages and features of their product. For some, this can be a daunting task. It's not unusual for participants to draw in rough before committing to the box. Too much time in rough and they are embarrassed by their box when it's time to show it to the rest of the group. Whilst others have engaging designs, these "do it in rough" folks have incomplete designs. More time is spent describing what they would like to have had on the box than what is actually on it.

Our challenge is to break the fear of getting started—to make them comfortable with a blank sheet of paper and confident enough to start brewing ideas. Overcome through starting small and easy. Recognise that sketching is not everyone's idea of fun and not everyone will be confident with it. ▪

PROTOTYPING THE EXPERIENCE

Prototypes have been used by various disciplines within the industry for years. The idea is that you make a quick and cheap prototype of your concept to iron out any issues before you go into production. In the physical product design world, this allows you to test both the concept and the details such as ergonomic factors (size, weighing, and controls) correctly configured. In digital product design, prototypes have the same purpose and benefits. They enable you to test and validate both the overall concept of the product and the key details of the experience.

So out of the customer journey we have sketched out some of the key design challenges that will make up our prototype. There are varying degrees of proto-typing that you can do, but for now we're just interested in very low-fidelity, rapid, sketch-based prototypes.

We're shortly getting to the stage where we want to validate our concept with customers. For this we want to make sure that our prototypes cover enough of the screen flows to support the primary customer goals. Walk through the journey and rapidly sketch up any screens that are missing to complete your flows. Now you have a prototype ready for testing!

PROTOTYPES AND SETTING EXPECTATIONS

A criticism of prototypes, especially from the agile community, is that they set unrealistic expectations, that stakeholders will see implementation detail that will never make the final cut of a product. Indeed this focus on implementation detail goes against what we've been talking about, on deferring decisions on *how* until we need to make them. That misses two points. Firstly, that if we're truly collaborating with open and honest communication then expectation management ceases to be an issue. Secondly, that prototypes provide a cheap and rapid tool for testing ideas, validating, or refuting them before committing to more costly code. Often this means we can reduce stakeholder expectations by demonstrating that features and functionality they believe are essential are inconsequential to customers in user testing. ■

VALIDATE

So we have done all this great work and we're feeling very proud of ourselves, but before we commit time, money, and resources to building our vision, we had better check that it's what the customers actually want. There are lots of ways that you can do this, but remember, we're all about the value and we want to be as fast, efficient, and lightweight as possible.

GRAB YOUR COWORKERS

A quick first pass would be to get feedback from within the organisation. This is where we want to involve the people who are closest to the customers: the front-line staff including sales, support, and customer service. Grab a handful of people and present your idea or ideas to them. Walk them through the customer journey, the moments of opportunities, and some of the quick sketches that you have done to elaborate, and explore your concept in more detail. These are the people who will be able to spot issues that you've not thought about (because quite honestly you just haven't had time yet). They will provide an external perspective but one that is quite close to the customers' own. Probe and ask lots of questions. You are looking to break your design. Use this feedback to quickly iterate. Modify the design based on the input and elaborate on the details that are missing.

Remember, it's only paper at this stage and that is because paper is much easier to change than code or shipped software. Don't be too precious about your idea, and be open to feedback and comments. Do be prepared to balance the needs of the business with the needs of the customers though. Sometimes the two needs can be in conflict.

TIME TO LEAVE THE BUILDING

Now it's time to validate the design with the people whose lives will be affected or who will have to decide whether they will pay good money for the product: the customers. In the same way that we left the building to test our assumptions, now we go out of the building to do *guerilla* testing of our concepts and designs.

GET IT OUT THERE

Testing your ideas with colleagues and customers will give you early validation; you could equally test it with larger numbers of customers by putting a dummy product onto the Web. Build a landing page that explains the benefits of your forthcoming product or feature and include an e-mail capture field for prospective customers to express their interest. There are now products such as unbounce.com that make this easy. It's possible to create a number of different versions to test different concepts. For example, if you're having difficulty identifying the basic feature set that will make the product attractive, place adverts for both and split test. One version has a long list of features, another has a short list, both with the same call to action: "I'm interested." Whichever has the greatest number of clicks may give you insight into which direction to pursue.

TESTING
EACH FAILED
HYPOTHESIS
LEADS TO A
NEW PIVOT,
WHERE WE
CHANGE JUST
ONE ELEMENT OF
THE BUSINESS
PLAN BUT DON'T
ABANDON
EVERYTHING
WE'VE LEARNED.

—Eric Ries

PIVOT

Organisations often find it culturally difficult to change direction. People do what they are measured and rewarded on, so to admit that the great idea you've got is wrong, without a framework to support that thinking will be difficult, if not impossible. By spending a little time envisioning and testing your insights with customers, you can change your mind early, cheaply, and often.

It's easy to get attached to your initial idea and continue to invest beyond when you should. Yet if you can get your ideas into the hands of customers early and often, the realisation that you're pointing in the wrong direction won't be so painful. It's far better to develop hypotheses around your product, then go out and test them than to assume you know what will work in the market. Then, based on those findings, either continue with what works or fail fast and *pivot*.

Doing envision activities enables us to address two fundamental questions: How quickly can you pivot? And how can you pivot?

The concept of pivoting is something start-up companies have been quick to embrace:

- Flickr, the photo-sharing website, started its life as a multiplayer online game which had a chat room that enabled sharing of photos.
- PayPal started out as Confinity, a tool for reconciling payments beamed between Palm Pilots.
- Gowalla, the location-based social network started out as a social game.
- YouTube started as a video dating site.
- Groupon started life as a fund-raising website. Its future looked bleak until they came up with a half-price offer for pizzas from the restaurant in their building.
- If you've seen the film you'll know that Facebook began as hotornot.com. Even as Facebook was growing, Mark Zuckerberg was working on other products.
- Twitter started its life in the podcasting company Odeo. It was an idea that came out of a brainstorming session; work started on it in March 2006 and it was introduced to the general public four months later.

And it's not just recent dot-coms that have changed their underlying business. Nokia started as a rubber company selling rubber boots; Lamborghini began as a tractor company.

GENERATING VIABLE BUSINESS IDEAS IN A WEEKEND

I (Marc) attended the Lean Startup Machine in New York earlier this year. It's a learning camp, where you're taught lean start-up tools and techniques, and a lean start-up competition. The team that won worked on the hypothesis that teachers spend a lot of time prepping classes, that they spend a lot of time searching for decent materials on the Web, and that they'd pay for a service that would provide them with quality teaching materials. Research with teachers validated the assumption that teachers spend a lot of time (thirty hours a week) preparing for lessons. But the idea that they display economically rationale behaviour was refuted. Teachers would not pay for the service. But their principals might. This was a pivotal moment. The team asked the teachers about lessons they have hassles preparing for—geometry was one example. So they built a minimum viable product that demonstrated searching for quality geometry resources. They trawled the Web to find the information, and on Sunday morning they called the teachers again and showed them the website they'd built. It may have been "smoke and mirrors," but it worked. The teachers loved it enough to recommend the concept to their principals—the people with money who would pay for it. All this in a weekend. ■

IN SUMMARY

In this chapter, we talked about envisioning success: how we can use design to rapidly produce a shared vision that has been tested, validated, and refined, and tangible artefacts that people can look at, nod their heads in agreement, and say "Yes! That's what we want."

Envision is about starting off on the right foot and giving us the best chance for success. We don't just want to jump at the first idea, or dive headlong into a solution; instead, we want to use what we learnt in discovery to inspire divergent thinking. We want to generate as many ideas as we can, because if our one idea turns out to be not so great then we have nothing left. Having generated lots of ideas we feel more confident that we can apply convergent thinking to refine the list of initial thoughts into one or two great ideas that we can take forward to the next level.

But that's not the end of the story. To ensure that we're developing the right thing for the right people, we need to rapidly explore our chosen idea(s) and add enough flesh to the concept. We want to rapidly create a low-fidelity prototype of the customer experience so we can validate our thinking with business stake-holders and end customers.

There is value in the envision activities because they spark ideas and help us refine our thinking. This is about doing just-in-time design to prove the concept before proceeding. There is as much waste (if not far more!) in spending time and money on an ill-thought-through, unvalidated idea that fails at launch, as there is in doing big, up-front design to specify and sign off on every last pixel. Now we're much more confident that we're building the right thing for the right people and are happy to elaborate on that vision.

COMING NEXT

Now that we have a vision and a design direction, we need to quickly elaborate and get to the next level of detail. What's more, we need to get ready for development.

ELABORATION: READY, STEADY, BUILD

8

"I KEEP THE SUBJECT OF MY INQUIRY CONSTANTLY BEFORE ME, AND WAIT TILL THE FIRST DAWNING OPENS GRADUALLY, BY LITTLE AND LITTLE, INTO A FULL AND CLEAR LIGHT."

—ISAAC NEWTON

In this chapter, we'll walk through the elaboration process, look at user stories and story maps to manage and prioritise stories according to customer goals, and prepare for the first iteration.

In this chapter, we'll get our vision ready for development and introduce a new aspect of agile requirements gathering: customer goals. You can't always get what you want, but you can use goal-oriented thinking to ensure the initial scope is in line with the design vision rather than a feature checklist. We'll also touch on how agile team's project management gets to the place where development starts in earnest.

As an experience designer, this talk of requirements and analysis may tempt you to skip this chapter. *Not relevant to me* you may be thinking. We'd urge you to avoid that temptation. Agile analysis is different from the old requirements specification and documentation process. It is inherently collaborative. By being involved in the story writing and project planning, you can ensure that the voice of the customer is heard and that customer goals are paramount in the management of the product backlog from which development will commence.

During elaboration we'll pull together the pieces of the puzzle that the team need to start actually building the product.

THE MINIMUM VIABLE PRODUCT

It's only natural, you want it all. You want to get a fully featured product to your customers, it's *what your customers expect*, isn't it? This is the wrong question to ask. The right question is what is the minimum that your most valuable customers need first. Rarely will they need *everything*. In 2006, the Microsoft Office User experience team published findings that just five commands accounted for 32 percent of all the command usage in Microsoft Word (Paste, Save, Copy, Undo, Bold).

If you focus on the minimum viable product, it means you get the bare minimum into the hands of customers and start learning from their real behaviour.

It needs to be viable and that includes delightful. There are a number of strategies you might use to get there:

- Get an initial beta into the hands of your most loyal and passionate customers, who will jump at the chance to be involved in your product development process.

- Do an initial launch to your internal staff, who are also customers.
- Go live with a product that is useful and desirable, supporting the most common goals with clear signposting of "coming soon" functionality. If customers click on this, you know it is of interest to them.

It can be harder to accept the concept of a minimum viable product when you already have a product in the marketplace that is being replaced. But even in this situation you should question the necessity of a "big bang" launch. You could keep the old product available in parallel with the new product, and retire the old product incrementally over time. For example, you could:

- Identify a discrete part of your product and focus on this first. For example, the *Guardian* newspaper website launched the Travel section first and then incrementally rolled out new sections learning as they went.
- Launch the minimum viable product to new customers (what your new customers don't know, they won't miss) and give existing customers the option to try the new version.
- Identify the most commonly used functions and launch those with the ability to return to the existing product for lesser-used functionality.

A BIG IDEA DOESN'T GUARANTEE SUCCESS

Eric Ries, the founder of Lean Startup, tells a story of how he worked for five years for a start-up with a hand-picked team of the great and good. When he joined they wouldn't tell him what the product was, just the names of the cool people he would be working with. The team was based in an aircraft hangar. The project was shrouded in secrecy. They were building the Big Idea, the future of the Internet. They generated excitement in Silicon Valley, the press were curious, and when the product finally launched it got column inches. But what it didn't get was customers. Five years to build the Big Idea with all the features, industrially strengthened, and then to fail. Not much wisdom in that.

This is a lesson repeated again and again, organisations shrouding their product development in secrecy, waiting until they've got the full feature set before hitting the market. The concept of minimal marketable feature set is alien to them. Painful as well. Why is this? ▪

THE MINIMUM VIABLE PRODUCT IS THAT VERSION OF A NEW PRODUCT WHICH ALLOWS A TEAM TO COLLECT THE MAXIMUM AMOUNT OF VALIDATED LEARNING ABOUT CUSTOMERS WITH THE LEAST EFFORT.

—Eric Ries, Founder, Lean Startup

PRIORITISATION

In consensus-driven organisations with multiple stakeholders, requirements are pushed by personal, siloed agendas. Marketing stakeholders will be pushing content management to the top of the pile, change management will be pushing training and support tools, IT will be pushing diagnostic tools, and the high priority requirements become a disjointed list of features that do little to address the business objectives.

Prioritisation is difficult. Bad experiences with IT often lead businesspeople to believe that anything given a low priority is effectively being descoped, and thus they are reluctant to mark anything low priority.

It doesn't have to be this way. The agile approach breaks functionality into user stories that are easily ordered. Agile experience design leverages this with story mapping as a tool for organising requirements around customer goals. We'll start by looking at user stories.

USER STORIES

DO YOU READ THE MANUAL?

Let's face it: when you unwrap a new product, chances are you won't read the manual. Manuals aren't read because people just want to start *using* the product. And besides, the product should be easy enough to use without a manual. When it comes to software development, documentation is like the manual. No one wants to read through reams of specifications; they want to start doing. Enter the user story.

WHAT'S THE STORY?

A user story is the fuel of an agile project. It is the requirement against which code is written and the project planned. Unlike the requirements documentation you may have seen in the past, a user story is very simple: a title and a sentence or two of plain English to describe it. Most importantly,

It is a *Placeholder*
for a Conversation

A user story represents a prompt for a conversation between the appropriate stakeholders as and when necessary.

This is because talking is more efficient than writing. It enables the requester of the requirement to be close to the people who are going to implement it. This is markedly different from the traditional approach to capturing requirements where the business analyst captures all the detail up front before development starts. When you have this closeness, you remove ambiguity and conflict.

Let's illustrate what we mean by a conversation.

Representatives of the business, experience design, and IT are in the room together talking about a specific feature at the point when it matters.

Introducing the product owner (PO), the experience designer (XD), and the developer (DEV) on an Internet banking project discussing what balance to display to customers on their account overview:

XD: We want to display an "at-a-glance" balance of their account.

DEV: We need to know which balance to display.

XD: Feedback from the existing site is that customers are confused with all the different balances we display. We'd like to go with just one, but what should it be?

PO: Good question. Cleared balance.

DEV: Thought you'd say that. We can get last night's closing balance easily, but getting a real-time balance out of the legacy system's going to take a lot more effort.

PO: How much more effort?

DEV: Well, we'd assumed using the closing balance, which is one point. To do what you want will be three points, and that'll mean taking something else out.

PO: OK, for this release let's go with last night's closing balance. I assume we'll be able to have some context-sensitive help to explain what this balance means.

XD: Yeah, no problem. Something like this? (sketches out his thoughts on paper).

DEV: We need to just make sure that's down in the acceptance criteria.

The experience designer was in the meeting and has stressed to the product owner that, for the customer, it's confusing to have many different balances on a checking account. They'd like to display the most up-to-date balance, that is, what the customer has in her account that is available to spend now (before the overdraft). Together they learned from the developers that that's a lot more effort than they'd anticipated. Now they've got a decision to make. They have two options:

- Do the simplest thing, which will not impact the timeline and will enable them to implement the full requirement at a later time.
- Choose to do the more complicated thing now, in which case they would have to descope something else to make it fit into the timeline.

The designer won't have to wait to see her designs butchered in production; she is part of the process and fully involved in the inevitable change and compromises that occur in the project life cycle.

SHARED

Being a discussion prompt card, the story serves multiple purposes for multiple stakeholders yet remains understandable to all:

- Business analyst: It captures the requirement and its business intent.
- Developer: It's something that can be estimated and developed against.
- Product owner: It's something that can be prioritised.
- Project manager: It's something that can be tracked.
- QA: It's something that can be tested.
- Designer: It's something that (may) need a user interface.

SAVING EFFORT

A story is not a document it's an index card (8.1).

With such a small canvas to write on, you're limited in what you can write. With such a simple mechanism for capturing requirements, it also means that they can be laid out to be seen in their entirety, be shuffled about, and be ripped up. An agile project can get through a lot of index cards, but before you question its lack of green credentials, spare a thought for those waterfall documents:

~This page is left intentionally blank~

8.1
You can't write much
on an index card with
a marker pen.

HOW IT'S WRITTEN

In its most elementary form the story card identifies who wants the story, what it needs to do, and why it is valuable: "As an X, I want to Y, so that Z." Don't worry, despite what you might hear, it's not compulsory to write your story in this format.

As a… This defines who the end user will be. The parallel with user-centered design approaches is obvious here: an understanding and appreciation of the user. The difference is that this is just at the role level.

I want to… Again, this is a common step with user-centred design approaches: an understanding of the customer (user) goal and tasks to achieve that goal. Addressing a requirement in terms of customer goals focuses development on what is needed.

So that… Why do we need it? What business objective is it trying to meet? Why should the customer care? What goal will it help her achieve?

AS A PERSONA

Is the user a persona?

For example, *"As Sue, the novice Customer Service Rep"* or *"As Mike, the experienced administrator."*

It depends on whether this adds value, detail, or context to the requirement. Often, the high-level role will be sufficient. For a generic requirement such as *login*, the requirement will be the same regardless of the persona. In other words, the persona is inconsequential to this story; all we need is the role. Other times the persona is a significant modifier to the story. For example, when a human context is critical to making a more informed decision on how the story may be implemented. Sue and Mike may both require the same functionality, but they'll interact with it in different ways, both by role, but also by ability. By identifying Sue, and knowing that she represents a large user base, we ensure that the user interface we design makes no assumptions of user expertise that we might otherwise make if we were designing only for Mike.

USING BUSINESS LANGUAGE

As far as possible user stories should be implementation agnostic. For example, the customer wants to store her details. We state the need to store information, but not the mechanism for achieving it (database, xml/flat file, and so on).

ASSUMPTIONS, NARRATIVE, ACCEPTANCE CRITERIA, AND OTHER ASSORTED ACCOMPANIMENTS

In the first instance, all we really need to do is capture the title and story details. We're working with the stories, we're familiar with them, and undoubtedly some are going to be ripped up or changed. There's a whole lot more to a story when it comes closer to development, but at this point it would be a waste to elaborate on them. At this point in the project life cycle, there's a good chance the stories we identify now will never be developed. They'll be split, changed, replaced, made redundant, or be found to be unnecessary.

WHAT MAKES A GOOD STORY?

Anyone who's been doing agile for any period of time will be able to chant the mantra "INVEST" when describing what makes a good story. They'll tell you it needs to be:

Independent: As much as possible user stories should work by themselves and be implementable in any order. That's not to say that stories can't be dependent on each other; to "delete a user from the system" there must be a story to "create a user in the system"; however, the dependency should not be intertwined and complex.

Negotiable: Remember the balance display story above? It was negotiable. The essence of the story was for the customer to know at a glance how much money she has in her checking account. There were a number of ways to make this happen. The negotiability of the story provided flexibility and freedom to work within the constraints of the project at the time of implementing the story.

Valuable: It's got to be of worth to the business requesting it or to the end customer. We don't need to build an enterprise messaging system or unified workflow engine if it's not going to deliver demonstrable value here and now.

Estimable: We need some sense of the effort required to build it. This is important when it comes to planning; we really want our stories to fit into an iteration.

Small: This goes hand in hand with estimable. If a story is large or epic we can have less confidence with how long it will take to produce, and with that largeness usually comes more uncertainty and ambiguity. For a designer, this can often be frustrating. What looks small to our design eyes could be large to a developer who is thinking about the third-party systems she'll need to integrate with and all the uncertainty that will entail. But more on that later.

Testable: In other words, you can easily articulate what *done* means; when the story is complete, given a certain state when an action is performed, a result will be produced. If you can't state this, how will you know the story is complete?

WHAT'S WRONG WITH THIS?

What we've just described is the agile practitioner's version of a story. But there's a mismatch going on here.

What's the value of something that is small and independent?

Value only lies in the broader product context. And here is one of the biggest shortcomings with agile stories. Independently they may be useful for development, but when they are presented as a collection of random stories in a backlog, there is no coherence or relationship to the overarching product vision.

The backlog is the list of stories, the requirements that have been identified but are yet to be developed. The order in which they are built is decided during planning meetings. When working in this way from the backlog, it's easy to lose sight of the vision.

Furthermore, because the stories are incrementally developed, the user interface will be emergent, aligned to development activities rather than the greater vision.

The alarm bells are probably ringing at that thought.

This is where you as an agile experience designer start to wield your influence on the project. For you, stories are going to be mapped back to customer goals. You're going to introduce a new level of acceptance criteria, that of the customer goal. But before we get to that, let's consider where user stories come from and how you can help drive the process.

DESIGN AND STORIES

We find that in performing teams the writing of stories is something that is everybody's responsibility and is a constant process throughout discovery, envisioning, and elaboration. Sometimes a sketch or wireframe comes first, with the stories being distilled from the design. Clearly this may result in relatively detailed and specific stories, but the important thing at this stage is to use whatever process is right for you and for the team. Other times, the story will be written and the design will follow. Again, there's no prescriptive way, it's up to the team to find which way works best for them. When developers and designers are closely collaborating, you soon get a rhythm. What is important is that the stories remain focused on business and customer goals. What follows is an illustration of how we can do that.

WEREN'T WE SKETCHING WHILST WE WERE ENVISIONING?

You probably were. That's why this isn't so much a linear, sequential process as one that is layered, doing what is required when it is required. As you developed different concepts in envisioning, through process flows, sketches, wireframes, or prototypes, capturing stories at the same time would have made sense if you had confidence that they were likely to make the final cut. But if you were just brainstorming, then capturing stories at that point would probably have been wasted effort. ▪

GOALS AND JOURNEYS

With clearly defined business objectives in mind, we turn to how these can be related to customer goals and the activities they perform to realise them. We may start with a persona and walk through a day in the life of their interaction with the product. The use of scenarios may inform the thinking. As we develop a customer journey for them, at each step we're capturing stories. At this point they may be just titles, prompts. Indeed at this stage we're looking at breadth rather than detail. Chances are they will be epics that we can break down into something more useful later when we start narrowing down on scope.

Let's take an example of online banking for a retail bank. We'll start with creating a scenario:

Alex is an administrative assistant for a logistics company. She is at work on her lunch break. She wants to check the balance on her checking account to see whether her salary has been deposited. If it has, she wants to pay money into her friend's account to pay for the festival tickets she bought for her.

We know this scenario is accurate because we have:

- Spoken to business SMEs and business analysts.
- Analysed web analytics data and identified these tasks as the most frequently used.

- Surveyed customers with a list of activities and asked them to indicate which they use most often.
- Interviewed/observed customers and seen this to be the most frequently used task.

Note our focus on goal frequency, but we could also consider goal importance. The ability to inform the bank that the customer is traveling may be an infrequent goal for most customers, but it is critical if the customer needs to use her cards overseas.

Let's break that scenario down.

Alex is an administrative assistant for a logistics company. She is at work on her lunch break. For the purpose of the story-generating exercise, this is sufficient. We can assume from the persona we developed for Alex that she will be reasonably computer/web literate and that she will be reasonably time poor—she wants to complete the task as efficiently as possible. We don't need all the detail of a persona unless it will add value to our scenario.

She wants to see whether her salary has been paid into her account.
Here we have her primary goal. This is important and will provide us with customer-oriented acceptance criteria later to ensure that the product we're building does what it should. It is also solution agnostic. As part of our process we can ask how it could be realised; each solution will come with costs and benefits. She could discover whether she's been paid:

- By checking her balance on the website.
- By checking her balance on her mobile device.
- By setting up an alert for salary payment and receiving it as an alert.

At this stage we have a conversation about the project constraints and expectations and build up our scope list. This ensures that we're recording ideas that could be in scope for the future, but we don't want to dwell on them now (8.2).

In scope

Balances on web

Out (for now)

Balance Alerts

Undecided

Balance on mobile device

8.2
Putting cards on the wall to indicate what is in and out of scope and undecided.

She wants to check the balance on her checking account to see whether her salary has been deposited. In our scenario we've identified the core activities she will need to complete to accomplish that goal:

- Check balance.
- Check a transaction.

In our scenario we identified another goal:

She wants to pay money into her friend's account to pay for the festival tickets the friend bought for her. This is another primary goal. In our scenario it is related to checking balance and transactions, but could just as easily be an independent goal.

We can write cards for what we've discovered and lay them out on the table (8.3).

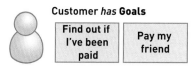

Customer *has* **Goals**

Find out if I've been paid

Pay my friend

8.3
The customer goals are written on cards and laid out.

With the scenario in mind, we need to go down to the next level and outline the tasks that will support the activities. We tell the story of what the customer does on the system, walking through the customer journey. If her goals are to check her balance and to move funds, there are a number of activities that make this possible. At this stage, we'll just consider these activities:

- Log in to bank account.
- View balance.
- View transactions.
- Move funds from her account to her friend's account.
- Log out.

We can map these out in a journey (8.4).

8.4
Decomposing the
goals into contributing
activities.

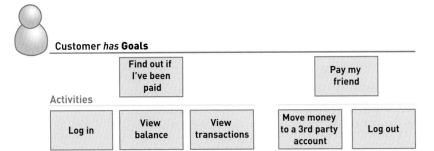

Now we can drill down into the tasks that will enable each of these activities to be realised (8.5). These tasks are the component stories that underpin the activity. For example, for "view transactions" we might have the following (we'll write these out as user stories):

As Alex, logged-in customer, I want to see the payee, date, and amount for individual payments so that I can see who I paid, how much I paid them, and when I paid them.

As Alex, logged-in customer, I want to see the depositor, date, and amount for individual deposits so that I can see who paid money into my account, how much they deposited into the account, and when the payment was made.

As Alex, logged-in customer, I want to sort the transactions by value or date view so that I can more easily find a specific transaction.

As Alex, logged-in customer, I want to search for a specific transaction by the payee or depositor's name so that I can find a specific transaction.

As Alex, logged-in customer, I want to refine the transactions shown by date or amount so that I can find a more specific transaction.

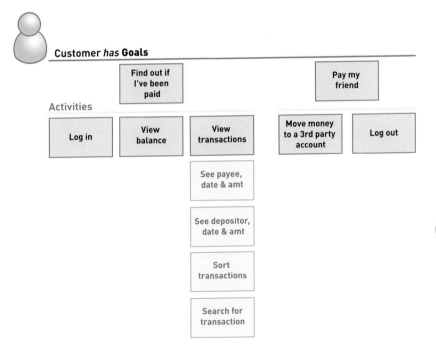

8.5
Breaking the activities down further into user tasks—the stories.

You'll notice that we're already introducing a concept of importance as we list the stories. We'll come back to that later.

💡 **TIP**

There will be some stories that don't fit; if a story does not support a customer task, question its relevance or importance. Even apparently technical or operational stories should relate back to a goal or activity.

A MAP OF STORIES

We've now got a bunch of goal cards laid out horizontally and beneath each of these a bunch of story cards laid out vertically (8.6).

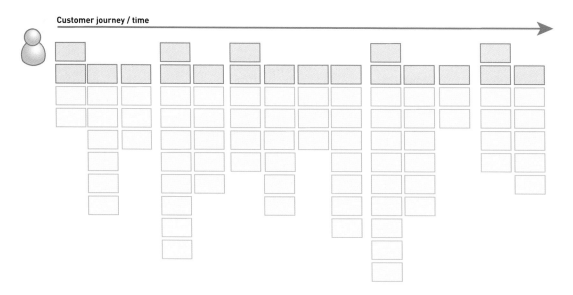

Customer journey / time

8.6

A customer journey with the goals laid out over time.

Whilst we've placed the primary goal cards on the top as a customer journey, what often happens is that because there are multiple customer journeys through the product, these goals essentially become functional areas. In this instance, the move from left to right becomes one of decreasing functional importance. We can illustrate that through another example.

Consider an ATM. It serves a number of purposes, satisfying the following customer goals:

- Withdraw cash.
- Deposit cash.
- Make a balance enquiry.
- Transfer funds between accounts.
- Withdraw foreign currency from an ATM in an airport.
- Top up your pay-as-you-go cell phone.

It's unlikely that a customer will do all those activities in one go! Then there are *hygiene* goals that are a precondition to the customer completing her primary goals, for instance, proving to the bank who she is (enter card and PIN).

Finally there are business goals:

- Provide marketing messages and cross-sell products.
- Prevent repeat card use for "bad" customers.

Here the concept of time no longer makes sense. We lay out the stories according to these groupings with the constituent stories beneath the goals or desired business outcomes (8.7).

8.7
The goals that a customer has with an ATM and the stories for each goal arranged underneath them.

Goals / outcomes →

Prove to the bank who I am	Withdraw funds	Balance enquiry	Prevent card usage	Marketing messages	Deposit funds	Transfer funds	Foreign currency	Cell-phone top-up

Remember that this is a collaborative exercise, together the team, (the BA, the developers, and the product owner) have identified the stories and together they seek to organise them by the goals and outcomes.

Don't think you're going to be able to do this on a desk. This activity requires space: the wall, a number of tables, or even the floor. You can get a feel for the scope of the project at a glance; it should be easy to look at any story and understand where it fits into the product vision. What you've just built is a story map (8.8). You can easily see the scope of the project and understand how stories fit into the bigger picture. It is still an abstract view—at some stage you'll need to tie them back to the interface they represent, but for now we've overcome the issue of a random pile of cards in the backlog. Better still, we've got a useful tool for helping us prioritise what is important. We'll talk more about prioritisation later.

8.8
Example of a story map covering a wall.

BUSINESS PROCESS

Similar to the focus on the customer's journey through the system, here we map out the business process. We'll still place the customer goal as paramount, but as a process it may be more efficient to consider the flow of data through the system. For example, the following of a work order through the system; it is *captured* by someone in sales, is *processed* by someone in accounts. It is *dispatched* by someone in the warehouse, it is *supported* by someone in customer service, and it is *serviced* by someone in engineering. Whilst the focus is on the business process, we still focus on the human goals (italicised verbs) again, extracting user stories from the flows as we walk through them. These may be developed on the wall or on cards on the table.

CROSS-FUNCTIONAL STORIES

As we walk through the customer journey, chances are we'll identify constraints or requirements that don't immediately pertain to functionality. For example, "A trader in Hong Kong wants to download the report quickly." Not a problem, we capture these, but always think on how we would test the story. In this case, "The report can be downloaded in any location in under two seconds." These nonfunctional requirements, discussed in Chapter 6, "Agile Discovery," are often referred to as cross-functional stories because their impact is felt across the system.

As well as performance, other examples of cross-functional stories might include: archiving, scalability, training, support, reporting, internationalisation, compliance, security, monitoring, and so on. This is also the place to capture requirements specific to design, for example, browser compatibility, accessibility, and so on.

THE UI DETAIL

When we sketch out interfaces, it's really easy to add detail that we feel is obvious or inconsequential but actually has a reasonable developer effort and will need to be called out as a separate user story. Similarly, there'll be stuff that as a designer we'll take for granted but which will make the developer suck through his teeth and say "you're gonna have to put that one into the backlog." Examples of these stories include:

- Table pagination
- Breadcrumbs
- Help
- Search
- Nonstandard page layouts that will require new templates

STORIES MAPPED

TIP

Rather than dwelling
in Visio or OmniGraffle,
work on the whiteboard.

The toolbox you use for understanding *process flows* and *customer journeys* provides a framework for enabling the team to capture better user stories. Identify the key goals and supporting activities—the customer journeys—then drill down into the component user stories. In this way you'll always be able to map the story back to its purpose. And that is important. It prevents us from descoping seemingly trivial stories without which the product becomes mediocre and functional rather than delightful.

THE NEW USER STORY BACKLOG IS A MAP.[1]

—Jeff Patton, www.agileproductdesign.com

| Find out if
I've been
paid |

| View
transactions |

| See payee,
date & amt |

| See depositor,
date & amt |

| Sort
transactions |

| Search for
transaction |

Hierarchy of importance

8.9
Stories for the goal;
order according to their
importance.

STORY MAPPING AS A PRIORITISATION TOOL

Let's return to the goals and the stories we laid out earlier on the story map. We identified a pretty full scope (8.6).

At first glance it's easy to say, "We need all of that." For each of those goals we've identified a number of stories. Let's look at one of those goals (8.9).

To view transactions there are a number of tasks or activities that will enable this goal to be achieved. Sure we'd love them all, but what if we can't? With them laid out in a story map we can visualise their relative importance to each other. Sorting and searching are valuable—they'll help Alex achieve her goal of seeing if she's been paid more quickly than having to manually find the transaction, but not having them is not critical.

---

1 http://www.Agileproductdesign.com/blog/the_new_backlog.html.

Rather than having a pile of user stories that we're prioritising in isolation, here we can understand the impact that our decisions have in the richness and completeness for delivering on the customer goal.

With this thinking in mind, we can now go through the whole customer journey and identify what a minimum viable product, a first release, will comprise (8.10).

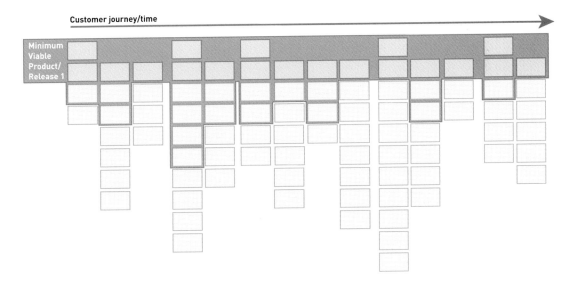

As we walk through the customer journey, we're covering the breadth but are also adjusting the depth of detail for each goal type.

When we have laid out our cards by overarching goals or outcomes rather than within the specificity of a customer journey as we did for our ATM example, then we can add a second dimension of prioritisation. For our ATM, it must do the basics of dispensing cash and balance enquiry. At a glance you can see that we're not including deposits, transfers, foreign currency, or cell-phone top-up (8.11).

8.10
Identification of the minimum viable product.

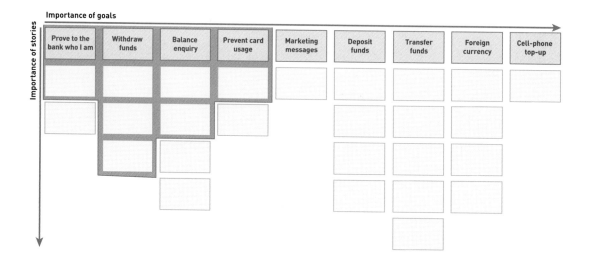

Importance of goals

Importance of stories

Prove to the bank who I am	Withdraw funds	Balance enquiry	Prevent card usage	Marketing messages	Deposit funds	Transfer funds	Foreign currency	Cell-phone top-up

8.11

Prioritising stories by
goal importance and
story importance.

HOW DO WE JUDGE IMPORTANCE?

At first glance it can be hard to deprioritise features, pushing them down the level of importance. There are a number of factors that may be considered to help inform your decision making on how important the feature is. Go through this list one by one, where we've tried to list them in order of priority. This is the sort of order we'd expect to see stories prioritised against.

Customer need: What if this feature wasn't available to the customer? What would happen? Would its omission have a catastrophic impact on the success of the product? Is it essential for the customer's goal to be completed? Is there a manual workaround or interim solution that would suffice? What if it came later, how would customers feel?

Business need: There are some features that the customer may not care about and have no impact on the customer experience, but there is a business imperative to have them included. Advertising is a good example of this. It delivers a critical revenue stream to the business but is not something that customers actively require.

Differentiator: Will this feature make your product stand out in crowd? Is it a marketable feature in its own right? Or is it just parity, doing what everyone else does? Remember that whilst it is tempting to drive your priorities by a need for feature parity (with the product you're replacing or with your competitor products) it's better to excel at what your customers really care about, even if that means removing functionality. This is something that Apple do really well.

Support: Does it prevent errors and enable the customer to complete their task efficiently and effectively? Things like data validation, process feedback, help. Consider the context of usage.

Frequency and volume of use: How often is the feature used and by how many people? If we believe it is (or will be) rarely used or is used by a minority of people, then maybe we can leave it till later. The exception to this is features that are demanded by high-value customers which can rise up the hierarchy of priority. In fact, high-value minorities are often a niche that can be served by a narrow subset of features tailored to them as an initial minimum viable product.

Delighter: These are often put at the back of the pile, but ultimately they are what makes a product compelling.

Another approach is to assign a score (1–5) for each of three factors: value to the customer, value to the business, and ease of implementation. Total scores for each story to find those with highest priority.

IS THERE AN ALTERNATIVE?

As you look at your stories, constantly ask if there is an alternative way of enabling the same outcomes to be reached. It would be great to have Chateaubriand, but if you're just looking to satisfy your hunger, a burger will do.

If we look at the ATM example, in our initial prioritisation we excluded marketing messages. To reach this goal of displaying relevant messages to cross-sell products to the customer, we assumed we would need to create and edit these and manage the supporting business rules. This would create significant scope but is not essential. All the complexity can come later; for the first release, we'll have a splash screen with promotional messaging that can be changed by the developer rather than the business.

Focus on what will meet the immediate business goal, with the full functionality to be delivered later.

THE PRIORITISATION EXERCISE WAS KEY, LEADING US TO FOCUS ON WHAT WAS REALLY IMPORTANT TO GET TO MARKET IN AN INITIAL RELEASE, AND WHAT FEATURES COULD COME LATER.

—Steve Pitman,
Head of Digital,
Which?

ESTIMATION

Even though we've prioritised what we believe the minimum viable product is, we've still no idea if we can deliver it for the time frame or budget we've allocated. The scope feels right, but is it doable? When the developers estimate the stories that have been identified, they will make assumptions. These will be geared around how they might implement each story in the simplest way. Design is probably not at the forefront of their mind, and it is for this reason that having a designer as part of the process, supporting the team in explaining what the story means for a customer, means that the developer estimates are informed by design.

 TIP

By being part of the estimation process, the designer ensures her vision for the stories is clearly articulated. This avoid estimate inflation later if design complexity is introduced.

As much as teams try to apply science to estimation, unless you've done exactly the same thing before, with the same people with the same knowledge and the same constraints, any estimate will be little more than a guess. How much of a guess depends on when you make it; the more information you have to hand, with less ambiguity, the more accurate it will be. At this stage of our process, we've got a vision of what we want and a collection of stories that will enable this to be built. We're comfortable with the fact that many of the stories we've identified may never be developed (it's change, remember), others will be split into smaller stories. But what we need right now is an idea of how big it is. After all, we need a budget to proceed and what typically happens is someone along the way has made a commitment to a date. We need to be clear whether we think that is achievable and, if not, give the bad news early.

Different teams adopt different approaches to agile estimation, but it should always be a collaborative exercise involving the developers who are actually building the product. It is typically a two-stage process, beginning with giving each story a relative size. This may be a number (often called points), or a T-shirt size. The story is described and they discuss the tasks they might undertake to complete the story. They then *simultaneously* state their estimate. Having a designer in the process helps spell out what the story means to the customer. Developers will look for the simplest solution, but this will often ignore user interface. Having experience design at the estimation table ensures this is not forgotten.

The next step in the process is to play a planning game. The team decide what team size is appropriate to work on the project. This will be informed by how they can parallelise work and how they can work most efficiently. They then identify stories they believe could fit into a single iteration. They tally up the total estimate size (for example, points) for all stories they thought would fit. They play this over multiple rounds and come up with an average estimate for the iteration. This average is the estimated velocity.

DOES THE DESIGNER PLAY?

In our experience, design effort is not included in the estimate, in the same way that analysis is not called out. The estimate includes only the critical path in a project, and development effort is central to this. Having designers involved in the planning poker game is beneficial for both sides. The designer can articulate her expectations for the story; the developers can raise issues early when they believe design expectations are going to have a significant impact on the effort to complete the story. The simplest way of developing the story sometimes will come at the cost of design. Only by you, the designer, being present at the session will you ensure that they are conscious of the need to delight as well as deliver.

There will be some projects where front-end design and development will become a bottleneck because of the scope of work to be done. For example, this can happen where there is graphic intensive work to be completed, such as with infographics. In this instance, it makes sense for these stories to be treated as independent of development effort and estimated by the design team in the same way. ▪

With an estimated velocity and team size, the team can now see whether their first prioritisation exercise was enough to cut the scope to something that will fit the time and budget allocated to the project. If it doesn't, it is time to return to the story map. When the stories have points associated with them (a price) and a total number of points that are estimated to be deliverable (budget), it is possible to play a further game, to "buy the release". The product owner is given coins to the numerical value of the total story points and places them on the stories that are important. When the money runs out, the release is bought. If we can't afford it, we'll have to cut more scope until the product is affordable. In this way, we can come up with an initial plan to take into development.

TIP

It is a fallacy that more developers will deliver a product faster. They'll often remind you that it takes nine months to have a baby, but nine women can't have a baby in a month

VELOCITY

It's basic math that you learn at school: speed equals distance over time. And that is at the heart of agile project management. The team's speed, or rather their velocity, is the amount of work they complete. It's a simple calculation. Take the amount of work (distance) they do over a given time period (an iteration or sprint). Once we know their velocity, we can predict how likely they are to reach their destination (scope) in the time scales we've given. This can be expressed as a simple chart:

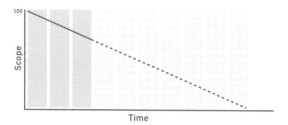

There's 100 points worth of scope that we plan to deliver in ten iterations. We're three iterations in, with a velocity of ten. It looks like we're going to make it.

But let's assume we're going slower than predicted:

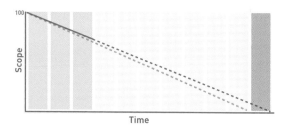

The orange line is what we predicted with a velocity of ten. Three iterations in and we're only delivering nine points in an iteration rather than ten. We extend the line, and we see that we're not going to make the date. At this point, the team have data to make an informed decision; either manage expectations that the scope can be delivered but it's going to take longer, or look to cutting the scope to make it fit.

There's another scenario that we can plan for. Three iterations in and whilst the team is hitting their planned velocity, we want to add more scope.

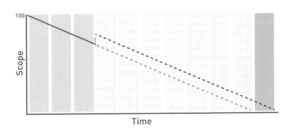

Instantly we can see the impact this will have on our ability to make the date. Again, we've got data to enable us to make an informed decision. We can push the date out, or we can remove something else to make the new scope fit.

What we've shown here is a *burn-down chart*. Many teams do it the other way round and present a burn-up chart—the concept is the same. This is a very simplistic view; you'll see a lot more added to these charts, and we'll explore this more in the next chapter on delivery. ▪

TIME, SCOPE, AND QUALITY: ARE YOU FIXING THE WRONG THING?

Design is all about the finished article, right? Unless you're a Michelangelo or a Picasso, your sketches or half-complete works are worthless. This thinking permeates through the industry and ties us into all sorts of knots. The traditional way of building software requires two primary design inputs before the construction phase commences:

▪ Defined scope articulated through requirements.

▪ Defined creative direction articulated through comps.

On top of this, quality is not going to be something we compromise on and there's only a finite budget for the project. We've fixed scope, quality, and time, so when things inevitably go wrong, one or more of those will have to give.

Rather than starting with unknowns as the primary inputs to the construction phase, (that is, scope and design), agile planning enables us to fix things we don't know and have control of: time and cost. There's nothing like having these set in your mind to help focus on what is really important and how to shape a compelling mini- mum viable product. Treat time and cost as an empty vessel into which you'll feed scope. With this mindset, it is easier to decide when you have built enough. ▪

IN SUMMARY

This chapter hasn't been so much about agile design as introducing the designer to the things that an agile project usually starts with. On an agile project, stories are the fuel that drives the delivery engine. In this chapter, we introduced how experience design can play a pivotal role in the development and prioritisation of stories. Rather than design and development working independently of each other with their own documents and deliverables, the user story is a shared artefact that has meaning and value to both practises.

The experience designer brings an emphasis on customer goals and journeys to the process of elaborating the product vision into something that developers can build from. We introduced the concept of the minimum viable product; if we start with the goal then decompose it down into supporting activities and tasks, we can better prioritise what is important. Rather than focusing on the breadth of functionality at a feature level, we can identify what depth we need to go down to in order to accomplish the customer goal and deliver a coherent and compelling customer proposition.

COMING NEXT

In the next chapter, the rubber hits the road as we start building the product. We'll look at what an agile project in full steam looks like and the role that design plays in it. We'll look to show how activities that you'd previously look to complete as input into the development process can now run in parallel. And we'll show you how designers work alongside developers and how usability testing is baked into the process rather than something that is a troublesome formality at the end of development.

9

INTO
DEVELOPMENT

"BY FAR THE BEST PROOF IS EXPERIENCE."

—ATTRIBUTED TO SIR FRANCIS BACON

Now we're ready to build the vision. Here we look
at the anatomy of an iteration and the life of a
story, how to burn down and not burn out, and
how to add experience design into the mix.

IT'S NOT
ITERATION IF
YOU ONLY DO IT
ONCE.

—Jeff Patton,
www.agileproductdesign.com

So far we've talked about getting ready. Now we'll turn to the heart of the process: iterative development. This is the nuts and bolts of agile software delivery. This is what it's all about: delivering working, production-ready code regularly and often. And this is where the worlds of the experience designer and the agile developer are most often in conflict. The designers complain that there isn't enough time to do what needs to be done. The developers complain that the designers just don't get agile. In this chapter, we'll look at how experience design and agile can be integrated on a daily basis. We'll start by looking at how we get from an idea that's been written down as a user story to something that works (and arguably could be put live, right into production). We'll consider the ceremony associated with agile. (In fact, there's far more rigor associated with agile than on a waterfall project). We'll cover a number of practises, both from the way that agile projects are managed and how developers work.

Throughout this chapter, we'll be using agile in the broadest sense of the word. This isn't pure Scrum or XP, but rather a distillation of what works best.

ITERATIONS: THE HEARTBEAT OF DELIVERY

Iterations, or sprints, are at the heart of an agile project. They're short, time-boxed periods in which the team organise and manage themselves. In essence, there are three parts to each iteration:

- The product owner asks for something of value to be done.
- In a short period of time, it is done.
- It is shown to the product owner to confirm that it's been done to his satisfaction.

Feedback, along with the ability to adjust to change as we go, is key.

This requires a spirit of collaboration and transparency. For every iteration, the team showcase is completed, and you get release-ready functionality. By keeping iterations short, the team avoids undertaking activities that may never be required. As the product emerges and is tested by customers, the inevitable changes are accommodated in the iterative process.

ITERATION ZERO

With the story-mapped backlog of user stories that we identified earlier, we're now ready to start turning them into a product. The project starts with iteration zero, an opportunity for the developers to get themselves set up and for the designers (visual and experience) to start work with the business analyst (BA) to flesh out stories in preparation for iteration one.

During iteration zero, the team should take care of logistical issues, especially ensuring that the team have an appropriate workspace and technology. This is when you set up hardware, software environments, source control, and project WIKI, as well as any tools you may need, such as development, tracking, and test tools.

The visual designers will have been working on creative options during the elaboration phase. At this point, they'll be looking for agreement on the high creative direction for the project.

ANATOMY OF AN ITERATION

Before each iteration commences, the team select the stories they want to play and then, in short, time-boxed periods, they elaborate on and develop the story. The objective is to produce something of value at the end of each iteration. This is what it looks like (9.1):

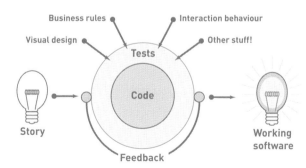

 TIP

Team workspace should include wall space for a card wall, whiteboards, and desk space that supports collaborative working—no cubicles or curvy desks, thank you!

9.1
The ingredients of an iteration.

Visual design is what the product will look like. We'll need creative artefacts that support the functionality. This may just be a wireframe, images to use in the story, or HTML and CSS into which the developers will build functionality.

Business rules are the logic behind what the system needs to do. These define or constrain what happens with inputs and outputs and how they relate to one another. Where there's a business analyst on the project, this is his realm, but business rules will have a direct impact on the experience design so, as we'll explore later, they're developed in conjunction with the user interface (UI).

Interaction behaviour defines how the customer will interact with the system. Again, this may be articulated in sketches or as HTML with placeholder JavaScript to illustrate the behaviour.

Other stuff may be required, depending on the nature of the product and the story itself. For example, writing by copywriters (let's stop leaving error messages to analysts and developers to write).

These inputs provide detail on *what* is required. But this is not sufficient for our agile developers. They need **tests**. Tests will enable the team to know *when* it's completed to the required quality. As we'll see later with test-driven development, testing is embedded from the start, rather than just at the end of the development process.

Finally, **coding** is at the centre of the process. As a non-techie person, it's easy to assume that coding is just sitting in front of a computer typing. That's like saying that visual design is just sitting in front of a computer with Adobe Photoshop® or Adobe Illustrator®. There's a lot more to it than that. In an agile process, the developers are doing the technical design as they go. They act as architects of the system as it evolves on the whiteboard rather than in a detailed specification up front. As they learn more and need to change and evolve their design, they *refactor* the code.

Throughout the development of the story there is continual **feedback**. We're done only when the story is complete (when it passes all the tests), so any formal sign-off in this loop is meaningless. The business rules, visual design, and interaction behaviour may have been captured, documented, or completed, but they may need to be revisited during coding. It is therefore incumbent on the owners of those activities to be actively involved in the development process. They're not just feeding the developers specifications to build from, they're active participants, *guiding what is built as it's built*. For the designer, this means that instead of design being something static that's created at the beginning of the project and not touched again, it's a continuous process.

At the end of an iteration the completed story is showcased to the stakeholders. With all being well, everyone is happy that the story does what is expected and the process repeats itself. When you're in a process of continuous design and continuous delivery, you'll almost certainly be able to release enhancements to your product at the granular story level.

More typically, stories are batched for release. A release has a similar anatomy. Customer goals are identified with the collated stories wrapped in tests, both at the code level (such as scenario testing) and at the experience design level (such as usability testing) to enable customers to achieve these goals (9.2).

 TIP

Remember, this is an iterative process and that means iterating, making changes to stories that you have already done.

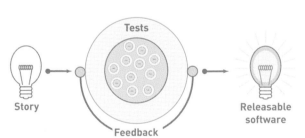

Story

Tests

Feedback

Releasable
software

9.2
The ingredients of
a release.

DO JUST ENOUGH

Let's return to the activities we need to do to turn the story into software. Just because this is an agile project doesn't mean we can skip the analysis. We have to get the business rules. We need acceptance criteria to test against. On a practical level the developers are going to need to know where to put functional elements on the page.

We need to reduce as much ambiguity and uncertainty around the story as possible before the code starts to be written, otherwise we'll be introducing the potential for wasted effort into the process.

For example, it's easy to specify what content you want on a single page, but until you actually see what it looks like, it's hard to be sure.

Take the description of a cell phone on a phone catalog page. There are dozens of attributes that could describe the phone: its size, display, memory, camera, and features. What phone criteria you present to the customer will be heavily influenced by their importance and value, but also by how they'll appear on the page. It would be inefficient use of developer effort to iterate the design in code. Far better to start with the design of the page first, experiment with that, then start coding.

This is not to say that you need to have all the analysis and design complete before the developers start writing the code. For example, if you have a list of titles for your customers (such as Mr., Mrs., Ms., Dr., or Professor), developing the story to create a customer on the system doesn't depend on whether or not *professor* is a title we need to capture. Coding can commence before this information is confirmed.

HOW LONG?

How long should an iteration be? For experience design to be successfully embedded into the process, an iteration should be a week or two in duration. This enables the team to regularly and rapidly provide feedback to the stakeholders; any longer than a fortnight and the benefits of the rapid feedback cycle become diluted.

With such a short time scale to write the code, it makes sense for the bulk of the analysis and design work for that story to be completed immediately prior to the story being played. When we're running at one or two weekly iterations, this can comfortably happen one iteration ahead. The fact that we're doing the analysis and design one iteration ahead means that it's ready for the developer to pick it up and start working on it without it getting blocked by lingering ambiguity over the requirement or the design.

In this way iterations should be treated as planning tools laid over the continuous process of design/analysis—develop—test rather than the batching-up of a set of stories to be pushed into development. We'll talk more about this later.

THE LIFE OF A STORY

Before we consider how design fits into the process, let's look at some of the core activities that occur during iterations in a performing agile team (9.3).

9.3
Core iteration activities.

Iteration planning meeting: The team start by planning the next iteration. They identify the stories they're going to play. During this meeting they'll review the team's velocity and agree on the amount of work they can commit to.

Analysis and design: This involves getting the meat onto the bone for the stories that have been identified for the forthcoming iteration. Here is where the bulk of the analysis and design is done—one iteration ahead of development.

Story planning meeting: In his book *The Agile Samurai,* Jonathan Rasmusson describes the story planning game as an opportunity to "review test criteria for upcoming stories… review estimates with the developers and generally make sure we've done our homework on the next batch of iteration stories." He adds that this is not an activity that's found in any formal agile method; rather, it's something he's found useful "for avoiding the waste that comes from starting an unanalysed story."

 TIP

Don't be cajoled into starting a story if you're not ready. If change is likely, it would be wasteful to build something. Either defer playing the story now or use cheap prototyping rather than iterating more expensively in the product itself.

Remember that agile is not a prescriptive methodology. You've got to find what works best for you and your team, and continually learn, adapt, and improve according to your own circumstances.

Design review meeting: Alongside the story planning meeting is the design review meeting. This provides an opportunity for people who aren't immediately involved in the project (marketing and branding, for example) to review the design.

On an agile project where design detail is emergent and subject to change, it's important to make sure that there is regular communication with all of the stakeholders to get their buy-in and feedback and to prevent potential bottlenecks from functions that aren't necessarily following an agile process.

Code: The developers write the code for the story.

Stand-ups: Every day the whole team get together and review what they've done and what they're about to do, and discuss any issues that are blocking the way.

Showcase: The team showcase the completed story back to the stakeholders. This isn't a prototype; this is real, live working code on a production-like server that could be made live if so required.

Retrospective: Immediately following the showcase the team review their progress and see what's going well (or not so well), solve puzzles, and determine how to improve. It is critical that the team take appropriate action based on the retrospective.

Test: When you showcase the story to the stakeholders, it's hard for them to be put on the spot and asked to agree that the story is done to their satisfaction. Giving them some time after the showcase enables them to evaluate the feature in their own time, and when a collection of stories is developed, ensure that the product is working as a coherent entity.

Analysis and coding are not activities that are performed in isolation. When the team is collocated and collaborating, the business analyst is focused on preparing the stories for the forthcoming iteration, but at the same time working with the developers on the stories that are currently in the iteration. Similarly, the developers in the current iteration input into the stories in analysis as and when the analyst has questions.

Whilst these activities appear linear and sequential, in practice they're not. Analysis needn't be completed before coding commences; stories may not always be finalised in the iteration.

In many respects the concept of the iteration is a management tool, overlaid on activities to ensure the regular heartbeat of delivery. It's up to the team to decide how to work best.

ADDING DESIGN INTO THE MIX

When we take this just-enough, just-in-time approach to writing stories, we already have a precedent for introducing design into the process. The analyst works closely with the stakeholders (and developers where necessary) to flesh out the story. This will include:

Acceptance criteria which indicate what the story must or must not do. Once these statements are passed, the developer knows that he's done.

A narrative which describes the story. This may include business rules, inputs/outputs, validations, data—anything that the developer needs to know to deliver to the stakeholders' expectations.

A wireframe which shows how the feature described in the story will appear on the UI.

There's a familiar word: wireframe! So design may already be part of the process; what we now need to do is make it an explicit and integral part of it. What if we were to pair design with analysts? What if, in the same way the team capture acceptance criteria and business rules as input into the story, the design was solidified at the same time? This is the first role of the experience designer, to work with the analyst and *look forward* to ensure that the developers will have the necessary detail to code with. The next role is to *look now*. They work with the developers as they code to support them as they develop the application. Then the experience designer *looks back* to review the work that's been completed and test it with customers. Finally, the experience designer *looks out* to explore future concepts and ideas to maintain the evolving vision (9.4).

In many respects, this is how a business analyst works on an agile project. He's part of the development team, yet he has his own discrete activities to undertake. It's the same with experience, creative, and visual design. Design is not a separate track that sits both operationally and physically apart from development, only to interact at iteration planning meetings and showcases. The designers are an integral part of the team.

 TIP

Keep communicating with the developers! Don't slip into your old waterfall ways, designing in isolation an iteration ahead. Being agile requires being responsive to the immediate needs of the team whilst maintaining an eye to the future direction of the product.

9.4
The role of the designer
in an iteration.

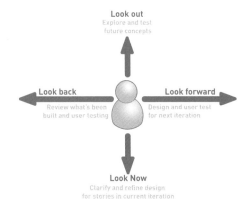

There are four requirements for successful integration of experience design into the agile process:

- Design is integral to the process and not just a supporting track.
- Design supports the developers during the development iteration.
- Detailed design is done just in time for coding rather than being batched up more than one iteration in front.
- Conceptual design runs alongside development to reduce the risk of developers doing the wrong thing.

How this works in practice is illustrated in the model below (9.5).

9.5
Design works just
ahead of development,
supporting
development, testing
ideas, and validating
future concepts.[1]

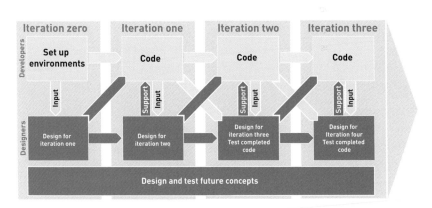

---

1 Download Desiree Sy's 2007 paper "Adapting Usability Investigations for Agile User-Centered Design" at http://www.upassoc.org/upa_publications/jus/2007may/agile-ucd.html to read how this approach was used at Autodesk.

WORKING AS A TEAM

Building a successful digital product is a team exercise and there is no place for functional silos in the process. No one likes being presented with a *fait accompli*; each team member wants to have input at each step along the way. The designers must have a relationship with the developers on their project; they need to be on first-name terms! They participate in the planning meetings and in the daily stand-ups. As we'll see, they support the team in four ways:

- **One in front:** Providing design and defining interaction behaviour for the stories.
- **Clarifying:** Supporting the developer in the iteration with the design.
- **Testing:** Testing the story with customers.
- **Design spikes and the evolving vision:** Defining and driving the vision to ensure design coherence and creative integrity.

 TIP

When you work in a shared space, teamwork is natural. Designers sketch and engage developers about feasibility. Developers get a feel for product vision and what's coming next.

PROBLEMS IN THE PROCESS

Sometimes process gets in the way of sense and can harm the results. Sometimes we get attached to the way we've always done things, regardless of whether it's still necessary or needed. Two common, wasteful practices that we often see are:

- Documentation created long after it is needed. For example, producing specifications, wireframes, and comps after the product is complete because the process mandates those deliverables for success.
- The business stakeholder insists on signing off only if designs are presented as comps. He wants to see the design for every page as it will appear, not as it evolves. Shedding the attachment to the formal, high-fidelity mock-ups of UIs can be a tough nut to crack, but it's essential if you're going to drive agility through your whole process. ■

ONE IN FRONT

The business analyst and designer work together just ahead of the developers, capturing requirements, defining acceptance criteria, refining the design, and producing creative artefacts for the stories that are about to be played. We want to be sure that when the developers have finished the story (assuming it needs no further iteration), it's complete. We want to avoid a situation where the functionality is done, but we're still unsure how the customer will interact with it or what the visual design will look like.

CLARIFYING

This probably represents the biggest shift in the way the designer works. As the developers are coding, the experience designer is supporting and regularly communicating with them. Typical areas for clarification are:

Interaction behaviour: If the developer and designer are working in close proximity to each other, there's no point in the designer creating a detailed specification that describes how the interface should behave. The communication of this detail could be just as easily managed through a conversation.

Visual design: Once we have core page templates designed, there's little point in the designer creating detailed Photoshop comps for every subsequent page that is just a variation on a theme. Individual pages will of course need creative collateral; however, these should be created on a just-in-time basis.

TESTING

Unlike on waterfall projects where testing is a formal checkpoint, an expensive and time-consuming piece of overhead toward the end of the project, in an agile project the experience designer can test upcoming concepts in preparation for forthcoming iterations and completed stories as the product evolves. There's no reason not to get customer feedback and do usability testing (formal or guerilla) with three to five customers on every iteration, and making it part of the project DNA. With such testing you don't need video. The team accept your insights and recommendations at face value—they don't need to be backed up with footage.

Running a usability test can be hard work and mentally draining. We've found benefit in having the participant, facilitator, and an observer in the same room, the observer being the BA, who sits well behind and out of view of the participant and makes notes throughout the test. At the end of each usability session, the facilitator and observer walk through the screens the participant interacted with and write down key findings on the flip chart. In this way major usability issues are easily captured. The following day at the morning stand-up, the results of the test are briefly recounted. The team may identify quick fixes that can be absorbed in the current iteration with no impact on team velocity. Alternatively, new stories or bugs are raised to be prioritised accordingly at the next iteration planning meeting. It's important that these are not placed behind upcoming stories for new functionality, but assessed immediately for their impact and necessity.

Usability testing will mean iterating. Something's wrong if you test for usability but ignore the results.

DESIGN SPIKES AND THE EVOLVING VISION

There's more to the life of the designer than just feeding the developers with specific design for the specific UI elements of the specific story that will be played. There's also the bigger picture design work to be done before the developers write a line of code, namely:

- The overarching *visual identity* and creative direction of the product.
- The development of *creative ideas and options* for specific problems.

VISUAL IDENTITY

Compelling aesthetic design can take time and is an iterative process in itself. Whilst we could have customer journeys sketched out and a story list ready for development in a couple of weeks, the visual identity is often more subjective and subject to flux as different stakeholders provide input into it. If the visual identity and overarching look and feel of the product are still in flux, working from these inevitably leads to code rewrites when the design finally materialises.

Stung by having to rewrite code because the user experience (UX) doesn't match the story, developers insist that the UX be signed off on before they get started. This can result in rushed design or delayed development. There are a number of things we can do to address this issue.

Ask why: It may be possible for design to happen quicker than you'd imagine. Look at your current design process. Why is it taking so long to get sign-off? Why do you need to produce comps of every page? It's possible that the visual identity—even for a completely new brand or product—can be developed far faster if you're more collaborative in your approach and focus on what's important: overarching visual identity and key templates rather than individual yet repeated elements.

Buy time: Agile projects typically start with iteration zero; this is a period when the development team set themselves up. No development is happening and this is the first opportunity to buy time for design. Developers typically like to tackle the technically complex stories first. These will often have few design requirements, giving you more time to address the creative.

Design in the browser: Rather than separating the design from the code, when you have a front-end developer working closely with the designer it's often possible to design in the browser, getting the programmatic structure of the page complete and removing the dependency of the design, which can be handled separately in the style sheet.

CREATIVE IDEAS AND OPTIONS

When a developer faces a complex problem that he's unsure of (especially when estimating unknown stuff), he validates his approach with a *spike*, a deep dive through a solution to confirm it works. Designers also use the concept of spikes to explore different design solutions to specific problems. For example, an e-commerce website might have a requirement to mark products as sale items with a price markdown. For the developer this is a flag and a new price, but for the designer there are options that need to be explored for visually differentiating and promoting sale items.

DESIGN DOCUMENTATION

PROTOTYPE

Sometimes you can really only validate a design or a feature when you see it in the flesh. Comps look great on paper but often fail to transfer with such impact in the browser, particularly on pages that pull stock product images from a database. Interactivity can be described, but only when it's built can it truly be experienced. Innovative concepts sound great in the brainstorming session, but what will they be like in practise? A prototype can be treated as a spike to address these questions, provide the team with a facsimile vision, and reduce the need for rework based on changes to the UI.

Moneysupermarket.com had this cool idea to display the number of car insurance quotes the system was searching, with the number decreasing as the customer revealed more information. For example, when a driver in his forties entered his date of birth, providers that specialised in older drivers would be removed from the quote set. As a solution it was sketched out, and the team thought it was great. A quick mock-up was produced and it was tested on customers: it consistently bombed. This large number decreasing every time data was entered was a distraction. But more importantly it failed the "so what" test. Customers didn't see the point. In a couple of days the idea had been built, tested, and trashed before impacting the development team's velocity. Consider how much cheaper this was than building the functionality over several iterations and discovering it wasn't really required.

Using a prototype as a design specification can overcome many of these issues. Wireframes produced in drawing packages such as Visio or OmniGraffle are static and they're still handed over to the designer.

DESIGN IN THE BROWSER

Whilst the wireframes, prototype, Photoshop files, style guide, and everything else that the UX team produce are all very helpful, they usually describe the same feature, just in different detail. Prototyping tools get closer to the real thing,

 TIP

Tools such as Axure and Balsamiq are great for providing a greater level of interactivity and for testing concepts and walking through customer journey mock-ups.

but at the end of the day they're still artefacts that are thrown away, used as scaffolding to build our thinking rather than contributing to the product itself.

Even if the team are working collaboratively, it can be hard to ensure that everything is synchronised. If the product owner wants the "Buy now" button to read "Add to basket" but tells only the visual designer, who doesn't share this with the BA or the experience designer, then quality assurance (QA) will find it hard to validate what is right.

This is especially true if the different design artefacts have a life of their own, for example, if the BA is writing stories independently of the experience designer who in turn is producing wireframes in isolation. It's easy for the experience designer to add a design element to the wireframe without considering its impact. Take pagination on a table, for example; it's easily drawn, but harder to implement.

Then there's the visual designer who can't do his design without wireframes. He uses wireframes to produce comp layouts in the form of PSDs or Illustrator files. He also needs to keep the project style guide document up to date to ensure a degree of consistency. This designer, being creative, will make changes which probably need to be reflected not only in the wireframes but also in the stories too. Finally, the developers get to start on building their live code. It's not until the feature has been built that the product owner and the QA get to see it actually working on the screen. Technical constraints such as screen sizes, browser inadequacies, and interaction behaviour *without* JavaScript often don't come to light until development of the story is completed, resulting in unscheduled redesigns or dropped features.

LIVING PROTOTYPE

The living prototype is an interactive HTML prototype that has the benefits of prototypes but also shares common code that the developers can work with. Indeed it enables the back-end developers to work on the heavy lifting, which they're good at, whilst the front-end developer can support the creative design and information architecture, which they're good at.

THE FRONT-END DEVELOPER

Agile has its roots in the creation of software systems where the UI was not a differentiator. It needed to enable customers to meet their goals efficiently and effectively, but the design aesthetic was not something that took priority. Flash forward to
customer-facing web applications where the interface is the product. The UI brings
a requirement for a new set of skills around HTML and CSS. To build beautiful products (not just functional ones), the Java or .net developer has to get layouts pixel
perfect, understand accessibility, and ensure they work across different browsers
and devices. Some developers can do that. But for many teams and projects, it will
be more efficient and effective to have a front-end developer who's responsible for
the UI. At first this sounds like we're introducing specialisation and will result in a
functional silo in the team. It need not be like this. Being responsible for the living
prototype and design in the browser, the front-end developer becomes the bridge
between design and development, increasing the team's efficiency and reducing the
risk of rework as the product evolves. ▪

The experience designer still creates the initial wireframe sketches, but as the
team agree on the basic elements that will go on a page and the core structure,
the front-end developer writes HTML to support these concepts. For example, on
a cell-phone shop we might have the following:

- Device pages
  - Device list
  - Device details
- Plan pages
  - Plan list
  - Plan details
- My Packages pages
  - Packages list
  - Package details
  - Edit package

The experience designer has illustrated these on a sitemap and sketched out on paper what these look like—not a detailed wireframe, just a sketch. Pairing with the front-end developer they produce a basic HTML mock-up without any styling.

The front-end developer writes HTML to support the basic data structure:

```
<div class="device">
  <h3>device name</h3>
  <ul class="device-features">
  <li>feature 1</li>
  <li>feature 2</li>
  </ul>
  <p class="call-to-action">
  <a href="device.htm">view</a>
  </p>
</div>
```

With this in place, the front-end developer can start creating placeholder CSS to lay out the page, essentially creating the wireframe for the experience designer, *designing in the browser*. He might use quick and dirty JavaScript to represent interactive behaviour. Once this is completed, we can start designing in the browser. We no longer need to rely so heavily on wireframes to inform the design (9.6).

In Figure 9.6 we can see that the navigation is left as placeholders. The page needs only to support functionality as it's created, yet it has the visual framework to ensure its layout and design integrity.

Because of the way the HTML has been semantically structured, if the designer decides to use columns rather than rows to display the phones, this can be changed in the CSS with little or no change to the structure of the HTML. In our example, the phones are displayed in the DIV class "device." How this DIV is displayed is controlled by the CSS.

9.6
Example of a wireframe
designed in the browser.

The visual designer then pairs with the front-end developer to work on the creative treatment. The beauty of CSS is that making changes to the design is relatively straightforward and impactful (as a visit to www.csszengarden.com will testify). Rather than having to refer to the wireframe in the story, the developers have a better medium to work with. They drop their functionality into the HTML produced by the front-end developer. The images, CSS, and JavaScript live on top of both the living prototype and the live code. Both share these assets.

We're now less reliant on wireframes and visual designs. The living prototype serves the same purpose and should be a supporting document to the story. In practise, the living prototype enables the team to spike different concepts. As the design matures, a common UI framework emerges, as illustrated in diagram 9.7.

Shared vision	Design spikes						Compelling Customer Experience
	Design & analysis	Design & analysis	Design & analysis	Design & analysis	Design & analysis	Design & analysis	
	Code	Code	Code	Code	Code	Code	
	Test	Test	Test	Test	Test	Test	
	Common UI framework						

9.7
The evolving design through spikes to a common UI framework.

WORKING WITH THE PRODUCT OWNER

The product owner on an agile project has a lot to think about. If he's commercially minded and driven by the desire to get *features* shipped, design and the focus on the customer experience often slips. Pairing the experience designer with the product owner as a product steward helps to ensure that the yin of the business is balanced with the yang of the customer.

Agile software development is inherently democratic. We let the product owner decide what is most important to him, what will deliver the greatest value and then build that first. The problem with this democracy, with this *unleashed choice,* is that the product owner doesn't always know what's best. He's not always the best person to choose.

There is a difference between domain knowledge and what we'll call *experience* knowledge. When prioritising requirements, the product owner will typically wear his commercial hat; he's thinking about targets, and those are based on shifting product. He's invoking his domain knowledge. But other than price, cold commercials are not what shift products. It's the experience that does. For that you need experience knowledge. This is what the experience designer brings. Thus, the experience designer pairs with the product owner to:

- Bring the voice of the customer to the process (the real customer, not the agile customer!).

- Ensure that delivery is pursuing the vision.
- Maintain the focus on customer goals over independent features.
- Set creative direction and ensure that it's followed.

WORKING IN ITERATIONS

We'll now look at the core agile practices that you'll see in an agile iteration (pairing, testing, debt and refactoring, stand-ups, backlog, burn-up, showcases, and retrospectives) and look at what they mean to the designer.

PAIRING

Writing code is all about the typing, right?

Take a look at your sketchpads, your scribbles, your doodles. It takes a lot of ideas, a lot of thinking to make a design you're ready to share. You probably bounce ideas around and seek inspiration. The same is true with writing code. The typing is only part of the story. A good developer thinks about the solution he's building and continuously looks to simplify it and make it better. Two heads are better than one, and this is certainly the case in software development. Two developers work on the same code, one taking the role of the driver whilst the other is the observer or navigator. The driver is at the keyboard writing the code whilst the navigator guides and supports, pointing out errors and bugs whilst suggesting how the code could be better constructed. The roles are regularly rotated. This is not two people doing one person's job; watch two developers pairing and you'll soon realise that it's an intense activity with little time for the distractions and procrastination that can occur when working alone.

So what does this mean for the designer? You probably do it already but don't call it such. You're working on a tricky problem, or have a specific design challenge and you'll call on a colleague to work through ideas with. In the agile experience design, don't see another designer as the go-to person every time. Go to the team.

PAIR WITH THE DEVELOPERS

Paired programming is a gift for the designer who wants to engage the developers on his project. In pairing, people are naturally more receptive and open to ideas. Remember that coding is more than just typing; there's no reason why the designer should not pair (or triple) with the developers to work through ideas. On a performing team this pairing works in two ways:

- The developers call on the experience designer to clarify design detail, or walk through alternative ways of implementing the design.
- The experience designer takes a gnarly design problem ahead of development to inform how it might be implemented.

PAIR WITH THE BAs

There's a lot of crossover between the role of the BA and the experience designer, and it's unfortunate that these are often organisationally poles apart—the BA sitting in IT and the experience designer sitting in the business. We described earlier how having them work together minimises interruptions with stakeholders. Rather than each questioning stakeholders individually, they do it together in one go.

The BA focuses on business rules whilst the experience designer focuses on the experience. Both think about process flows. We no longer leave it to the BA to specify how the customer will interact with the application; it's a paired activity. By pairing with a BA you potentially make his job easier, as he doesn't then have to interpret the detail to put into the story narratives because he'll have the understanding firsthand. Equally, by pairing with a developer you'll inject technical constraints and opportunities into the process. When acceptance criteria are defined, pairing ensures that acceptance criteria for customer goals and the UI are included.

PAIR WITH THE QAs

QAs have an annoying knack of asking difficult questions and exposing flaws in your well thought-out interaction model. Your designs will typically accommodate the happy path; the QA will help identify corner cases and ask, *"what happens if?"*

QAs will typically look to ensure that the story is functionally complete. By pairing with the QA, you can support him in ensuring that the story is aesthetically complete and, when taken with other stories, enables the customer to meet his goals.

PAIR WITH YOUR FELLOW DESIGNERS

It can get lonely being a left-brained single designer in a right-brained ocean of IT. Design inspiration is often found through interaction with other designers. When you're embedded in an agile team, there can be less opportunity for this collaboration and pairing with your peers. Remember that there's no one proscribed way of doing agile; it's adaptive and you must do what is right for your team and your organisation. If you feel that you're losing the connection to your fellow designers, do something about it:

- Organise a weekly design studio where you all get together to share challenges and look for creative solutions.
- Rotate designers through the different projects to spend a couple of hours each week pairing on a project.
- Get the whole design team to sit in the same place as IT.
- Get the project team to sit closer to the business team where the designers sit.

TESTING

For many experience designers, testing just means usability testing. There's a lot more to testing on an agile project, where you're delivering quality throughout the process rather than fixing it at the end. Instead of focusing on what we need as an open-ended question, acceptance criteria enable us to ask how we'll know we're done and testing helps to answer this question. Seen in this light, testing should become interesting and relevant to the work of the experience designer.

In waterfall projects, a significant amount of time at the end is spent on manual testing. An army of testers have test scripts and try to break the software to ensure that it works. On an agile project, the team strive to automate the testing as much as possible. With automated testing and the ability of stakeholders to interact with the application as it's built in an as-live environment, testing at the end becomes a short formality if it's required at all.

TEST-DRIVEN DEVELOPMENT (TDD)

In test-driven development, the developer writes the test first. He describes what the software will do before writing the code to make it happen. In doing this, he's baking quality into the solution. In the first instance, these tests are known as *unit tests,* that is, they test the individual components that the developer is working on. These unit tests come together in a test suite and can be run against the whole application as it's built. The tests are written based on the acceptance criteria that the analyst captured in the story. The analyst could describe the conditions by which the test will pass; however, there's a better, more consistent way of writing this using a format and philosophy known as behaviour-driven development.

BEHAVIOUR-DRIVEN DEVELOPMENT (BDD)

Given *a context or scenario*

When *something happens*

Then *there is an outcome*

Acceptance criteria that are stated like this transcend the concept of a test at a granular level and becomes a statement of the *behaviour* we expect from the completed code. In thinking of behaviours we can move beyond testing at the discrete unit level and test the system as a whole. This concept was first introduced by Dan North[2] and is supported by development tools such as JBehave and NBehave.

With an understanding of this simple concept of BDD, the experience designer can now use a consistent language for articulating user-interaction behaviours. Rather than a wordy specification for how dynamic interactions should be implemented, BDD provides a common vocabulary for expressing what you want to happen.

As a designer, you should be comfortable with these concepts; developers like Dan North have purposely striven to enable business and technology to use the same language and vocabulary. This means that even if you know nothing about curly brackets and *public voids*, you should be able to look at the code and get an idea of what it's trying to do.

---

2 http://dannorth.net/introducing-bdd/.

EXPERIENCE ACCEPTANCE CRITERIA

Tests are based on acceptance criteria that state what is acceptable and what is not. In the design world we have something similar: we produce a style guide that does the same thing from a design point of view, a statement of what is acceptable and what is not. Unfortunately, we often lose sight of who we're producing the style guide for. We create it as a document for marketers, who sign off on it, happy that it will direct compliance for all brand assets. Developers don't really do this sort of documentation. Are we expecting a time-pressed developer to care that buried in the style guide are instructions on the use of capitalisation? When the developer creates a Save for later button, how do we prevent him from coding it Save For Later. The answer is clear. *Design should be part of the acceptance criteria.*

If we capture design behaviour in our stories, there are two immediate benefits:

- We can be more certain that the design will be implemented as we intended. We don't have to assume that the developer will refer to the style guide (they don't) as they implement the story.

- The developer can write automated tests that ensure the style guidelines are followed. The style guide becomes part of the suite of tests that are run. For example:

  - **Given** *there is a button*
  - **When** *it has more than one word*
  - **Then** *the first word is capitalised and following words are in lowercase*

- This test is written once and can be automated to be used across the entire application. Clearly, if proper nouns are used, the criteria will need updating, but in one simple test we've ensured that the style will be adhered to automatically. That's one less thing the QA needs to police for.

GOAL COMPLETION ACCEPTANCE CRITERIA

An issue with automated testing is that it's formative, that is to say it's diagnostic and concerned with the quality *of* the system. But we also need to ensure quality *for* the system, that is, it achieves the goals it sets out to meet. We need a way of doing summative testing to verify the product does what it sets out to do.

Remember how we used customer scenarios and goals when we elaborated our stories? We can return to these in development as a tool for ensuring design coherence and confirming that the product does what we intended it to do.

Just as we wrote acceptance criteria at the story level and tested these, the team should create customer scenarios and test at the goal level. Let's return to the banking example we introduced in Chapter 8, "Elaboration: Ready, Steady, Build," and the scenario we wrote:

Alex is an administrative assistant for a logistics company. She is at work on her lunch break. She wants to check the balance on her checking account to see whether her salary has been deposited.

In that story we have the context of usage (needs to be completed quickly), the goal, and real data. Ultimately, the success of the application depends on this scenario being possible; the scenario becomes a test. The passing of any number of tests at the unit level is irrelevant if the overarching goal cannot be achieved. Only when the customer can meet her goals can we have confidence that done really is done.

DEBT AND REFACTORING

Developers talk about technical debt. They write some code that is not perfect, and like financial debt, they have to pay interest on that debt later in the form of extra effort. There's nothing wrong with incurring a little debt on the way, provided that you pay it off. For developers, that means refactoring. Experience design can incur debt as well. This can be due to several reasons:

- **Starting without a clear UI direction:** Functionality is built without thought to how the customer will interact with it as a complete and coherent proposition.

- **Compromising usability through intentional scope prioritisation:** To deliver customer-facing functionality, the team decide to trade off seamless, integrated back-office tools.

- **Compromising usability through unintentional scope prioritisation:** Despite the experience designer's best efforts, the product owner is driven by the need to deliver features over experience quality.

- **Inconsistency through emergent design:** As the design evolves and the team introduces new and more complex features, inconsistency creeps in as new creative thinking supercedes the old.
- **Pages that don't work as intended:** More (or less) content or functionality appears on a page than was originally planned.
- **Product pivot:** As you learn from your customers, or market forces dictate changes to the product, the UI needs to be updated.

Like developers, the experience designer should be comfortable with refactoring the design to pay down this design debt.

Martin Fowler describes refactoring as "a disciplined technique for restructuring an existing body of code, altering its internal structure without changing its external behaviour." As the codebase grows, it often gets more complicated, and as you learn more, refactoring is an approach to simplifying it. It's an admission that you're not going to get it right first time. A similar approach can be taken with design, especially when the product is in the early stages of development and early beta. Successful refactoring of the UI depends on good team communication and strong management of the process. Changes at a superficial level may be easily addressed in the CSS, but more structural changes are likely to have an impact on the team's velocity and be assessed for their impact. Having good rationale for the change, for example, feedback from user testing, helps support the case.

STAND-UPS

The team come together at the daily stand-up (which is just that—a meeting held standing up). The team assemble in a circle, often near the card wall. A token is passed around; only the person who holds the token can speak. That is not to say there can't be conversation; the conversation follows the token. But if it seems to be turning into a dialogue between two people, there will be a suggestion that it be continued after the stand-up.

The person holding the token tells the group what he did the previous day and what he's going to do today. He lets the team know of any issues he may have. Other team members will make suggestions, or one developer will offer to pair on solving the problem.

When he's done talking, he passes the token to another team member. When all team members have said their piece, the stand-up is done. It's a democratic form of sharing knowledge and reporting team issues, ensuring that they can be addressed as they occur.

BACKLOG AND CARD WALLS

We introduced the backlog and the card wall way back in Chapter 4, "Setting the Scene," as a visual indicator of the team's progress. It indicates the backlog: work to be done, work in progress, and work completed. Within this flow more discrete stages may be included. The following list indicates the stages that a story might go through on a project:

- **Backlog:** This is the backlog of all stories that were identified during discovery, envisioning, and elaboration. It's the holding bay.
- **Identified:** These are stories that have been prioritised for development.
- **Design elaboration and customer validation:** Often there are a number of different ways a story could be manifest in the UI. This can take time and may be included on the card wall. We may also look to validate the story with customers. This may include testing them as part of a prototype and undertaking *guerilla usability* testing on them.
- **Analysis and design:** This is where the necessary detail such as acceptance criteria is captured for development. Design work happens at the same time.
- **Analysis and design complete (Ready for Dev):** This is inventory for the developers to pick up and work from. There should be only a few stories appearing here at any given time. The team should be looking for *flow*; if this is becoming a backlog, there's every chance that the effort to create this backlog may be wasted as things change during development.
- **UI complete:** Particularly when working with a living prototype, some teams may have the front-end developers complete the HTML and CSS in preparation for development.
- **In development:** The developers pick up the story card and start work on the code. The developers, front-end and back-end, organise themselves and their tasks to do what's required for the acceptance criteria to be met and the story

to be marked as done. Sometimes an additional user interface design step may be included. For example, the user interface may require complex styling or interaction models that are developed by the front-end developer rather than the core back-end team. Wherever possible the team will collaborate, but sometimes this specialisation will be required for efficient workflow.

- **Dev complete (Ready for QA):** The story passes the tests as described in the acceptance criteria. For the developer, it's done. This is the inventory for QA to pick up and work from. Like Ready for Dev, a large backlog here is something to be concerned about.

- **In QA:** The QA picks up the story and ensures that it meets the requirements. This may include manual testing for that story, and exploratory testing to ensure the product works as a coherent entity; for example, whether it meets customer goals, looks and feels right, and supports real-world customer behaviour (such as cross-browser compliance, use by those with visual or motor impairments, or unexpected actions like multiple clicks on a button.

- **QA complete (Ready for User Acceptance Testing—UAT):** The QA is satisfied that the story is complete. At this stage, it will be made available in an environment that mimics the live environment. All stakeholders are now able to interact with the product.

- **In UAT:** UAT gives the business an opportunity to play with the functionality as live to ensure that it meets expectations. Asking for sign-off on a story at the showcase can often be unrealistic. Showcases are contrived with a specific purpose of demonstrating the stories that have been completed in that iteration. They rarely last longer than an hour and that is often not enough time for the product owner to digest what he's seeing and how it works in the bigger picture of the emerging product. Thus an agile project UAT should be a formality that is conducted throughout the process rather than a long period at the end of development.

- **UAT accepted:** The product owner marks the story as completed and done.

This is the life cycle of the story. It's important to note that it's a *pull system,* or *kanban,* that is, tasks are undertaken on demand. You only do analysis for stories that are about to be developed. When seen in this light, the notion of the iteration and strict adherence to what happens when becomes less important. It's more important to be concerned with the critical path of developing agile software and reducing inefficiency in the process. But that also means that there is no reason why other supporting activities can't occur outside this immediate process. This is why the broader design vision activities should not appear on the developer's card wall. Testing broader concepts and exploring different interaction approaches can occur outside the card wall if they're not part of the development critical path. In this instance, the designers may develop their own card wall to manage their workload, but this is separate and independent from the core development pipeline.

KANBAN

Chris Fleetwood, Agile Project Manager, ThoughtWorks

Kanban typically manifests itself in work limits on a card wall, a continuous flow of tasks and a culture of pulling rather than pushing tasks into downstream functions. Work limits prevent functional areas from accepting new tasks until current tasks have been completed and passed downstream. The pulling culture requires functional teams to signal when they're ready to accept new work, rather than have it accumulate at their doorstep. A consequence of this, across the breadth of the story wall, is to limit the total amount of work in progress at any one time and by doing so, increase throughput, lead-time predictability, and customer confidence.

These features of Kanban needn't be limited to the development and technical testing columns on a story wall. When agile teams began to adopt Kanban, a story wall was likely to have consisted of analysis, development, and testing columns, and work limits were applied against those functions. Introducing work-limited UX columns to the left of development completes the picture.

This means that tasks are prioritised to feed the UX activities to the left, before being pulled into development toward the right—as opposed to the established practise of prioritising directly for development. The time a task spends in the UX domain becomes clearly visible and doesn't artificially inflate development times. It tells us if UX activity is causing a bottleneck, or suffering a bottleneck. Work limits force us to tightly couple the UX and development functions, leading developers to think about design and designers to think about development. It reveals invaluable information about the end-to-end flow of work, opening doors to *Kaizen*— a culture of continuous improvement. ■

BURN UP

With the stories identified and the project team working through them, the project manager can produce a graph showing the team's progress, and this can be illustrated at a granular level for each of the steps in the card wall (9.8). Scope more than doubled after four weeks. Five two-week iterations in and we can see scope has ballooned and the team is going to miss the target (green line).

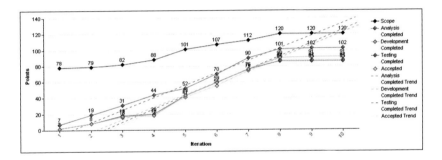

9.8
Burn-up chart
produced using the
project management
tool Mingle.

The use of burn-up or burn-down charts indicates the progress of the team and serves as a guide to whether we'll make it. This works on a story level. What it doesn't tell us is whether the scope we're covering is delivering the customer goals. To do this we need to illustrate goal burn-down. The following diagram shows a subset of the goals for an entertainment website. At a glance you can see which goals can be achieved, which are partially complete, and which are outstanding (9.9).

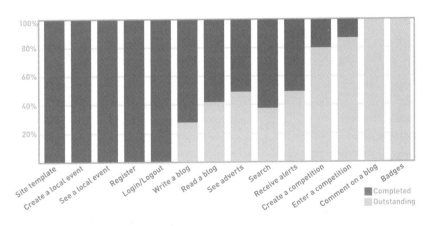

9.9
Chart showing goal
completeness.

SHOWCASES AND SHOW-AND-TELLS

There's a lot of ceremony (and expectation) around the showcase. This is when the team demonstrate to the stakeholders what they have built over the last iteration. Avoid the temptation of impromptu usability testing. Similarly, don't let stakeholders get caught up on design issues, which should be registered in the meeting but not dwelled on; treat them as bugs to be fixed in later iterations.

Inviting senior stakeholders to a showcase that demonstrates the clicking of a button and the pulling back of data from a legacy application may not be the best use of their time, and if they've not been close to the process it can appear to them as lack of progress. Some teams therefore replace the showcase with regular show-and-tells to close off the iteration. This focuses on the immediate stories developed in that iteration, with a larger and longer showcase reserved for demonstrating the completion of customer goal-orientated functionality to the wider audience.

Whilst showcases are not usability tests or design reviews, they do present a great opportunity to highlight customer opinion to the project team and the wider business. People who have had little exposure to customer-centred design don't always appreciate the benefits until they've seen it for themselves. Present the highlights (what worked) and the lowlights (what didn't work) and if you have video footage edit a couple of very short clips and show customers in the wild. Then present the recommendations and intended actions as a result of the testing.

TRUE STORY
by Michelle Bennet, User Experience Analyst

I was working with an international bank on a new Internet-only product. We spent a decent amount of time on the customer journey from the home page (or other SEO landing pages) through the product information pages and then onto the online product application pages. We had a disagreement with the marketing department about the call-to-action. They wanted a big, graphic, banner-ad-style link positioned on the right hand side of the page. Based on good usability practise and lots of experience with usability testing, we advised that a different style of call-to-action embedded in the body of the page would be more effective. We took both designs to customers and tested both scenarios. There was a wide margin separating the results. The banner-ad-style call-to-action failed dramatically; no one could find the link. We talked marketing through the results and they were astounded but appreciative of the insight, to the extent that they asked us to show the customer video at the next showcase, where both the CEO and CIO were making a guest appearance.

The video was an absolute eye-opener for the entire team as they watched customers berate the bank's brand "because they made it too hard" or they were "trying to hide things to sell more things" and all because the link they were looking for was in an advertising blind spot. Both the CEO and CIO, who had never been exposed to customer testing, immediately realised the significance of the exercise and the potential impact to their business of getting the design wrong. Without any hesitation the CEO declared, "It's one thing to make mistakes, that's part of doing new business. But it's another thing to make mistakes when they can be avoided. We should do customer testing at every opportunity and build it into our future processes." ▪

RETROSPECTIVES

Retrospectives are an opportunity for the team to get together to figure out what parts of the project are working and what parts are not working so well. Depending on the safety of the group, topics can range from working hours to process to team integration to lack of confectionary supplies in the team biscuit tin. There's no specific flavour of retrospective for designers, but it's a good place to work out how well design is integrating with the rest of the team.

Before running a retrospective, especially if there are people in the group who have not participated in a retrospective before, it's a good idea for the facilitator to make sure everyone understands the prime directive of a retrospective:

"Regardless of what we discover, we understand and truly believe that everyone did the best job they could, given what they knew at the time, their skills and abilities, the resources available, and the situation at hand."[3]

 TIP

It's best to have someone from outside the project team run the retrospective. The facilitator should not participate by writing comments; he should simply facilitate the groups by talking about the comments.

3   Kerth, Norman L. *Project Retrospectives: A Handbook for Team Reviews.* Dorset House Publishing, 2001.

IN SUMMARY

In this chapter we introduced the iteration: how the team work iteratively and incrementally, delivering working software in short, time-boxed periods. We looked at the life cycle of a story, starting in the iteration planning meeting and then, just enough analysis and design for coding to start.

Agile projects are collaborative. The experience designer is part of the team. We introduced the experience designer's activities: to look forward, designing and validating the design with customers for the upcoming iteration; to look back, reviewing and user testing what's been built; to look now, working with the developers within the current iteration; and, finally, to look out, exploring and testing future concepts to ensure that the right path is followed.

It's possible to bring design much closer to development by designing in the browser. This may not suit every situation, but it is a way to synchronise design and development by sharing common elements across the prototype for testing upcoming ideas and providing a UI framework for functionality to be dropped into.

We discussed how the experience designer should pair with the different members of the agile project team. We explained why testing is fundamental, and that it should be automated wherever possible. The experience designer brings a new focus on testing, to ensure that the product meets experience quality and enables the customer to accomplish his goals. Finally, we described the card wall and how stories are managed through the project.

COMING NEXT

In many respects, getting the product to market represents the first step in the product development process. So far we've stressed the value of starting with a minimally viable product. In the next chapter, we'll show how the product evolves from that. We'll describe how agile itself is evolving to focus on continuous improvement based on learning and feedback from customer behaviour. And we'll see how there is no one design, but rather multiple options that can be tested to deliver the optimum customer experience and the greatest benefit to the business.

BEYOND
AGILE
TO
CONTINUOUS 10

"LIKE A PETRI DISH, THE INTERNET HAS ITS OWN CULTURES THAT EVOLVE AND INTERACT...THE IDEA IS TO USE THE NET'S DYNAMICS, SOCIAL AND TECHNOLOGICAL, AND APPLY IT TO BUSINESS AND ORGANISATIONS....IT MAKES SENSE TO APPLY ITS WORKINGS AND TOOLS TO COMPANIES TO STIMULATE COLLABORATION, CREATIVITY AND ULTIMATELY INNOVATION."
—ADRIANA LUKAS,
SELF-HACKER AND FOUNDER OF
THE BIG BLOG COMPANY

Let's look beyond the project framework to life after launch and see how we can measure and learn from customers to inform continuous product improvement.

The new product development process that happens within a project framework is only part of the story. For most product owners or product managers, *life begins at launch*. Now more than ever, performance and development are driven by strategic objectives and tightly tied back to business benefits and return on investment. Now we recognise that even seemingly insignificant changes to product or service design and implementation can have massive financial impact for better or for worse.

Customers are merciless in their pursuit of value for time and money. Two fundamental changes have contributed to customers having businesses at their mercy. The first is the plethora of convenient choices. If you can't deliver what customers want, when they want it, and how they want it, a competitor who can is only a click away. The second is that customers now have a voice and multiple platforms on which to broadcast their voices. They want you and the rest world to know exactly how they feel about your product or service. So you had better start listening.

In this chapter, we'll look at the powerful combination of the social Web and advances in measurement and analytics. We'll also look at seismic changes that are happening behind the scenes in IT: how some organisations are moving away from infrequent, big bang code releases and instead streamlining and automating their process to allow continuous delivery with frequent releases multiple times a day.

To embrace these new ways of working, organisations adopt the philosophy of Kaizen (a Japanese word that translates as "good change" or "continuous improvement"). This means engaging in continuous improvement through the combined efforts of continuous design and continuous delivery. But it's not just a matter of buying some new tools and adding a couple of new processes into the mix. Changing a company philosophy and its associated behaviours, activities, and processes requires large programmes of change and will affect everyone from the boardroom to the front line. Harnessing the power of continuous design and continuous delivery to constantly evolve products and services in line with what customers need and want will not only make the design and development process more effective and potentially increase success, it can also exponentially improve customer experience management—and ultimately boost your bottom line.

We recognise that as experience designers or product managers you might not be in a position to make these changes. However, we bring them to your attention so that if some of these things are already starting to happen within your organisation, you can recognise them and start to take immediate advantage of them. If they don't already exist within your organisation, we hope that you'll see the benefits and evangelise about them to the people in your organisation who *can* make these changes.

WHAT DOES LAUNCH LOOK LIKE?

Launching a new product is no small feat. There's an awful lot of effort and people involved and there are late nights, weekends, and too many cups of coffee—no matter how well you plan. In terms of launch strategy, there's a sliding scale of effort running from the traditional full-scale, big bang launch to simply launching a holding page for a website to measure interest (10.1).

10.1
Sliding scale of launch strategies.

BIG BANG THEORY

Cosmology theory tells us that there was a time when nothing (as we know it, Jim) existed. Then there was a massive explosion of matter and the universe was born. Many products are born this way. Explosions don't just happen; a great buildup of energy is required for an explosion. With a big bang launch the idea is to create as much buzz and anticipation for the product as possible so that you're guaranteed customers on the day of the launch. Think about the various iPhone and iPad launches around the world. Apple are masters at big bang launch. However, it's not an undertaking for the faint of heart or the light of wallet. It takes months of coordinated PR and marketing effort to create the hype and the excitement needed for a launch of that magnitude. It's also fraught with peril. What happens if your campaign isn't big enough or doesn't have the reach and only a handful of customers turn up on launch day? What happens if the campaign was ultrasuccessful in generating interest, but you disappoint your customers because some part of the product fails or doesn't work as intended, or worse, you have to delay launch due to a major technical hitch? A big bang launch has to be carefully orchestrated to be successful.

As well as the risks associated with big bang releases, a major drawback is that sustaining the product development team during the project up until launch takes a large investment of capital. A return on investment can't begin until after launch, so it will be a long time after the start of the project before any return on the original investment is realised. It will be even longer to the break-even point, where your returns have covered your initial investment, and you start making a profit. Every day that your product isn't in production is a day's revenue lost and another day for new entrants and competitors to steal market share.

ROLLING RELEASES

Rolling releases let you get to market much quicker. The idea is that while you might have a grand vision of the end state, you release a small subset of the vision to start with and build up to the full vision over time. It can take between 10 and 24 months to design, build, and test a fully baked website with all the bells and whistles and then launch it, but you can launch a static home page in a few hours with minimal activity.

Obviously, along with the sliding scale of functionality is the sliding scale of value to the customers, so one could ask what's the value in launching a static home page? Ask Just Cages, an Internet start-up (powered by Forward3D) that built a new product vertical and took it to market in just a day. Compare this with the companies that spend hundreds of thousands of dollars to design shopping experiences that offer little more than the Just Cages experience. And whilst those companies spend lots of money on getting the big up-front design right, Just Cages are quietly optimising and improving based on the data and customer usage. In fact, the concept for the product was conceived from data: they looked for trends and opportunities in Google searches. They sought a high-value product that was highly searched for, yet had few paid-for ads and identified parrot cages as a potential product. People were searching for parrot cages, but there was no obvious retailer for them. So they set up an experiment. They built a landing page, mocked up some product pages, and drove traffic to it through Google AdWords. They then waited to see what would happen. When sufficient traffic was driven to the site, they built an e-commerce website. By generating enough user traffic just from a static home page they proved the business case and used the evidence to build the real product (10.2).

This is where the minimal viable product really comes into play. Anything you think you know about your customers is really just guesswork until your product goes live and customers start interacting with it. That's when product life and learning truly begins. So why wait? Why burn up lots of time, effort, and money developing a comprehensive product before launching, when you can continue to create small sets of high-value features and release them frequently for customers to use?

One advantage of this approach is that the sooner it's released, the sooner you can start making a return on your investment. Start small and scale big. You need minimal funds to get going, and then once you're up and running, the returns can be ploughed back into further development.

Another advantage is the ability to fail fast and fail cheaply. If you've spent only a small amount of money and a minimal amount of time and the product fails, it might dent your ego, but your actual losses are much less than if you fail with a fully baked product. Lessons learnt from small failures can lead to bigger successes, but big failures are much more difficult to recover from, especially financially.

A large organisation might argue that this approach is less appropriate for them because launching a half-baked product could be detrimental to the brand based on customer expectations about quality and coverage. However, we've worked with big brands and large, well-established organisations that have taken this approach and it has proven to be highly successful.

If you go down the rolling releases path, consider making the future road map one of the features of the website. Show your customers what's coming to keep them interested and coming back. You can even involve them in the creation of the road map. Use interactive methods or social media to get them to suggest features that would be valuable to them and help improve the website. After collecting a catalogue of customer suggestions, get them to vote on the suggestions to help you prioritise the features for the road map. It goes without saying that the actual road map has to take into account technical complexity and business value, but you'll have a much easier time justifying costs and priorities if you know these features are what your customers want (10.3).

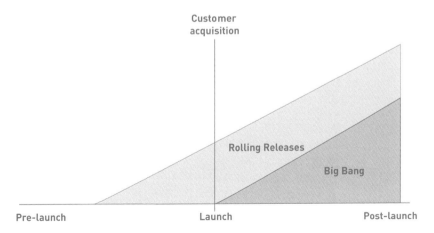

10.3
Customer acquisition.

A BIG BANG WITH ROLLING RELEASES

Another approach is a combination of the two methods described above. For brand or other reasons you might need to do a big bang launch, but to reduce risk, increase acceptance, and generate some pre-release buzz you can embark on a series of pre-releases to a limited, closed audience. It might be as structured as doing an alpha and beta pilot, or it could be as unstructured as doing continual releases to a test site that you use as your experiment lab. Either way it still allows you to test, learn, and remove the big boulders before the big day.

To do this you need to cultivate a customer development panel and get the panel to use and evaluate your product while you're still in development. If you have an existing website and an established customer base, then you can profile your ideal customers from the larger group and cherry-pick new ones to join the panel. You can spin the recruitment message so that your customers perceive this invitation as a privilege, whereby they get to help develop the next generation of product and see it and use it before anyone else. Combine your recruitment strategy with *social CRM* (see below) to target customers who are influencers in social networks. You can use their position to help spread the message virally when the time is right. Another advantage to using existing customers is that because they are already loyal to your products and services you may not even have to pay them to get involved.

If you don't have an existing product, then recruiting a customer development panel will be more of a challenge and you may need to offer incentives to get prospects involved.

If you'd welcome customer involvement prior to the actual launch, consider building up the social communities in advance of launch. Create a blog to generate interest, use one of the big social sites such as Facebook or LinkedIn to create a community and get people talking, create an e-mail or Twitter campaign to spread viral messages about your product, and provide articles or blog posts on affiliate websites where your potential customers hang out. By doing this, you'll have a much better conversion rate on day one than you would if you just open your doors onto a cold and uninformed marketplace and hope that customers will come and find you.

BEYOND RELEASES TO CONTINUOUS IMPROVEMENT

All of the approaches mentioned above share the concept of a release, the batching up of functionality and features before making them available to customers. What if you could go beyond this, go beyond agile and the project framework and continuously evolve your product? This new approach takes real-time learnings to continuously design and continuously deliver the product.

CONTINUOUS DELIVERY

Another groundswell that's happening in IT is continuous delivery, which is all about the continuous deployment of software to the live environment. The movement was born from frustrations that affect highly efficient, cross-functional agile project teams who have designed and developed a great product, that's now ready to ship, but who get held up because the rest of the deployment pipeline isn't as agile (10.4). Instead, there's a long and laborious quality assurance process to endure first. Following QA there might be a lengthy process as the product is pushed through the IT Operations group responsible for the deployment pipeline. What could be more frustrating for a project team than to have gone from start to code complete in less than six months, only to have the product sit on the deployment conveyor belt for another six months?

> I LOVE DEADLINES. I LIKE THE WHOOSHING SOUND THEY MAKE AS THEY FLY BY.
>
> —Douglas Adams

AGILE PROJECT TEAM
Analysis & Design
Test & Build
Wall → **Quality Assurance** Wall → **IT Operations** → **Live**

Last mile

Continuous delivery doesn't mean releasing updates monthly; it means releasing whenever an individual statement of value is ready to release, which could be multiple times a day. This requires a new way of thinking and a new confidence. For example, rather than releasing to a test environment, you test in production.

10.4
The last mile to live can be as long as the project.

You learn from real customer feedback rather than from opinions in showcases. Design becomes a set of hypotheses that we look to test. We deploy our design hypothesis and, through a process of testing and measuring, we adapt and improve the product. Companies like Netflix and Facebook take this approach: they continuously release and monitor impact. Feedback is real time and continuous; they immediately have insight into whether a change is successful, if it's being used, and if customers like it. This small and incremental approach means it's easy to roll back changes that don't have a positive impact on revenue or experience. With such a fast-paced approach, design takes on a new flavour.

Continuous delivery creates a fully automated, repeatable, reliable deployment process for getting changes to the live environment as quickly as possible. Instead of having centralised functional teams of quality assurance (QA) and operations, it's about having decentralised cross-functional delivery teams, where testing is built into development and combined with operations. Jez Humble, coauthor of *Continuous Delivery,* stated during his presentation at InfoQ that there are three key benefits:

- **Fast customer feedback:** The quicker you release to live, the quicker you can get customer feedback on the product and begin to optimise the product based on real data.
- **Reduced release risks:** When you deploy large-scale changes, lots can go wrong and pinpointing where the problem lies can be difficult. If you're doing small changes frequently, it's much easier to understand where and what the problem is and act on it.
- **Real measure of project progress:** The only measure of project progress is working software that customers are using. Any other measure such as "code complete" is not delivering value to either the business or the customer.

High-profile companies like Flickr, the online photo-hosting and sharing website, are already doing this. According to Yahoo! advertising solutions, Flickr has 51 million registered members. It takes an awful lot of effort to keep that many customers happy, especially when there are so many other great photo-hosting services out there. What Flickr has done is to optimise the production and deployment pipeline so that the site's development team can make updates and improvements as often as they want or need to (10.5).

The screen shot taken from code.flickr on the day we wrote this section shows that the last deployment was only just over an hour ago, and that in the last week there were 61 deployments consisting of 572 changes made by 21 people. A little bit different from the once-a-year code release!

CONTINUOUS DESIGN

For a short period at the beginning of Internet history there was a misconception that you could build a website, launch it, and forget about it. Website owners quickly realised that this didn't make any sense and that, like any business, online businesses need to make sure that service is timely, that content is updated and replenished, and that the environment is refreshed from time to time. The reality is that life begins at launch and you have to stay on top of the game if you want to survive and thrive.

Continuous delivery lets us get serious about doing continuous design. Continuous design takes usage data and context to look for vital insights, patterns, and

---

1 http://code.flickr.com.

anti-patterns, and to apply product vision and design thinking to continuously evolve the product and drive continued success. It's an active state of mind, one in which we're no longer looking for perfection in isolation but rather using validated learnings to bring new creativity to the fore. Where once the designer would present three alternative treatments for the client to choose the safest one based on subjective opinion, it's now possible to test them all and let the data decide.

Usage data and context provide vital insights, patterns, and anti-patterns that help the team to continuously evolve the product.

This represents new kinds of challenges for designers though. Once all you had to worry about was fending off the overly subjective opinions of non design-educated senior stakeholders. Now you have to worry about the collective opinion (uneducated and educated) of the groundswell of consumers and what the data is saying about your creative efforts.

Doug Bowman was the first visual designer at Google but eventually parted company with them, citing the following reasons for leaving:

"When a company is filled with engineers, it turns to engineering to solve problems. Reduce each decision to a simple logic problem. Remove all subjectivity and just look at the data. Data in your favor? OK, launch it. Data shows negative effects? Back to the drawing board. And that data eventually becomes a crutch for every decision, paralysing the company and preventing it from making any daring design decisions."

He went on to say:

"Yes, it's true that a team at Google couldn't decide between two blues, so they're testing 41 shades between each blue to see which one performs better. I had a recent debate over whether a border should be 3, 4 or 5 pixels wide, and was asked to prove my case. I can't operate in an environment like that. I've grown tired of debating such minuscule design decisions. There are more exciting design problems in this world to tackle."

Despite the current excitement about analytics, we don't believe that data is everything. Data is just noise unless you know what to do with it. Clive Humby, Founder and Chairman at leading UK retail experience company Dunnhumby, is often quoted saying, "Data is the new oil," likening data to one of the world's most valuable and essential commodities. And indeed it is. Without data we have no idea whether what we're doing is effective or not, whether our investment is making a return or not. However, to complete the full context Michael Palmer, Executive Vice President of the ANA (Association of National Advertisers), said:

"Data is just like crude. It's valuable, but if unrefined it cannot really be used. It has to be changed into gas, plastic, chemicals, etc., to create a valuable entity that drives profitable activity; so must data be broken down, analysed for it to have value."

We still believe there's a place for the creative talents of the designer to work in conjunction with the visionary talents of the product owner, because the key to success is data combined with context and insights. What's more, a single instance of data and context does not give you true insight. Consumers often pivot on a whim, a promotion, or discount, but whims and pivots can be short-lived. Therefore, we need to gather insights over time by using the data and context to recognise patterns of success and failure (10.6).

The key to creating a successful customer experience is to combine data with context and insights.

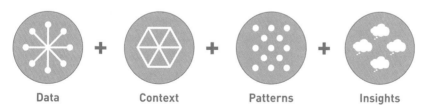

| Data | + | Context | + | Patterns | + | Insights |

10.6
The continuous design equation.

CONTINUOUS IMPROVEMENT

As mentioned earlier, Kaizen is a philosophy that actively promotes and encourages change. In organisations that have embraced Kaizen, improvements are suggested and implemented every single day. This is a stark contrast to the change philosophy of most Western organisations, one in which change requests are catalogued but implemented only periodically. Kaizen is a collaborative effort without hierarchical or functional bias. Everyone from every department, in every role from the CEO to the clerical staff to the bathroom cleaners, is invited to input suggestions for improvement. The ideas are sorted, prioritised by value, and then implemented. It's said that Kaizen offers a great advantage both in terms of employee satisfaction and retention and in terms of continuously improving ahead of the competition rather than reacting to the competition.

To embark on our journey of Kaizen, we join the dots between lean startup, continuous design, agile, and continuous delivery, and embrace the concept of continuous improvement. Where agile is all about fast, yet rigorous software development, lean startup is all about fast, yet rigorous entrepreneur-style thinking for product development. Lean startup focuses on ensuring that there's a market for the business opportunity and on using customer feedback to validate and expand on the thinking.

We've talked about what we mean by "done," and in this world of continuous improvement it may be that done is never actually done. It's a continuous evolution based on the forces of change. By accepting this mindset we can get the minimal viable (desirable) product out into the real world as quickly as possible so we can fail fast if we're not heading in the right direction, or scale fast if we are (10.7).

10.7
Fast and furious methods combine to create Continuous Improvement.

Our notion of continuous improvement covers all the bases:

Business: It explores the business case for product development by understanding the value proposition in light of market opportunities and threats.

Customers: It injects customer context and insights, allowing product concepts to be validated with customers from the outset and throughout the process.

Technology: It helps us determine the most appropriate development and delivery method for the organisation, taking into account the brand, the IT organisation, and technical environment with a view to getting to market as quickly as possible. If the organisation, with some investment, can support continuous delivery and it's appropriate for the brand, then we would certainly advocate it as the best way to get your product to market quickly.

This isn't about getting a project out the door but rather about embarking on a continuous journey of evolutionary product development, one in which we use quantitative and qualitative data as well as passive and active feedback from customers to test and learn quickly and respond and adapt to the changing needs of customers, to market forces, and to advances in technology.

LISTEN AND MEASURE

With any amount of change you have to consider the impact on existing customers and be able to measure the impact of the changes. With large-scale changes you increase the risk of alienating customers and it's much more difficult to understand where the problem lies. With small, incremental releases it's much easier to measure the impact and roll back to a previous version if necessary.

We might have high-tech tools at our disposal, but the rules of business are still the same. To achieve success we have to listen to customers, measure our efforts, and make informed decisions about the actions and adjustments needed to maximise potential opportunities.

Until recently, measuring was a mind-numbing, laborious activity done by marketers and bean counters. Likewise, listening to the customer has always been a direct quantitative activity that was done only on a small scale by frontline sales or support staff or by field experts. What's more, the information gathered has remained within the domain of the division affected by or instigating the collection activity, rather than being shared with a wider audience who might also find it valuable.

The information age is a period unprecedented in history for many reasons, not the least of which is our ability to generate, measure, and mine data.

In February 2010, Wired.com reported about a study (conducted by market research company IDC and sponsored by EMC) in which it was estimated that there are around eight-hundred-thousand (800,000) petabytes of data currently at our disposal. (A petabyte is one million gigabytes.) To visualise this, a piece of standard A4 paper typically has 72 character per line and approximately 50 lines per page; that's 3.6 kilobytes per page. Therefore a petabyte is equal to 277,777,777,777 pages of text. Or a stack that would reach from earth three-quarter of the way to the moon!

With that amount of data available, today's analysts can cut paths through the 0's and 1's to tell us anything we need to know, if we know the questions we want answers to.

There's a plethora of different tools, techniques, and approaches available to us for measuring success. No one dimension should be the single measure. Instead, we need to combine a number of approaches to get a true representation of our success.

NET PROMOTER SCORE

The Net Promoter Score (NPS) is the customer loyalty metric popularised in Fred Reichheld's book *Ultimate Question*. The metric itself is a simple set of questions about how likely customers are to promote a brand, product, or service based on their experience. Of all the metrics of success, NPS is one of the most widely used. Net Promoter suggests that customers fall into one of the following three categories:

- **Promoters** are customers at the top end of the scale who are loyal and passionate advocates for the brand and repeat purchasers of products or services who actively refer others.

- **Passives** are customers who are satisfied with the experience, but are neither loyal nor passionate. These consumers may be swayed by competitor brands, products, or services where relative value is perceived to be higher.

- **Detractors** are customers who are dissatisfied with the brand, product, or service experience. There is a risk to brand, product, or service reputation from these consumers as they may be actively telling others about their negative experience.

To calculate the NPS you must first solicit customer feedback by asking customers how likely they are to recommend the brand, product, or service to a friend or colleague. Have customers use a ten-point scale, where zero is "not at all likely" and ten is "extremely likely" (10.8).

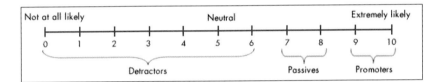

10.8
Net Promoter Scale [2],
npsloyaltyforum.com.

Calculate the percentage of promoters and then subtract the percentage of detractors to find out the NPS.

Net Promoter is billed as a complete enterprise framework and "discipline." Simply measuring is not enough to achieve profitable growth; instead, companies should adopt an operational model that puts the customer at the centre of everything.

Promoters of Net Promoter believe it to be a fundamental part of any customer relationship programme. It's easy to implement, has only a few key questions, and gets a high response rate, all of which increase its appeal and credibility.

On the flip side, detractors of Net Promoter claim that it has little statistical value or predictive power and that it lacks any real actionable detail.

Voice of the Customer (VOC) is the latest business buzz topic that talks about improving customer experiences by actively listening and engaging with customers. A VOC programme acknowledges and places strategic importance on the contribution that customers make to company success. Enterprise VOC programmes are different from previous customer intelligence activities because data comes from multiple sources and is accessible centrally. This enables

2 ® Net Promoter and NPS are registered trademarks of Bain & Company, Inc., Fred Reichheld and Satmetrix Systems, Inc.

different departments to take advantage of customer information that they might not have known about previously. In addition, a VOC programme will ensure that critical information is being *pushed* to the right people, rather than relying on them to discover the information for themselves.

A comprehensive VOC programme requires fairly sophisticated software to tune in to all the sources of information:

- **Solicited and unsolicited feedback:** Solicited feedback is deliberately requested. Unsolicited feedback is given without being asked. Feedback about a single topic can vary wildly depending on whether it's solicited or unsolicited.

- **Passive and active feedback:** Passive feedback is unsolicited feedback you receive from customers through a specific channel. Active feedback can be either the deliberate solicitation of feedback from customer groups about a particular topic, or actively looking for unsolicited feedback across many channels.

- **Structured and unstructured feedback:** Structured feedback follows a deliberate format designed to get answers to specific questions. Unstructured feedback is more organic; neither the content nor the outcome is predetermined.

- **Direct and indirect feedback:** Direct feedback is about the flow of information going firsthand from one primary source to another, such as a direct conversation. In indirect feedback, information comes via a secondary source or intermediary.

- **Qualitative and quantitative feedback:** Qualitative feedback is seeking information from the masses to provide statistically sound data; there is high coverage but low depth. Quantitative feedback goes into depth about a subject but lacks the breadth of coverage of quantitative feedback and is often not considered statistically significant.

VOC programmes take *all* the feedback and use the data to understand what customers are saying, both in terms of the implicit meaning and the sentiment. As well as getting the information to the parts of the business where effective action can be taken, it's also a goal of VOC to respond to customer feedback, where appropriate, to further facilitate the relationship. VOC programmes can be a critical component of continuous design and development as they provide much of the data needed to inform the evolution of the customer experience.

SOCIAL CRM

Voice of the Customer programmes are all-encompassing and reach across every channel, whereas Social CRM focuses on social networks and social channels. Customer Relationship Management (CRM) was once concerned with capturing customer details so that marketing messages could be pushed out to them. But since the birth of the social Web, the emphasis has changed: customers are no longer interested in one-way relationships in which they have no input. The social Web is much more about communities talking and sharing, and networks have become more organic. Organisations can't rely on the old static channels of direct marketing to reach customers; instead, they must go to places where customers congregate.

Some smart companies saw the business opportunities in social networking early on and sprung into immediate action. The reach of a single customer through the expansive platform of social media would astound the marketers of the last century. One small comment in the right forum or to the right network has the potential to have an explosive or implosive effect on a business.

The purpose of Social CRM programmes is to listen to what's being said, respond if appropriate, and encourage positive network growth through targeted campaigns. Social CRM specialists also have to consider a plethora of social channels, including the big social networks such as Facebook, YouTube, LinkedIn, and Twitter, as well as special interest group forums, industry specific networks, and even e-mail.

Through Social CRM programmes, companies can listen to what customers are saying, respond if appropriate, and encourage positive network growth through targeted campaigns.

There are three key Social CRM activities with which organisations get involved:

Listen and monitor: It's important to listen to what customers say about an organisation and its brands, products, and services across the Web and all the social channels. Learn where customers are on the Web to become a more active participant. Understand who the real influencers are within a community.

Pay close attention to influencers and, where appropriate, make them advocates and leverage their position in the community to create a positive buzz about new initiatives and social campaigns. By constantly monitoring the social Web it's possible to detect patterns and see trends and themes. This intelligence can be used to build positive campaigns or can diffuse or detract from negative buzz happening elsewhere.

React and respond: This is said with caution because react and respond doesn't mean jumping in and flaming any customer who says something negative about a company or its products. Emerging social etiquette suggests not publicly berating someone who posts a negative comment, even if it's factually wrong, but responding to her directly and giving her the opportunity to retract or amend what she said. Organisations can choose to react and respond directly in the same channel as the original conversations or via their own channel (website, blog, Facebook page, Twitter stream), or build a multichannel response campaign.

Reach out and engage: The aim is to engage and influence and ultimately convert people into buyers, brand advocates and extend reach to their contacts, friends, and followers. It's tough because everyone is vying for attention and consumers are getting smart about sifting the signal from the noise.

There are lots of sophisticated Social CRM systems out there that allow organisations to proactively launch multichannel campaigns and then monitor the effectiveness and make micro adjustments to improve results. Check out www.agileexperiencedesignbook.com for ten simple social guidelines that could help to increase the success of your social campaign.

CROWDSOURCING OPTIMAL DESIGNS

We're all about optimisation these days. We're constantly striving to ensure that we have the best-possible experience to suit our customers. What's great about working in the current digital environment is that you no longer need to rely on guesswork, hunches, or intuition to get closer to success. The other great news is that as a designer you can also take some of the subjectivity out of the decisions that your stakeholders are making.

There are a number of ways to work out the optimal design, where optimal means driving to get best results, whether that is driving increased traffic, increasing sales conversions, increasing your followers/members, or what have you. These include split testing, multivariate testing, usability testing, and using web analytics to inform decision making. Let's have a look at some of these techniques in more detail.

SPLIT TESTING

Split testing, also known as A/B testing, is the technique of splitting your web traffic and directing different portions of the traffic to different versions of a page. Let's say you want to determine the best design for a home page to drive customers to subscribe to your site. You can create different design variations, publish them to the Web, run your test, and then look at the results and base your decisions on statistical evidence.

The major advantage of spilt testing is that it's totally based on objective data, not subjective opinion. The customers flowing through the different versions of the pages have no idea that they are in a test situation. If you have clear goals and clear metrics, you can simply pick the design that stimulates the best performance. You can test different layouts, designs, button or image placements, or even two completely different look-and-feels to help you set design direction (10.9).

10.9
An example of changes made using split testing. (http://www.abtests.com)

A   **8.5% Conversion Rate**

B   **19.7% Conversion Rate**

The example above shows changes made through split testing at a wine merchant website. The conversion rate of the left-hand process was 8.5 percent versus 19.5 percent for the new tested version, a 131.2 percent increase. You can visit www.abtests.com to see more examples like this.

You need only do a quick search online to find a plethora of vendors offering A/B testing services backed up by case studies which claim anything from a 5 to 400 percent increase in clickthroughs or conversions. Google Website Optimizer is one of the best-known tools, perhaps because it's free and effective. It's also fairly simple to set up and doesn't require a background in software engineering.

If you're going to run split testing you might want to consider the following pointers:

- Try to anticipate what external factors might sway or bias your results.
- Present radically different versions if you're looking for a major win. Small variations in the design will probably produce only small variations in the results of split testing.
- Understand exactly what you want to measure before you start. Don't just think about sales. Also consider revenue per visitor or average order value and decide what's important.
- Don't take the data on faith. Make sure you analyse it and ask questions.

MULTIVARIATE TESTING

Multivariate testing is a variation of split testing. Where split testing is fairly binary, that is, it determines whether version A produces better results than version B, multivariate testing allows more granularity. With multivariate testing you can literally test the same design elements in hundreds of different combinations to work out the optimal design. Multivariate testing is most effective with high-traffic sites, as low numbers won't give you the statistics you need to prove the variations.

The variations could be as minimal as changing the size of a font, the position of a button, or the effectiveness of a headline. You can test individual modules or elements on a page or a variety of different elements. Obviously, the more variables you add to the test, the more complex it will be to understand which parts are working and which parts are not.

You can use both multivariate and split testing on almost anything in the digital space, from websites to banner ads to your social network pages to e-mail campaigns.

(ALL NEW) USABILITY TESTING

The International Organization for Standardization describes usability in ISO 9241-11 as "the extent to which a product can be used by specified customers to achieve specified goals with effectiveness, efficiency and satisfaction in a specified context of use."

Usability should be a product consideration from the start of the process and should be tested with target customers throughout design development. A number of different approaches to usability testing have developed over the last 20 years, but the intent to uncover usability issues is the same.

Formal testing: When we were rookies in this industry, nirvana for usability testing was a fully kitted out lab with one-way mirrors and expensive audio-visual equipment, all of which can make formal testing expensive. The sample size for usability testing is often small, which arguably is enough to uncover major usability issues, but it can be difficult to convince stakeholders that results are statistically viable.

Guerrilla testing: Throughout the book we have mentioned using quick and informal methods for taking concepts or rapid prototypes to the nearest willing volunteers to solicit feedback. Where time and cost might be a barrier to doing more formal research this approach believes that some research, even without formal rigour, is better than none.

Remote testing: Somewhere between formal and guerrilla testing on the high-tech scale is remote testing. Here you take advantage of cloud-based computing and software as service products for unmoderated remote usability testing. There's a range of different testing products available, so it's worth spending some time and playing with demo or free-trial versions to understand what you need before committing. See www.agileexperiencedesignbook.com for a list of evaluation criteria to consider when choosing a remote testing tool.

There are a few major advantages to doing online remote usability testing over doing moderated offline testing, including time and cost. However, there's a limit on the depth that you go to in unmoderated remote usability testing. In a moderated offline test, a session can last between 45 and 90 minutes and you can expect to cover the majority of the customer goals that require testing. Unmoderated online remote sessions need to be much shorter, around fifteen minutes, with a limited set of tasks, to retain the interest and focus of the participant.

We recommend doing a combination of both methods to get the best results. We've found that doing frequent but short online unmoderated remote testing, interspersed with more comprehensive offline moderated testing periodically, will give you enough coverage and the best results.

ANALYTICS: MINING THE LOGS

Analytics is a tool or set of tools used to measure and understand customer behaviour on a website for the purposes of optimisation. The analytics tools track how websites are used, traffic flow (numbers of visitors), where visitors come from and where they go to, how long a customer stays on a page, bounce rates, and conversion metrics, as well as all the vital financial information about how much they are spending, including revenue per visitor and average order value.

By understanding the picture that the analytics data paints, designers can enhance and improve customer journeys, information architecture, and interaction design, including placement of calls-to-action and page content and make the overall experience more engaging and fruitful.

Analytics is big business because data is a key difference between success and failure. Those who fail don't know how to measure, analyse, and act on the data. Conversely, those who succeed recognise the importance of data and dedicate teams to it. At the time we wrote this chapter, the breaking industry news was that Hewlett Packard had acquired UK-based multichannel analytics solution Autonomy "in a deal valued at US$10.24 billion." When Autonomy listed as a public company in 1998 the share price was £2.25; it is currently £25. If that's not proof that the industry values analytics, we don't know what is.

Let's look at how you as a designer can make the most of the data available from using an analytics tool to influence your designs.

First, find out what tool your organisation is using and see if you can get access to it. The majority of the analytics tools come with a dashboard that presents the statistics and trends. If you can't get direct access to the tool, then request specific reports from owner. While all the tools offer a variety of features and reports, they all have a core set of metrics. For the purposes of this chapter, we'll refer to examples from Google Analytics, as it's a free, easily accessible and comprehensive tool that many organisations use even in conjunction with other tools (10.10).

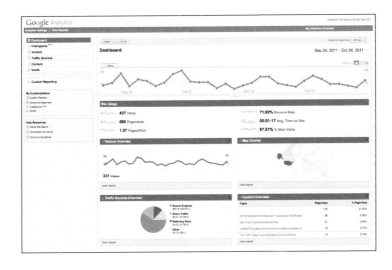

10.10
Google Analytics Dashboard.

So how do you mine the datalogs to understand how your site is being used and, more importantly, to know what needs design improvements?

ENTRY POINTS

Entry points are where the customers enter the website—and there can be many of them. They could start directly at the home page or enter the site at any page following a search-engine query or a social media "share," or they might enter on a landing page designed specifically to catch customers from a paid advert.

Don't assume that customers enter your site via your carefully optimised home page. Use the analytics to understand where the customers are entering and make sure that those pages in particular are optimised to allow customers to achieve their goals and then springboard to other pages in the site.

If you have an open site, meaning that the majority of the website has unrestricted access, consider that every single page could in effect be a home page or landing page. Therefore, all pages on the site should follow the AIDA principles: awareness, interest, desire, and action. Use this simple technique to guide the design and content to sell the rest of the website to the customer and increase conversion.

You can take a slightly different approach if the majority of your content is behind a paywall or registration process. In this case you need different design and marketing approaches for the pages that are outside the paywall as opposed to inside. Outside the paywall you'll need to spend a considerable amount of effort on marketing, design, and content to drive customer conversion to sign up, register, or buy a subscription. Once the customer has signed up, registered, or subscribed, content and pages inside the paywall can focus on cross-selling and upselling to other pages, content, and products within the site.

If your content is behind a paywall, you might also want to consider how this affects your search engine optimisation efforts. One way would be to enable the search engine and customer to see a part of the page. This could act as a teaser and potential springboard to conversion.

EXIT POINTS

Exit points are pages where customers leave your site. These are critical pages to look at. If you have pages with consistently high ratings for customers exiting, you need to explore why they are leaving on those pages. The reason might be that customers can't find what they're looking for, so check to see if the goal is obscured by clutter or noise from competing elements and content on the page. Perhaps there is no obvious call to action. Check out click maps and heat maps of the specific page to see if customers are even seeing the call to action. Perhaps it's in the wrong place, the design isn't strong or contrasting enough, or the message isn't strong enough. This is where you might consider using multivariate testing to experiment with some optimisation options. Even if your page isn't transactional, such as a simple content page, you ideally want to create links or calls to action that encourage customers to explore other content in your site.

If your exit points are the same as your entry points, then you're missing opportunities to convert customers and promote the rest of your site. This is even worse when customers are bouncing. Bounce rates measure when customers enter the site and exit from the same place without having made so much as one click, or where they've stayed dormant for a long period. In this case look at where the customers have come from and try to understand their goals and optimise the design accordingly. For example, if customers are exiting on landing pages from a paid advert, is the content on the page relevant to the ad? Does it have enough information to keep them interested and create the desire needed for conversion? Is the call to action strong enough? Is the process for conversion clear enough? Is there one simple path to follow (think of Amazon 1-click ordering) or are there confusing and conflicting options?

TIME

There are two dimensions of time to consider when looking at analytics. The first is *time on site*, the time stamp from when customers first enter the site to when they exit. Ideally if customers are engaged, they will explore different pages on your site. If the average time on site per customer is low, you'll need to reconsider your techniques and strategy, as well as your site's design and content.

The second is *time on page,* how long customers typically spend on one particular page. If you have pages where customers are spending a considerable amount of time (relative to the rest of your site), it could be a good sign that customers are engaged, but it's still worth reviewing the page to make sure that it's not a bad sign, that customers are spending more time there than they should because something is too complicated and they're are struggling to complete a goal.

TRAFFIC

Are you getting a high flow of unique customers but low rates of repeat visitors? The hardest and costliest part in the game of selling is acquiring new customers. Marketing theory tells us that it's easier to retain existing customers than to gain new ones. So if your customers aren't coming back, you need to look at why and try to build in incentives to get them to return. Is your site designed to attract new customers rather than value existing customers? Many sites fall into this trap, leaving customers who have invested time or money in your products and services asking, "What about me?"

Consider how you can make your website more sticky and what you can build into the site to engage customers. Do you have the sort of web environment where a community element would increase stickiness? Could you consider elements such as personalisation and customisation or provide facilities for customers to contribute and generate content? Could you include elements of gamification, that is, use game techniques such as incentive, reward, and competition to engage customers and keep them coming back?

CONTENT

Content is king. It needs to be timely, engaging, relevant, and directed at customer goals. You can use analytics tools to find out which are the most and the least popular pages, analyse the differences, and then use this to understand what's working and what isn't with regard to content. Content can consist of text, images, multimedia, widgets, and so on, and can also be closely tied to events. On less popular pages, start with the page itself. Analyse the content and the structure of the page. Ensure that the content is:

- Original, well written, and well designed
- Clear and concise with a heading which piques the customer's interest
- Structured in a journalistic, or inverted pyramid, so the value of the content is explicit from the top of the page not buried in the detail somewhere at the bottom of the page

If you've followed all these guidelines and have a perfectly designed page with great content, then look at optimising the page from a search-engine perspective to make sure that people can find it and look for opportunities to link to that page from other pages in the site and outside the site (10.11).

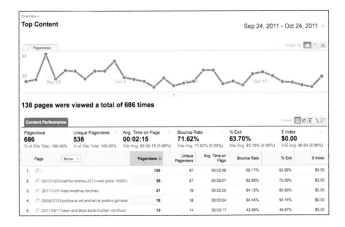

Google Analytics: top
content data view.

EVENTS

Events are the activities or actions that customers can do on a website. Events include clicks, hovers, downloads, forwards, shares, prints, and so on. Most analytics tools will measure both events per page and events per visit. If you have pages with a low rate of events, you might need to analyse the content and make sure that it's engaging. Even if it's a blog or editorial piece, which elements can you include on the page to encourage customers to interact? Can you include images or charts that they can manipulate or annotate? Is it appropriate to include a simple voting/rating or comments/feedback widget? Can you incorporate social media widgets that encourage customers to share your content with their friends and network?

CONVERSION

Conversion is that all-important term, the holy grail of digital marketing. The Web Analytics Association describes conversion as "a visitor completing a target action." In e-commerce it's used to describe the final commitment of a customer to make a purchase. On a nontransactional site it can mean registering, completing a profile, personalising, signing up for a newsletter, sharing with a social network, and so forth. Whether or not the website is transactional, conversion is the measure of success of the website: the more conversions, the greater the success. So it's not surprising that there's a lot of noise about the conversion process. Analytics can help you understand how many customers start out on a conversion path compared to how many customers complete and convert. This is commonly referred to as the conversion funnel (10.12).

10.12

Google Analytics Conversion Funnel.

The pie chart (10.13) shows that 20,143 customers viewed the product and that 3,466 (17 percent) actually proceeded to the shopping cart page. Having compared a number of sources, it appears that the average conversion rate for e-commerce sites is between 2 and 3 percent, with some of the top performers achieving between 12 and 23 percent and rare outliers achieving up to 40 percent.

10.13

Google Analytics conversion data.

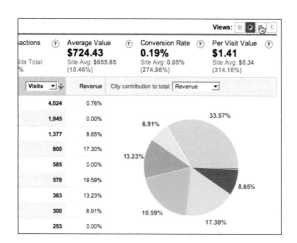

Look at the analytics to understand exactly where customers are dropping out. Cross-reference events on pages where customers are dropping out. Look for where customers have stopped clicking, had a period of inactivity, or stopped filling out a form. Analyse those events and activities in detail and see how they can be improved.

The key conversion activities to look out for include registration, account creation, and shopping cart processes. As a designer, you need to design these conversion processes to be efficient and as easy to complete as possible. Remove any barriers (such as asking for information that's not mandatory) and any distractions (such as clicks to other pages) during the process itself. Also arm customers with as much information that will help them complete the process, without interruption, before they start. To minimise abandonment partway through the process, tell customers about any additional costs or conditions such as shipping and returns before they embark on the process.

VISITOR DETAILS

Visitor details include some pretty important stuff for a designer to consider. Visitor details tell you about operating systems, screen resolution, access devices, and the geographic area that your customers come from. As a designer, you need to optimise the designs for the most-used browsers and operating systems as well as screen resolution. You might have your favourite browser, but if you only consider that when designing, your design might be suboptimal or even unusable when displayed on other browsers if it's not optimised for them. Screen resolution will also affect the layout and structure of your site.

USING ANALYTICS

When you decide to take this approach, to use data to support your design decision making, it's important to ask the right questions when you're viewing historical data and make sure that you eliminate any factors that might skew the result. More importantly though, it's essential to create a baseline from which to operate and then record exactly when you made changes and what those changes were so that you can measure and analyse the future impact of those changes. Don't just assume that because you've changed something that the performance will improve. It's not always obvious how to solve a problem, especially when you're dealing with large volumes of traffic. As with the stock market, the value of your investment can go up as well as down. You might have to try several different options in isolation or in combination before you hit on the winning formula. Therefore, we recommend that you use an analytics tool in combination with an optimisation tool.

 TIP

Establish a baseline by taking a snapshot of the situation immediately before publishing any changes. Record exactly what you change and monitor the response to ensure that the changes are having a positive effect.

TIP

Before publishing your design changes, make sure there's a rollback plan just in case the changes have a severely negative affect.

TIP

Be willing to ride out the storm. If the change has a negative impact, consider waiting a short period before you roll back. Your customers just might need a short period of adjustment before they accept them.

DO THE NUMBERS ADD UP?

There is a danger with using only analytics to shape your digital product and experience development. You could tweak everything based on every little whim, but it takes a good product visionary to really understand how and where to drive innovation. A/B testing is like the 1980s Coca-Cola versus Pepsi challenge all over again. At the outset of the blind taste test, the majority of participants said they preferred Pepsi over Coca-Cola. This campaign had seismic effects for Coca-Cola, yet through additional research Coca-Cola proved that the winning strategy is much more than the initial taste.

Be careful before jumping to conclusions and acting on the results. You might be tempted to act immediately when results show that an overwhelming majority prefer version A. However, you might want to consider whether the results are due to the Pepsi Challenge syndrome, which delivered instant gratification but didn't win out in the long-term taste test. Or is the popular choice the most familiar and therefore appeals because of customers' instinctive resistance to change? Consider that the least popular option in the short term could be the most effective in the long term. Analytics and business intelligence are essential, but it's far more important to understand how to read the data and then use it to make informed decisions.

This issue is not a new one or endemic to current experience analytical testing methods. Usability testers also had (and still have) the same problem. A good design researcher shines not in the report of their findings but in their recommendations. Almost anyone can observe, listen, and record verbatim what customers say, but insights come from understanding the real problem behind the words and coming up with a creative solution that solves the problem.

Avoid jumping to conclusions or asking the wrong questions about what the data tells you. We worked recently with a large online financial services comparison site that panicked when their sales of car insurance dropped off fairly significantly one week. They assumed it was related to recent changes that had been made. They went back and reviewed all the recent changes and came very close to rolling back some of them, when someone on the team mentioned the weather. On further investigation they noticed a direct correlation with the drop in sales and an unexpected and severe snowfall, which had crippled the UK roads. As people weren't driving, car insurance wasn't forefront in their minds. The online site waited before making any changes, and sure enough, as the weather improved, so did sales.

Here's another scenario. You're refreshing or rebuilding your website. You're introducing new functionality and features, and sweeping away the old. You've done usability testing of your new concepts and the results are positive. With success baiting, you go live. Yet it doesn't go quite as you expected. You expect that the numbers and feedback will go on an upward trajectory from day one, but they don't. What you didn't expect was the dip (10.14).

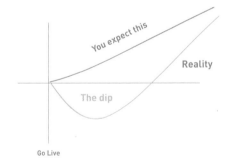

10.14
Resistance before adoption of change.

In October 2009, Facebook redesigned their newsfeed. Customers were up in arms, groups were formed, and noisy negative feedback abounded. When the BBC redesigned their news page, 60 percent of commenters hated the BBC News redesign and there were volumes of comments including: "A silly waste of licence-payer's money and another example of the relentless advance towards turning the Web into a Fisher-Price wonderland for simpletons."[3]

Resistance to change is almost always inevitable. Brace for dissent, especially if you have a vocal and loyal following. Professional speaker, writer, and consultant Peter de Jager states: "Most people are reluctant to leave the familiar behind. We're all suspicious about the unfamiliar; we're naturally concerned about how

---

3 From Martin Belam at www.currybetdotnet.

we'll get from the old to the new, especially if it involves learning something new and risking failure."[4]

What's interesting is what happens next. Hold your nerve and you'll get over this initial dip. We've seen a number of projects recently where this phenomenon occurred; numbers drop and negative feedback is loudly heard. But this dip is ephemeral and to be expected. The challenge is in planning for this and setting expectations accordingly. Telling your CEO that the new design has resulted in a drop in conversion rate will be a painful conversation unless you've set expectations beforehand.

DECIDE WHERE TO INVEST YOUR TIME

Having explored the different methods for testing the effectiveness of your digital experience, you might be wondering where's the best place to focus your time and money and which method might yield the best results?

The following chart from Econsultancy shows the different methods for understanding customer experience, which techniques are used the most, and which are considered the most effective. User testing is a clear winner in the measure of effectiveness but used by less than half the websites using web analytics. Also interesting to note is that, of the companies using web analytics, only just over one-third saw that technique as being a very effective method for understanding customer experience. The outlier is "session replay technology," which captures the user's view to be replayed later and is fairly new on the scene (and probably the reason for the low adoption indicated in this study). However, it gets a high score for effectiveness compared with other commonplace practises such as split (A/B) and multivariate testing.

Graph 10.15 illustrates illustrates that there is no silver bullet. Our recommendation is that you use a variety of the techniques in combination. The data from analytics will give you one perspective, while customer testing (both remote unmoderated online and moderated offline) will give you another. The more techniques you can employ, the higher the resolution picture you'll create of your customers and their motivations, behaviours, and actions.

---

4 De Jager, P. Resistance to change: a new view of an old problem. The Futurist, 24-27.

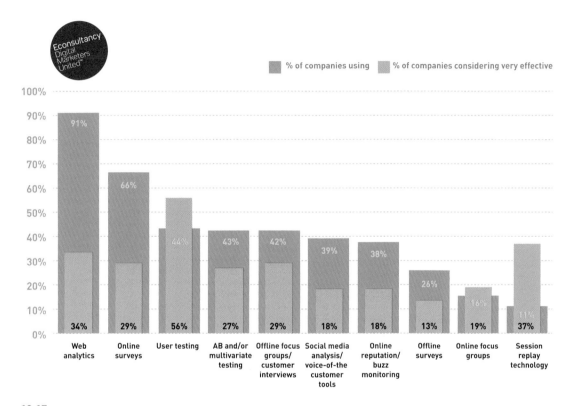

10.15

Comparison of customer experience assessment methods.

Source: econsultancy.com/uk/reports/reducing-customer-struggle.

PRODUCT EVOLUTION AND MEASURES OF SUCCESS
Janelle McGuinness, Head of eBusiness at an international
direct retail bank

As the owner of websites for a direct bank, the performance and effectiveness of
our sites is paramount to the success of our business. Our websites not only have
to attract new customers and allow them to open a new bank account online, but
also service their ongoing needs. Those different functions mean a lot of different
measurements. Choosing the right measures is crucial to support decision making.
There's no point in having measures that have no real value or having masses of
insightful data that you don't have the systems or time to analyse.

It is not worth making a significant investment in a change unless you can measure
the outcome. Without measurement you have no idea if your actions have resulted
in improvement or failure. Exposing yourself to scrutiny requires bravery because it
doesn't leave a lot of room to hide when it doesn't work as planned. However, being
able to measure results is exciting—whether the results are favourable or not, at
least you have the information to do something about it.

Before determining the measures to use it is important to be clear on what you
are trying to achieve. Set clear goals for the change and avoid ambiguous phrases.
Either you met your target or you didn't. "Increase conversions to 75 percent by 1
January" is a clear target. "Get better conversions soon" is not.

Clear targets help determine how much you should invest in measurement. So assess
how important the change is and then determine what level of investment in measurement is appropriate. As well as deciding on the absolute number of measurements,
you can increase or decrease the investment by altering the accuracy of your measurements. For example, ask yourself, "Do I really care how much time each customer
spends filling in each question, or am I most concerned about how long they spend
on each page?" Keep in mind though: just like the absolute number of measures, the
degree of accuracy alters how much weight you can place on the results.

We use a number of different metrics to assess the customer experience. One of
these is Net Promoter Score (NPS), which helps us determine customer satisfaction.
While this is a powerful measure from a general business context, as a web owner
it doesn't give me specific, actionable information. The brand, the latest advertising
campaign, product pricing and features—things that are beyond my control—can
significantly affect the NPS score. The opening of bank accounts via our website is

a key area that I do have control over, and we measure it intensively. However, we don't look at the total number of accounts opened as an absolute number. Again, the number of people driven to our website is affected by external factors such as brand, price, and marketing.

To really determine the performance of our account-opening process, we measure conversions. This is the ratio of people who start the account application process versus people who submit the completed application. The closer this number is to 100 percent, the more successful the application form is. We make an assumption that a customer who is willing to start the account application process is serious about seeing it through to the end. If they don't complete your application the problem is likely with your site, not the customer. For us, understanding both the conversion rate and where customers drop out during the application process is critical.

The key is in knowing what to do with your measurement data once you have it. If your goal is to improve conversion rates, and your results are falling short, then you have to look at ways to improve the process. The right quantitative measurements are crucial. But this sort of data won't always provide a lot of context or meaning. It tells you how many, but not why. Qualitative measures like customer surveys, focus groups, and usability studies can provide insights into where customers are getting confused. But qualitative data can be tricky to read and not always representative of the larger customer community.

Once you have determined where the problem is, the next step is to try out solutions to fix the issue. Measurement plays an important role in honing solutions to solve the problem. Understand what impact you are expecting from your change and how much you want to invest in measurement. If you are investing significant effort in wholesale change to the structure or flow of business-critical applications, then it is worth investing the time and money to measure the changes. However, if you are just tweaking the words in a line of help text, a quick sanity check with a colleague is probably sufficient.

You won't always have a complete data set to draw accurate conclusions, and sometimes will just have to go with gut instinct. This is part of everyday business. But if you are going to make the effort to make a change or try something new, having meaningful ways to measure impact gives you the information you need to make decisions. It also provides the proof for senior stakeholders about the success of a change. Where the Web is concerned, everyone believes they are an expert and are happy to tell you their opinion. However, hard data is irrefutable and defeats any subjective debate. ■

IN SUMMARY

This chapter stressed that while launch might be the end of the project, it's just the beginning of a new life for the product or service and it's where the real learning begins. From here it's essential to embark on a programme of listening to customers and measuring the rate of success to prioritise and focus on improvements that will deliver the most value.

There's a wide range of tools and techniques that you can use to measure and assess digital product success. However, data and logic is not always enough on its own to make an informed decision. Instead, we recommend that you use a combination of qualitative and quantitative tools to gain a holistic view and inform a programme of continuous improvement.

With real-time data available to help businesses understand where the strengths and weaknesses of digital products lie, businesses also need mechanisms to respond quickly. Continuous design combined with continuous delivery gives businesses the opportunity to continuously improve products and push them out to the live environment as frequently as multiple times a day, rather than releasing them once or twice a year. With this shift in mindset, we can continually optimise the product to increase customer satisfaction and business success.

This might amount to evolutionary product development, but it's a revolutionary change to the way we once designed and built software.

COMING NEXT

That's all, folks! Well, not quite. As you turn the page, you'll enter the Toolbox, a collection of tools and techniques that we view as the most valuable in our daily pursuits of creating engaging, desirable experiences in a continuous and agile way. Many of the tools started life outside of agile, so what we've done is to describe the original method and objective and then describe how the execution might vary slightly if you apply it in an agile framework.

PART THREE

THE TOOLBOX

What follows is a collection of essential tools, techniques, and activities that all experience designers should keep handy. These tools aren't necessarily specific to any method; many of them, in fact, existed long before agile. But what we've done is describe the techniques in terms of what they are, and why, when, and how you apply them in the agile world. For the fledgling designer and the would-be designer, learning, practising, applying these tools will set you apart from those who say they can do agile customer-centred experience design and those who actually *can*. A seasoned experience designer is likely to be familiar with many of these—but it's all about how the technique varies when it has an agile flavour.

There are many great tools out there, but these are the ones that we consider the most essential. Some additional resources are listed at the end of the chapter as well.

The difficulty in compiling this section is that in a world of continuous design and development, many of these activities could be applied and repeated at any and all stages of product development.

Some of these tools will change with time, application, and technology. Let us know about your favourite, most successful, or newly developed tools and techniques by any of the various contact methods listed in the preface and we'll endeavour to share them.

AFFINITY MAPPING

What is it?

It's a quick-start, low-fidelity method for organising a magnitude of low-level information points into key themes that can help you see the hundred-foot view rather than the one-centimeter view.

Why do it?

Do it when you've too much information, but you don't know how to sort the keynotes from all the noise.

When to do it?

Do it whenever you've lots of manually collected data points that require a manual process to sort and understand.

How to do it?

- Transcribe your notes onto sticky notes using the one-point-per-sticky-note rule.
- Stick your notes to the wall and ask, "So what?" to help you understand why the note is important. Don't just take your first answer, keep asking "So what?" until you understand the real issue.
- When you find a few notes that are about the same issue, group them together and give the group a label that summarises the issue.
- Check your grouping. If you've large groups, try to break them down into smaller themes or issues.

The agile flavour

Don't wait until you've collected all the data. Map it incrementally. Do it as you go along while it's still fresh in your mind.

Don't worry about writing up your findings in a long document. Just communicate the headlines (the real issues) and capture the detail with photos. Better still, invite people to "walk the wall."

Get the team to collaborate on the process so everyone understands.

ANALYTICS

What is it?

Analytics are data sets and tools that measure customer, business, and web performance.

Why do it?

We want to learn from historical data about what has worked well and hasn't worked so well so we can make informed decisions about the future.

When to do it?

Do this at the start of a project and as an ongoing activity to see how the patterns change over time.

How to do it?

- Find out which data tools or data sets your organisation currently uses. There might be lots of them buried in less-than-obvious places.

- Once you've identified who holds the data, see if you can get access to the tool itself, then you can decide what's important.

- If you can't get access to the tool, see if you can get some specific reports related to your questions.

- Look through the data to find trends and anomalies. Where are the spikes and the dips? See if you can understand what caused them.

- Focus your data analysis on the activities that you're hoping to drive. Understand web analytics such as popular content, entry and exit pages, pages with high bounce rates, conversion rates and conversion drop-off points.

The agile flavour

Unless you have a background in data analysis, this isn't always an easy task. Try to make it a team activity, not only so you can all share in the understanding, but also because people from different functional areas will look at the data in different ways. Project the reports or the tool onto a large screen and discuss. Write key points on sticky notes. They might spot things that you wouldn't have done, or offer a perspective on the trends that you might not have considered on your own.

AS-IS EXPERIENCE DESIGN REVIEW

What is it?

It's an expert review of the customer experience of an existing product.

Why do it?

Do it to understand what works and what doesn't from a customer experience perspective.

When to do it?

Do it at the beginning of a major redesign project, in the early stages of a new product development project (evaluating competitors), or afterward as part of evolution.

How to do it?

- Grab your personas and their goals and get ready for some role-play.
- Immerse yourself in the persona and try to complete the tasks to achieve the goals from each persona's perspective.
- Consider all dimensions that are essential to creating a good experience, including usefulness, usability, desirability, value, findable, engaging, sticky, gamification, interaction, content, informative, efficient, integration with social media, user-generated content, and so on.
- Revisit the session, pulling out highs and lows in the experience.

The agile flavour

Make it a team activity. As the experience designer, you can play facilitator and get different people on the team to play different personas. Project the website on a large wall so that everyone can see. Have everyone else write important observations on sticky notes and do an affinity map (discussed later in this chapter) to finish.

 TIP

Use the think-aloud protocol and either video-capture the results using Silverback or a similar tool, or have someone else take notes as you say them out loud.

AS-IS/TO-BE PROCESS MAPPING

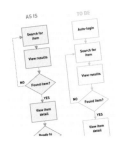

What is it?

This is a visual way of mapping tasks that a customer does when using a specific system to achieve a specific goal.

Why do it?

Do it to record and understand either the existing (as-is) process flow or to design the future state (to be).

When to do it?

The as-is map is done at the beginning of the new product development process to understand existing process flows and identify opportunities for improvement. The to-be process map can be done at the beginning of the process to understand the macro processes and throughout design and development to work out the micro process for smaller goals.

How to do it?

- Start with your persona, his characteristics, and one of his goals.

- To create an as-is map you need a good understanding of the existing process, ideally through direct observation. Plot the activities in the process on a flow chart using sticky notes.

- To create a to-be map take your persona and any as-is maps and brainstorm improvements for the process. Again, plot the activities in the process on a flow chart using sticky notes.

- A variation on this is the lean version of value-stream mapping. Take your as-is process map and add times to the value-added activities, then plot the time between the activities. This lets you see where time is spent on low- or no-value activities. Use this map to identify areas of improvement.

The agile flavour

Make the exercise collaborative and time-boxed. If you have a large team, divide into smaller groups and give each team a different process to investigate and map out. Regroup and present the as-is maps to get a shared understanding, then as a whole group, brainstorm the opportunities for improvement.

CAMERA AS DOCUMENTATION

What is it?

It's using your camera as a documentation tool.

Why do it?

Seriously, who spends time reading epic tomes of documentation? So if no one reads them, why waste your time writing them? If all you need is a record of the activity, findings, and the outcome, then make the outputs of the activity visual and take a photograph.

When to do it?

Do it whenever you create something visual that you need to record for prosperity. Everything from a scribble on a sheet of paper to sketches on a whiteboard to process mapping and affinity mapping can be captured with a photograph. It saves missing or mistranslating any detail, too.

How to do it?

- Dare we share point-and-shoot? You don't need a snazzy camera, just one that can capture the detail well enough that you can read it later.
- Point your camera, frame your shot, shoot the picture, and—most important— check it before you walk away. Zoom in and check that you've the detail and that it's not blurry.
- Download the shots from your camera frequently (daily, or at the end of each session) to a central space that the whole team can access. Or you can publish the pictures to a photo-hosting site and share them with a closed group.
- If people insist on some level of documentation, use your preferred presentation software, insert the photos, and then annotate by pulling out the highlights.

The agile flavour

To be honest, it doesn't get much more agile than this, except to say that everyone can take photos and share: it's not the responsibility of the project photographer, as long as you all keep checking that someone has captured the moment.

COLLABORATIVE DESIGN

What is it?

It's using a small team of people to work together to create the design.

Why do it?

To generate more solutions, to be more efficient, to apply specific domain knowledge to the emerging design, to understand the context of activities to the design, to get buy-in, and shared understanding from the team.

When to do it?

Do it early in the process to generate the initial design vision, then do it through-out the process to get the next level of detail or next iteration of design.

How to do it?

- Decide who you are to collaborate with. Include anyone from the project team, domain experts, content specialists, product owners, and real customers.

- Ensure that everyone feels that they can contribute equally and stress that the idea is to design, not critique. You don't need to be an artist to contribute: if you can draw a box and a stickman, then it's all the talent you need.

- Work as a whole group, or divide into smaller groups.

- Each group should have access to design artefacts such as personas, scenarios process maps, or the customer-journey map.

- Give each team a design challenge and ask them to generate six quick alternative ways of solving the problem.

- The team reviews the six options and selects the strongest candidate. Present back to the whole team to get feedback and a shared understanding.

The agile flavour

Collaborative design has always been a process for rapidly exploring low-fidelity design options with groups of people. It doesn't get much more agile than that. The key is to complete the activities within a limited time period and to do just enough design thinking to get you to the next step in the process. This isn't about big, up-front design but about rapid solution generation through design thinking.

COMPETITOR REVIEW

What is it?

It's a review of your direct and indirect competitors and their offerings.

Why do it?

It helps you understand threats and opportunities for your product or service, market, customers, and business by looking at competitor strengths and weaknesses.

When to do it?

Do it during the early stages of the project when you're looking at the business or the market context. Repeat any new competitors as they emerge.

How to do it?

- If you have to do it yourself, first talk to business stakeholders to identify key competitors. Prioritise the list and then pick the top three to investigate.

- Look at the direct lines of competition, such as the comparable products, and compare yours against theirs feature by feature to understand strengths and weaknesses.

- Look at official sources of market research and media reviews to understand the industry opinion and ratings about their product/service compared to yours.

- Look at user-generated content, including customer reviews, customer ratings, and special-interest consumer groups.

- Do a SWOT analysis of each competitor (strengths, weakness, opportunities, and threats) to map out your findings.

The agile flavour

You're a designer on a team of business analysts, developers, and project and product managers. None of you are market researchers, so the task should not fall solely to you. To speed up the process, identify the competitors and distribute the task of investigating each competitor between the team members. Complete the task within the time-boxed period, then reconvene to share your findings.

 TIP

You're a designer, not a researcher, so look to leverage internal and external research done already.

 TIP

If you can't find any relevant research, speak to the product owner about budget to commission research.

CONTEXT SCENARIOS

Denise logs onto her compu
launches her browser windo
clicks on bookmarks and sel
bookstore.com. She searche
authors name and was pleas
see that although she spelle
wrong there was a suggesti
the author she wanted. She
that the author has a numb
books that she din't know
One in particular has a five
review. She decides to rea

What is it?

These short narratives describe the activities done by customers to achieve
goals in the context and environment in which they're performed.

Why do it?

They help you understand the broader customer context, including motivation for
use, and explore design solutions and requirements.

When to do it?

As with personas, it's ideal to create scenarios at the beginning of the process
to inform design.

How to do it?

Scenarios should be informed either by direct customer research or by someone
in the team who has direct involvement with customers.

- Start with your persona, his characteristics, and one of his goals.
- Use plain English to describe the scene.
- Describe the tasks that the customer needs to do to accomplish her goal.
  Refer to process maps if you already have them.
- Avoid specific references to technology or particular interactions, unless it's
  a known constraint, as this could constrain your thinking to one solution.
  Remember, the idea is to give you some context to explore your options.
- Add details such as inputs and expected outcomes.
- Include context beyond the boundaries of your product as it's helpful to under-
  stand motivation. For example, if you're working on a website, how did the
  customer find the website and where did she land?

The agile flavour

Divide up your project team into pairs or small groups. Brief the groups on writing
scenarios and give each group a persona to base their scenario on. Have each
group complete the scenario within a specified time limit. Present the results
back to the group to share and critique the scenarios.

CONTEXTUAL INQUIRY

What is it?

It's a means to observe people in action in their natural environment.

Why do it?

Do it to understand customer behaviours, motivations, processes, actions, and the environment or context in which they are undertaken.

When to do it?

The results will influence your understanding and the design, so do it at the beginning of the project. Do it again once you're live. Repeat after launch to see how things have changed.

How to do it?

- Identify your target customers.
- Grab your notebook, sticky notes, and camera (photo and video ideally).
- Reassure them that you're not assessing them or their performance.
- Explain exactly how you'll use your research, photos, and videos and ask them to sign a release or consent form.
- Make notes and take photos and video of the environment, including the desk and any artefacts on the desk. In particular, look out for artefacts that they refer to during a task, such as a notebook, cheat sheets, or sticky notes.
- Ask what they're doing and why. Ask why they're doing it in that way or that order. Is there a logical or mandatory sequence of events and which ones are critical? What are the customers' pain points? What are the things they like?

 TIP

The clue in the title is "contextual." This should be done in the context of the actual environment where customers perform their work or tasks.

The agile flavour

Try to get some cross-functional representatives to observe the session. A business analyst might be able to shed light on issues that arise from the business domain. A technical engineer might be able to give context to issues that are a result of technical limitations and system constraints. A business or product manager will get an understanding of his customers firsthand. Limit numbers to two or three, including yourself. Brief the other observers on observation etiquette and give them the job of scribe or cameraperson.

 TIP

Be mindful of "observation etiquette." As tempting as it can be, don't judge, give any opinions, or criticise. You're there simply to observe, understand by asking objective questions, and record.

CUSTOMER EXPERIENCE/JOURNEY MAP

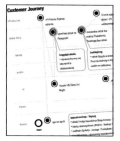

Source: jasonfurnell.
wordpress.com.

What is it?

It's a way to visually represent all the channels, touchpoints, activities, and experiences that a customer has when trying to achieve a specific goal.

Why do it?

Do it to analyse the current customer experience or to help envision the ideal experience for the future. Use it to understand customer experience across channels and to identify opportunities and challenges for your product.

When to do it?

Do it at the start of the process to help kick-start design.

How to do it?

- Create the canvas and the key steps or phases across the horizontal axis.
- Option one: On the vertical axis place channels such as website, phone, customer service, and so on. Plot your journey on sticky notes and add a smiley or sad face to highlight good or bad experiences.
- Option two: Have an "experience rating scale" as your left axis ranging from high to low. As you plot out events make a note of the channel.
- Using either method to plot the journey, take a persona and write one event per sticky note and add it to the map either aligned with a channel or with the experience scale.
- With smiley faces or events that rank high on the experience scale, this is the stuff we want to keep doing. With the sad faces or low-ranking events, explore opportunities for improvement.
- Also identify moments of truth or opportunities where you can improve, excel, or create a real point of difference in the customer experience.

The agile flavour

Make the mapping exercise collaborative and time-boxed. Brainstorm the events as a team and have the facilitator plot them to the map. Ask what the customer does or might do next. Once you've identified pain points and moments of truth, brainstorm opportunities for improvement or making a point of difference.

CUSTOMER TESTING

What is it?

It's getting direct feedback from customers who use your product or service.

Why do it?

There's no better way to understand what your customers truly think of your product than to find out firsthand from the customers themselves.

When to do it?

Do it throughout the life cycle of the product, especially when considering change.

How to do it?

There are books devoted solely to customer testing so we're not doing the subject justice by giving it one page to talk about four different techniques. However, consider:

- **Guerrilla testing:** When you've little budget or time, simply grab your designs and take them to the nearest person. The idea is that some feedback is better than none at all. You could test something as small as a specific interaction or something as big as a concept.

- **Concept testing:** Use this method to get feedback on the macro-level ideas or mental models and compare different concepts.

- **Moderated usability testing:** You need customers who match the target profile, test tasks/scenarios, and a prototype or system to test on. Ask the customer to complete tasks using the system and probe to understand the customer's behaviours and thought processes. Success or failure is based on the task completion rate and the customer satisfaction.

- **Remote unmoderated testing:** Based on the above, however. This uses cloud-based or client software instead of a moderator. Participants are recruited to match the customer profile and are given specific tasks to complete.

The agile flavour

Guerilla testing is probably the most agile flavour of customer testing as it's quick, relatively easy to do, and free. Divide the project team into small task forces to get more feedback from a wider range of people in a shorter amount of time.

DESIGN REVIEW MEETING

What is it?

It's a meeting of stakeholders to assess design work in progress.

Why do it?

Do it to socialise design progressions and solicit objective feedback from different functional experts and stakeholders to get to the next stage of development.

When to do it?

Do it frequently, at least once during every iteration and ideally while work is in progress.

How to do it?

- Set up a recurring meeting to happen at a regular time and place. Limit the meeting time to an hour or less.
- Socialise the artefacts for review in advance to make the meeting more productive.
- Ask the invitees to send a delegate if they're unable to attend or to send their feedback about the designs to you advance of the meeting.
- At the meeting introduce the designs and what stage they're at in the development process. Use whatever medium is appropriate for the project and the audience.
- Work through each design in turn, soliciting feedback from all the attendees. The most effective method is to provide each attendee with sticky notes and a pen and ask them to write one comment per sticky note. If you're presenting printouts of designs, attach the comments to the relevant design. If you're showing electronic versions of the designs on a computer or project, make sure that the sticky notes clearly identify which design element they refer to so that it's easy to identify later.

The agile flavour

This is about as agile as a design review meeting can get.

ELEVATOR PITCH

What is it?

Elevator pitch is a technique for distilling the product value proposition into a discrete, easy-to-remember, compelling, and repeatable phrase. It's like a mission statement, but it has a specific formula and is created in the context of being on a brief elevator ride with your boss, investor, or company VIP.

Why do it?

Do it to clearly and concisely to articulate the unique value proposition that you intend to deliver with your new product.

When to do it?

Create your elevator pitch at the beginning of a new product development process and revisit it throughout development to help you stay on the right track. Re-evaluate again after launch or before any period of significant change.

How to do it?

There are a number of variations on this theme, but the one we like best comes from the book *Gamestorming*[1] by Dave Gray, Sunni Brown, and James Macanufo, which suggests the following framework:

- For (*target customer*) who has (*customer need*), (*product name*) is a (*market category*) that (*one key benefit*). Unlike (*competition*), the product (*unique differentiator*).
- Before crafting the phrase, answer the questions denoted by the words in italics above—for example, who is the primary target customer?

The agile flavour

Make it a collaborative effort involving business stakeholders and the cross-functional project team. Display the results in a key location in the war room and refer to it throughout the early phases of the project to keep you on track.

 TIP

If you've a large group, consider breaking into smaller groups then comparing and contrasting results.

 TIP

Wordsmith if necessary after the group session to make the pitch coherent and easy to repeat.

---

1 *Gamestorming* by: Dave Gray, Sunni Brown, James Macanufo Published by O'Reilly Media, Inc. Copyright © 2010 Dave Gray, Sunni Brown, James Macanufo. All rights reserved. Used with permission.

ETHNOGRAPHIC RESEARCH

What is it?

This immersive research activity is similar to contextual inquiry, except that it requires you to get involved with the activity, rather than just observe.

Why do it?

It helps you gain firsthand experience and a true understanding of customers' cultural, social, and motivational behaviours in the context that they happen.

When to do it?

Ideally, do it at the beginning of the project because you want the results of the study to inform your design solutions and project requirements.

How to do it?

- **Get native:** Identify your target customers. Go and watch them do their thing in the place that they're doing it. Get native and join in.

- **Be a customer:** To understand the customer experience, become your customer and try to complete some of his or her goals. You can do this in the physical world or online or ideally both to compare the experiences. For example, what's it like to purchase a mobile phone online and in-store? What's it like to open a bank account via the Web or in a branch?

- **Go on a service safari:** This looks beyond a specific product and thinks about the overall service experience. Go out into the wild and think about the service supporting your product. What are the different phases? Who are the people involved and what contribution do they make? What touchpoints do you interact with? What is the space or environment like?

The agile flavour

Get as many team members involved as possible. Divide into small groups and try one or all of the approaches above. The more people on your team who are empathetic toward the customer situation, the better chance of everyone contributing to the development of a product based on empathetic insights. If everyone gets it, you don't have to waste time explaining yourself or justifying your customer-centred design decisions. At the very least, show the team the videos during the showcase.

TIP

It's hard to write sticky notes when you're immersed in this activity. But don't rely on memory and write the notes after the event because you could forget key information. Try to video or audio record the process to leave you hands-free to join in.

HOT AIR BALLOON

What is it?

A hot air balloon is a visual discovery tool.

Why do it?

It can help you understand the constraints and advantages that might hold back or propel an opportunity.

When to do it?

Do it at the beginning of a new product development process or at any point in product development when you're considering sizeable change.

How to do it?

- Draw (or print) a large hot air balloon on paper or on a whiteboard.
- Distribute sticky notes and pens to all participants.
- Get everyone to brainstorm the ropes—things that hold us back—and the fuel—things that can help us fly.
- Group the sticky notes into common themes.
- Talk through the groups and prioritise to understand the key issues, any mitigating factors, and key opportunities that can be acted on.

The agile flavour

Keep this exercise time-boxed and short. Make it a collaborative effort between the project stakeholders and the cross-functional project team for richer results.

IDEA GENERATION

What is it?

A creative way to generate multiple options before deciding on a solution.

Why do it?

By generating multiple options, you've a better chance of hitting on the right one.

When to do it?

It's typically done during the early stages of the process, but you can use this approach whenever there's a design challenge.

How to do it?

There are hundreds of different techniques to help you unleash your creative thinking. Grab a group of people and warm up the session with an icebreaker to get everyone talking and brains ticking. Stress that the point is quantity not quality, and not to be constrained by what you know.

Here are some to get started:

- **Brainstorm:** Get everyone to think of ideas to solve the design challenge and write each new idea on a sticky note. Get participants to build on each other's ideas until everyone has run out of ideas.

- **Ask "what if?"** Asking "what if" will give a different frame to the challenge. You can also append "what if" questions to "how might we." For example, ask "How might we solve this challenge if we had to deliver tomorrow, if budget was unlimited, if we were constrained by X, if we had no constraints, if it was to be nominated for an award, if it was to have social impact," and so on.

- **Word games:** There are lots of word games that you can play to help unleash ideas, including word association, random word games, combining words. Frame the design challenge, pick a word game, and go nuts!

The agile flavour

Get the whole team involved. In a cross-functional group there will be many different styles of thinking and approaches to problem solving. The more you include, the more interesting the results will be. Keep it time-boxed, and either have a session scribe or use low-fidelity methods to capture the results.

INFORMATION DESIGN

What is it?

It's a visual model that represents the categorisation and flow of information across and within an application to meet customer expectations and goals.

Why do it?

Do it to understand the best way to present information to customers to help facilitate achieving their goals.

When to do it?

Do it continuously, throughout the product development life cycle.

How to do it?

Start with the macro information design—that is, the overall structure of your information flow on your site or application and then drill down to the micro page-level information design.

- **Card sorting (macro):** Write the major content topic areas onto cards or sticky notes. Group into categories of similar topics and give each category a name. Or start with the group name and add content to the corresponding group.

- **Site map (macro):** Create structure for your site by creating a site map around content. Write content on sticky notes and group into a logical structure.

- **Content inventory (micro):** If you're working with existing content, create a content inventory to understand the current content set and then mark areas for deletion that are no longer required and add in content that is missing.

- **Content mapping (micro):** Grab your site map, content inventory, personas, process maps, and page templates and map the content to specific pages ensuring that you support customer goals and tasks.

- **Split and multivariate testing (micro):** After mapping your content, use split or multivariate testing to test the right information design for your customers.

The agile flavour

All the activities can be done by cross-functional teams. Involve the product owner (or content specialist), business analyst, experience designer, and front-end developer.

INSIGHTS

What is it?

Insights are deep understandings of the real issues and design challenges.

Why do it?

To understand the root cause of the issue so you can consider the right solution.

When to do it?

Insights are typically done at the beginning of the process when you're considering problem statements and understanding the challenges.

How to do it?

There are a number of different methods for getting to insights, including:

- **So what?** When you find an issue ask "so what?"; keep asking the question of each answer until the question can't be answered.
- **Five whys:** Ask why it's a problem and keep asking why of every answer until the question can't be answered.
- **Affinity mapping:** Use affinity mapping (earlier in this section) to find related issues and understand the macro issues.
- **Explore cause areas:** Consider the problem from the point of view of the business, customers, and technology.
- **Fishbone diagrams:** Draw a horizontal line, write your problem on a sticky note, and place the note on the left of the line. Draw branches off the horizontal line of macro areas related to the problem—for example, people, process, budget, and brainstorm-related or contributing factors on sticky notes.

Use any of these methods to come up with overarching statements that describe the problem space, ideally phrased as a positive opportunity. We can then use these statements as the design challenges in an ideation or collaborative design session by asking, "How might we solve this design challenge?"

The agile flavour

Collaborate with the project team and subject-matter or domain experts. The more perspectives and the more cross-functional minds that are looking at the problems, the the better the chance of getting to the real insights.

LOOK INSIDE

What is it?

It's the process of exploring your organisation to see if a challenge like yours has already been tackled.

Why do it?

Why reinvent the wheel? If someone has knowledge that you can leverage, then why not make your life easier?

When to do it?

Do it at the early stages of the project.

How to do it?

There are multiple methods and techniques for this, including:

- **Stakeholder interviews:** Ask key people what they know and what they think you need to know before you start the process. Consider all the different channels that might be involved, including sales, operations, and so on. Find out how the project/product strategy is tied back to company strategy.

- **Hunt the data:** Find out which departments are measuring anything that might be relevant to your project and try to get access.

- **Hunt the research:** Many large organisations have research departments or contracts with research agencies, so ask the questions you need to know and see if they have already done the research or if they could do it for you.

- **Know your customers:** Find out who the key customer advocates are within the organisation, such as marketing and customer service, and find out every-thing they know about customer wants and needs.

- **Get to know the brand:** Find out who owns the brand and get a copy of the brand guidelines to know what it stands for and to guide your product development.

The agile flavour

Discover activities focused inside the organisation can be run in a number of ways to make them more agile. Instead of holding individual interviews, you could run a workshop. Instead of doing consecutive activities, split up the team and run them simultaneously, making sure you all get back together to share the findings.

ME AND MY SHADOW

What is it?

It's working alongside someone to find out exactly what he does and how he does it.

Why do it?

There's no better way of understanding customers, their work practises and behaviours, and the environment than doing it firsthand. This is similar to contextual inquiry, except instead of being the inquirer, you're actually doing the task yourself.

When to do it?

This is most suitable for complex Web or desktop applications. Do this at the beginning of the project to gain an in-depth understanding of the customer and the tasks.

How to do it?

- Organise this activity in advance. You'll likely need permission from a line manager and someone who has agreed or been nominated to be the person that you'll shadow.

- Brief the person you're working with. Tell him exactly what you're doing and why and reassure him that you're not assessing his performance in any way. Ask him to go about his daily job exactly as he would if you weren't there. Ask him to treat you like an apprentice that he's training.

- Try to repeat the tasks he undertakes, noting which parts are straightforward, rewarding, or difficult. Use your skills as an experience designer to evaluate how you could make improvements. Ask the person you're shadowing what things he would like to see changed.

The agile flavour

It will be hard to take notes as you're doing this activity. If appropriate, have a scribe work with you; if not, then download your thoughts onto sticky notes imme-diately after the session before you forget the detail. Also video the activity if you can, so you can share it with the team later.

PERSONAS

What is it?

Personas are profiles based on customer research, that bring customers to life.

Why do it?

Personas are artefacts that can be used to inform product decisions.

When to do it?

Create personas at the start of the product development process.

How to do it?

Create believable, credible personas, which encapsulate understanding and empathy, and include context and goals.

- **Customer characteristics:** Name, role, brief characteristics, reason for using the existing or new product and their values.
- **Use:** The customers' technical ability, their familiarity with technology, and frequency of use.
- **Goals:** List the goals this type of customer would want to achieve using your product and prioritise based on importance and frequency.
- **Current pains:** List reasons why trying to achieve these goals is painful today.
- **Needs and desires:** List the customers' needs, wants, hopes, and desires for the new product.
- **Scenario:** Describe a brief activity scenario that provides motivation and context around the customers' reasons for using your product.

Just be sure to avoid stereotypes or generic segmentation descriptions.

The agile flavour

Hold a workshop that might include people within the organsation who once *were* the persona types that you want to create. Include people who have done direct customer research, people who work with customers on the front line, people who are responsible for the product positioning, and even actual customers. If you can't get customers, validate the details when you get a chance. Have participants brainstorm the details and record them on sticky notes.

PRODUCT BOX

What is it?

It's a fun and visual way of exploring the unique selling points of your product.

Why do it?

It helps you position your product in the marketplace against competitors and make it appealing to potential customers.

When to do it?

At the beginning of any new product development or before any significant change.

How to do it?

The following is based on Luke Hohmann's *Product Box* from *Innovation Games*.[1]

- Get your project team and business stakeholders and form small groups.
- Give each group a blank box coloured pens and sticky notes.
- Each team needs to design the product box. Imagine it on a supermarket shelf next to the competition. Think about what would persuade a customer to buy your product and not the competitors'. Consider name, nutritional info, marketing slogans, offers, price points, and so on.
- Introduce an element of competition. Set a tight time deadline and tell each team they need to prepare a five-minute pitch (Dragon's Den style) and that the best one will win a prize.
- Assemble a panel of external judges. Each judge should play a customer or investor and decide which product they would buy or invest in and why.
- After the time limit is up, invite each team to present in turn.
- Consolidate the feedback from the judges and announce the winner.

The agile flavour

Make it a time-boxed and collaborative effort involving business stakeholders and the cross-functional project team.

---

1 *Innovation Games* by Luke Hohmann, Published by Pearson Education, Inc. Copyright © 2007 Luke Hohmann. All rights reserved. Innovation Games® is a Registered Trademark of The Innovation Games® Company.

PROTOTYPING

What is it?

It's a visual model that represents a possible solution to the design challenge.

Why do it?

Create prototypes to rapidly and cheaply explore design ideas and solutions, to facilitate feedback from customers, team members, and stakeholders.

When to do it?

Do it continuously, throughout the product development life cycle.

How to do it?

There are a few different flavours of prototyping to consider:

- **Paper prototyping:** Use paper, pens, and sticky notes to rapidly sketch the user interface. Great for initial concepts and designing templates.

- **Low-fidelity prototyping:** Use a low-fidelity prototyping tool such as Balsamiq or even PowerPoint to create the user interface. Ideal for moving beyond the concept/template stage when you need to reuse patterns and elements.

- **High-fidelity prototyping:** Create the prototype in the tool or programming language nearest to that of the end product. Use the tool to do "design spikes" to test that an interaction style will work as intended. The idea is that this isn't meant to be comprehensive or usable code but to give you more confidence in the suggested solution.

- **Living prototyping:** Unlike high-fidelity prototyping, the living prototype isn't meant to be thrown away. It's an evolutionary expression of the interface that is built incrementally and represents the design detail as it emerges.

The agile flavour

Prototypes are tools that can be developed collaboratively (see collaborative design tool) and can be referenced and shared by all the team. The description above refers mostly to the use of the various types of prototype within an agile environment. The key agile takeaway is to do just enough to get you to the next stage of development without doing big, up-front design.

RETROSPECTIVE

What is it?

A retrospective is a quick, feedback-driven method to review team.

Why do it?

Do it to understand what can be improved.

When to do it?

Do it continuously throughout the process.

How to do it?

- **Safety check:** If this is the first time you've run a retrospective with this team, you need to run a safety check to see if everyone is comfortable to give feedback. Read and display the "prime directive":

  "Regardless of what we discover, we understand and truly believe that everyone did the best job they could, given what they knew at the time, their skills and abilities, the resources available, and the situation at hand."[1]

  Ask each participant to write a number between 1 and 5 (5 being high) that represents how comfortable they feel giving and receiving feedback. If the numbers are low, be sure you understand the issues before running the exercise.

- **Running the retrospective**
  - Remind the participants to respect one another's opinions.
  - Dimensions could include: **Did well** (and should keep doing), **could improve** (things to change), **start doing** (things we aren't doing that might be useful), **what puzzles us** (things that we don't understand).
  - Collect the sticky notes and attach them to the relevant dimension.
  - The facilitator, who is ideally impartial to the project, groups the sticky notes into themes and then encourages group discussion.
  - The facilitator should collect any actions and assign each action to an owner.

---

1 Norm Kerth, *Project Retrospectives: A Handbook for Team Reviews.*

SHOWCASE

What is it?

A showcase usually marks when the team demonstrate the working software.

Why do it?

Do it as a checkpoint to solicit feedback from the product owners, customers, and project stakeholders.

When to do it?

Toward the end of each iteration, or short period of development, where a small, demonstrable chunk value or working software is showcased.

How to do it?

- Invite your audience, including product owners, stakeholders, and other interested parties. Also invite members from the project team. It's good to have everyone involved as they can hear the feedback firsthand and have cross-functional representation to answer any questions from the product owner or other stakeholders.

- Set their expectations about what they will see. This is important, as you might be demonstrating an HTML-only version of working software whereas the vice principle of marketing might be expecting to see the full visual treatment.

- Demonstrate the work developed since the last showcase.

- Ask for feedback as you go through the demonstration. Give one person the responsibility of recording the feedback.

- If appropriate, give a progress report saying what you have or haven't achieved against the intended plan and highlight any major roadblocks.

- Explain what you intend to work on for the next development period and when to expect the next showcase.

- Ask for feedback on the format of the showcase so that you can adapt it to make it more productive, valuable next time.

STAND-UP

What is it?

A stand-up is a short, periodic status meeting for the project team and other interested parties. Also known as a *scrum* or *huddle*. It's called a stand-up because everyone literally stands for the meeting as an incentive to keep it short.

Why do it?

Do it to connect regularly with the broader team and get a shared understanding of progress and blockers.

When to do it?

Do it daily throughout the process!

How to do it?

- Decide on a regular time that works for most people.
- Nominate a talking stick or similar object (balls are good because they can be thrown to random people in the stand-up and create a good sense of energy).
- The person with the talking stick starts by saying the **progress made** since the last stand-up, what they **intend to work on next,** and **any problems** that are preventing them from making progress. It's the facilitator's (or scrum master's) job to see if anyone can help with the issue and to decide to take it offline if it's going to derail the stand-up meeting.
- After the first person has finished speaking, they pass the talking stick to another person, who repeats the process until everyone has had a chance to speak.
- The last person with the talking stick keeps it until the following day and becomes the first person to speak.

STORYBOARDING

What is it?

It's a way to illustrate customer activity scenarios or customer journeys.

Why do it?

It can help to illustrate a concept prior to development.

When to do it?

You can use a storyboard to depict both the as-is process and the to-be process and even use this method to draw comparison. Create storyboards during the early stages of the product development process when you want to explore or communicate the key benefits of a particular concept.

How to do it?

- Think about any good comic books that you might have read and what you'll remember as key events in the story illustrated and captioned. This is the kind of thing you're aiming for.
- Start with sticky notes to work out the key activities and events of the story.
- Write the captions to inform the content of the image.
- Create the corresponding illustrations, which can be as simple as a hand-drawn sketch, as heavyweight as a Flash animation, or anywhere in-between.

The agile flavour

Collaborate as a team about what the scenes should be that tell the story. Even if few people on the team can draw, they can still brainstorm the flow of the story, contents of illustration, and the captions.

STORY MAP

What is it?

It's organising stories to show both how they support the system and customer goals and the relationship that they have with each other.

Why do it?

Do it because it enables the team to see how the stories fit together and can be prioritised to deliver a minimum viable product.

When to do it?

It's used during elaboration to help prioritise stories and then in delivery alongside the story backlog.

How to do it?

- Identify key customer goals.
- Organise the story cards that have been captured during story writing under these goals.
- Prioritise these stories according to their importance in enabling the goal to be accomplished.
- Draw a horizontal line. Stories above the line are in scope; those below are out of scope for the immediate release.

TASK ANALYSIS

What is it?

Task analysis helps you understand the tasks needed to achieve goals. It's similar to customer journey mapping, value stream mapping, and as-is/to-be process mapping but focuses specifically on customer goals.

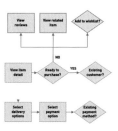

Why do it?

Do it when you need to understand the tasks required to accomplish a goal that will inform information and interaction design.

When to do it?

Use it to evaluate existing products or to brainstorm ideas for new products. It's particularly valuable when you're doing goal-driven product development.

How to do it?

- Grab a persona and a list of his or her goals (collected using customer research activities and persona development).

- Brainstorm about the persona's motivations, pains, and so on. For each goal, make a list of tasks that the persona would need to do to complete them. Use sticky notes to record the tasks in case you want to change the order of the tasks.

- Use the results as a design artefact to help shape information and interaction design.

 TIP

You might need to break large tasks down into subtasks.

The agile flavour

Make it a collaborative effort involving the cross-functional project team. Don't worry about documenting the results, just display them in the war room and photograph them for record and wider distribution.

300

TRADE-OFF SLIDERS

What is it?

Trade-off sliders help to visually prioritise project or product dimensions.

Why do it?

When everything is equal, it's hard to focus your attention. When you're developing a product, you need to understand and prioritise the most important dimensions and then focus your time accordingly.

When to do it?

Run this exercise during early project stages. You might need to rerun it if there are any dramatic changes in the project landscape during development.

How to do it?

The following is a variation on the theme from *Radical Project Management* by Rob Thomsett.

- Ask business stakeholders to brainstorm a list of important project/product dimensions, such as scope, time, budget, quality, customer experience, or other measures of project success. Agree on a short list of six to eight dimensions and write them in a vertical list on a large sheet of paper.

- Now draw a horizontal line next to each item and add gauges to create a scale. The number in your vertical list will determine the number of gauges in your horizontal scale.

- Ask the business stakeholders to place a sticky note on the scale where left is least important and right is most important. The trick here is that no two dimensions can have the same measure of importance.

The agile flavour

Make it a collaborative effort involving business stakeholders and the cross-functional project team.

TIP

This task seems simple enough, but it may require a good facilitator when business stakeholders don't agree on project priorities.

INDEX